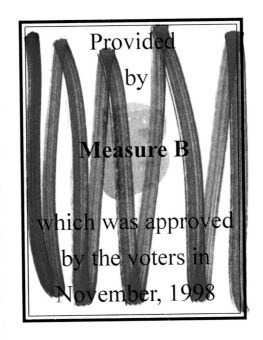

SHUTTERBABE

SHUTTERBABE

Adventures in Love and War

Deborah Copaken Kogan

VILLARD   NEW YORK

Title page photo: Reuters/Grigory Dukor/Archive Photos
All interior photos: © Deborah Copaken Kogan

Library of Congress Cataloging-in-Publication Data

Kogan, Deborah Copaken.
    Shutterbabe: adventures in love and war / Deborah Copaken
Kogan.
        p.   cm.
    ISBN 0-375-50364-1
    1. Kogan, Deborah Copaken. 2. News photographers—United
States—Biography. 3. War photographers—United States—
Biography. 4. Women photographers—United States—Biography.
I. Title.

TR140.K64 A3 2000
070.4'9'092—dc21   00-038179
    [B]

Villard Books website address: www.villard.com

Printed in the United States of America on acid-free paper

9 8 7 6 5 4 3 2

First Edition

Book design by Barbara M. Bachman

CONTENTS

AUTHOR'S NOTE

Throw ten photojournalists in front of a burning house, and I guarantee you'll get ten different pictures of that house. One of them will snap a wide shot of the whole fiery mess. Another might focus in on a single window, a singed teddy bear smoldering on its sill, while a third might get distracted by the young couple who, oblivious to the blaze, are making out under a streetlight in the far distance.

This is a work of nonfiction. But this is also my story, my slide show, my burning house. Enter it knowing that, beyond a few name changes here and there, every flame is real.

SHUTTERBABE

PART ONE ·

DEVELOP

SANGLAICH VALLEY, AFGHANISTAN, 1989

PASCAL

THERE'S A WAR GOING ON, AND I'M BLEEDING.

An unfortunate situation, to be sure, but considering it's 2 A.M., fresh snow is falling and I'm squished in the back of an old army truck with a band of Afghani freedom fighters who, to avoid being bombed by the Soviet planes circling above, have decided to drive without headlights through the Hindu Kush Mountains over un-paved icy roads laced with land mines, it's also one without obvious remedy. I mean, what am I supposed to do? Ask the driver to pull over for a sec so I can squat behind the nearest snowbank to change my tampon?

I don't think so.

It's February 1989. I am twenty-two years old. My toes are so cold, they're not so much mine anymore as they are tiny miscreants inside my hiking boots, refusing to obey orders. In my lap, hopping atop my thighs as the truck lurches, as my body shivers, sits a sturdy canvas Domke bag filled with Nikons and Kodachrome film, which I'm hoping to use to photograph the pullout of the Soviet troops from Afghanistan.

Actually, I have no idea how to photograph a Soviet pullout. Though this is my second story as a professional photojournalist, I'm still not clear on what it is photojournalists actually do in a real war.

The first story I covered, the *intifadah*, was more straightforward. Organized, even. I'd take the bus early every morning from my youth hostel in Jerusalem to the nearby American Colony Hotel, where all the other journalists were staying (and where I eventually wound up staying when my clothes were stolen from the youth hostel), and I'd go straight to the restaurant off the lobby. There, I'd ingratiate myself with any photographer I could find who had information about the day's planned demos, his own rental car, and a basket of leftover Danish.

After eating, we'd drive around the West Bank and wait for the Palestinian kids to throw rocks at Israeli soldiers, which we knew they would do only once a critical mass of journalists had assembled. Then we'd record the resulting skirmishes onto rolls of color slide film while trying to evade arrest and/or seizure of our exposed films by the soldiers. Next, we'd all rush back to Jerusalem to the Beit Agron, the Israeli press office, where we would lie about what we'd just shot ("religious Jews," we'd say, or "landscapes,") and get our government-issued shipping forms stamped and signed accordingly. Finally, we'd head to the strange little cargo office at the airport in Tel Aviv to send our film on a plane back to our photo agencies in Paris. Simple.

JERUSALEM, ISRAEL, 1988

But here in Afghanistan the situation is more obscure. I'm alone, for one, which among other things means I have no one to help me figure out basic puzzles like how to get my exposed film out of the mountains. Or how to write captions when no one around me speaks English, and I have no idea where, exactly, these photos are being taken or what it is I'm actually seeing. I'm just assuming that at some point, someplace, I will see some dead or bloody mujahed, or some dead or bloody Russian soldier, or some mujahed firing off his Kalashnikovs, or one of those great big Soviet tanks whose names I can never remember, or, well, *something* that looks vaguely warlike that I can shoot and send—again, it's murky to me exactly how—back to my photo agency in Paris.

I look over at Hashim, who's rearranging blankets, knapsacks and boxes of ammunition to clear more leg room on the crowded truck bed. He yanks my maroon nylon backpack from the center of the pile, fills in the newly empty space with a green metal box, mimes "Can I sit on this?" while pointing at my backpack, and, when I nod yes, he wedges it into a corner and plops his 180-pound rump right on top of it. A gentle crunching sound ensues, followed almost immediately by the smell of rubbing alcohol. Shit. My mind races to try to recall what else, besides the bottle of alcohol, I packed in that outside zippered pocket.

Then I remember. My box of Tampax. My one and only box of Tampax. Well, now. I'm fucked.

Oblivious, Hashim slowly inhales a Winston cigarette and kneads his amber worry beads through his ragged fingers. Trained as a journalist, he's the one Afghani among my forty-seven escorts who actually speaks a few key English phrases such as "Food soon," "Danger, stay in cave," and "Toilet time, Miss Deborah?" But even though I know he will probably understand me if I say, "Please get off my bag," he definitely won't understand "because my tampons are exploding." And because "Please get off my bag" sounds sort of rude, and because the squishy backpack does look like a comfy place to sit while all of us are scrunched together on the back of this rickety old truck heading God knows where, and because my hygiene woes do not hold a candle to the miseries of jihad, I say nothing. Besides, I'm covered from head to toe in an electric-blue burka—an Islamic veil, worn like a Halloween ghost costume—which tends to hinder communication. Not only does it muffle my speech, it makes it impossible to guess, for example, that underneath all this rayon, under my shiny blue ghost costume, I cannot stop crying.

What on earth possessed me to come here?

In a word, Pascal. It's Pascal's fault I'm here all alone, and when I get back to Pakistan I'm going to kill him.

THE FIRST TIME I noticed Pascal it was from afar, at a café on the rue Lauriston near the Sygma photo agency. That would have been in late September 1988, about two weeks after I'd arrived in Paris, ready to start my life. Every day, I'd go to that same café and spy on the photojournalists eating lunch there. Most afternoons, I'd order a *croque monsieur* and place my portfolio ever so casually on the chair in front of me, hoping that the sight of my work along with the Leica around my neck would somehow draw a photographer over to my table. In my fantasy, the photographer would ask to take a look at the pictures and then, duly impressed, he'd invite me to come join the rest of his gang at his table for an *île flottante* and a round of espressos. I'd sit down and, after modestly refusing to do so, I'd be persuaded by the other men—they were all men—to pass my portfolio around the group, one of whom would be an important photo editor who'd want to send me that very same afternoon to go cover a war. It didn't really matter which war because I knew better than to be picky. Any war would do.

But that was just the fantasy. In reality, I had to settle for eating my sandwiches alone and in silence.

On that first day I noticed Pascal, he strode like a bulldozer into the café, pushing in the cool autumn air from the outside with his angular torso. With what seemed like a single fluid motion, he unhitched the camera bag from his shoulder, placed it in the pile of sacks already there on the banquette, greeted his colleagues with an ironic *"Salut, les potes!,"* pulled off his blue cashmere crew neck, knotted it around his shoulders, lit a cigarette and sat down to fondle a menu. His features were sharp and finely chiseled, his eyes sparkled with what appeared to be a touch of mild insanity, and his lips had corners that turned up when he smiled, like the Joker's in *Batman.* When his steak au poivre arrived, he sliced into it with the grace of an aristocrat, the tines of his fork facing down then up as one by one the freshly cut morsels disappeared into his mouth, each effortless bite punctuating the rhythm of his fraternal chatter. He is magnificent, I thought.

Pascal was an up-and-coming war photographer, and I admired his work. His pictures didn't just show action, they screamed action. Bombs exploding, young children crying, soldiers cowering, grimacing, dying. Exactly the kind of images that I was desperate to start shooting, if only I could figure out how.

After two weeks of getting nowhere with my portfolio-on-the-chair ploy and spending far too many francs on *croque monsieurs,* I realized I'd been going about it all wrong. With my shaky French, I called the general number for Sygma and asked to speak to Claude, the editor in charge of news photos. For whatever reason, perhaps because he couldn't understand me on the telephone, perhaps because it was a slow news day, he agreed to a meeting. The next afternoon, when I arrived at his desk, he started to laugh. "You're the little girl from the café," he said. A few of the photographers I'd been stalking, Pascal included, stared and tittered from behind the glass wall of the photographers' room.

As Claude flipped through my portfolio, which was bulging with photographs of strip clubs and the men who visit them, his eyes opened wider and he began to shake his head. Then he muttered *"Putain!"* I knew *putain* meant "whore," but at the time I did not know it could also be used idiomatically to mean something more tame, like "wow" or "holy cow." But before I could figure out where the epithet had been directed, at the strippers or at me, Claude looked up and said, *"Tu voudrais aller où?"*—"Where would you like to go?"

I cocked my head. I crossed my arms. "Israel," I said, more of a dare than a word.

Claude smiled and, to my amazement, replied, "Fine." We made a deal: I'd pay for the trip; Sygma would pay for my film and development costs and then distribute the pictures upon my return. A break. At last.

As I turned to leave, Pascal caught my eye and winked. Whenever I thought about that wink afterwards, I'd shiver.

The next time I saw Pascal, it was two months later. I'd just arrived back from Jerusalem. Chip, my colleague and occasional lover, an American who'd lived in Paris for most of his adult life, invited me as his date to a dinner party Pascal was throwing with his live-in girlfriend in Paris. The live-in girlfriend part should have tipped me off, but then Pascal cornered me in the living room and challenged me, with his mischievous smirk, to a staring contest. No problem, I thought. I'll beat him hands down. But after what must have been less than sixty seconds of locking eyes with the man, I didn't just lose. I was hypnotized, rendered incapable of higher thought. Or even medium thought, like "Stay away. Girlfriend shares his bed."

Within minutes of losing the staring contest, and battling an overwhelming urge to sniff Pascal's neck, I cooked up a plan. It was a simple plan, really. One that would solve what I was beginning to understand would be a constant dilemma: companionship on the road. With our cameras in hand, we'd leave Paris, our worldly possessions, the live-in girlfriend, and my less sexy lovers behind. We'd spend the next couple of years traversing the planet, bouncing from coup to insurrection, war to revolution, passing our days shooting pictures and our nights under the stars, making love to the gentle thrum of incoming mortar fire.

Afterwards . . . well, I wasn't exactly sure. I didn't think in afterwards.

Okay, so I had an active fantasy life, but this time I could smell the thoughts as they popped into my head. Or maybe it was just the big slabs of steak that Élodie, the live-in girlfriend, was preparing in the kitchen. In any case, while Élodie was off in the kitchen preparing the meat, while Chip was embroiled in another conversation, Pascal suddenly turned to me, blew a puff of his cigarette into my face, and said, "I'm going to Afghanistan next week. Why don't you come with me?"

I sucked on my own cigarette, choked on it really, and blew the smoke back into his face. Then, composing myself, I shot him a conspiratorial smile. "Sure," I said. "Let's do it."

It was as simple, and as complicated, as that.

Early the next morning, I quietly slipped out of Chip's bed and went directly to the bank to take out three thousand dollars, almost all of my savings, to pay for my trip. I'd started my postcollegiate life in Paris with seven thousand dollars, saved from a summer job shooting photographs for a *Harvard Lampoon* parody, a semester waiting tables, an academic prize, a *Washingtonian* magazine photo contest I'd won, publishing my thesis in *Boston Magazine* and a mercy assignment from my parents, who'd asked me to shoot and print black-and-white portraits of my grandparents. But rent, food and the trip to Jerusalem had set me back. Plus Sygma had dawdled in getting my pictures out to the magazines and had yet to sell a single photo. I'd just sold some of my old black-and-white work to *Photomagazine,* but that money—a little over a thousand dollars for eight printed pages—would not be coming in for another month.

After decimating my bank account, I jumped on the Métro and rode to the appropriately named Nouvelles Frontières—"New Frontiers"—Travel Agency, where I booked and bought my ticket to Peshawar, Pakistan. That night, I was on the floor of the tiny apartment I shared with three room-mates, frantically reading back issues of newspapers and magazines, try-ing to figure out who was fighting whom. What's a mujahed anyway? I wondered. Where's Peshawar? What's a Stinger missile? Why did the Americans give Stinger missiles to Islamic fundamentalists? Is Pascal a good kisser? What kind of a name is Gulbuddin Hekmatyar?

My knowledge of world events at that time was woefully scant. Pa-thetic, even. While I had spent a lot of time in college either studying ob-scure historical topics or playing catch-up with the prep school kids—plowing through Shakespeare, *Beowulf,* Kant, the entirety of evolu-tion, studying the Russian revolution in intimate detail, learning more than I cared to know about the monuments of ancient Japan—I'd spent hardly any time reading newspapers or focusing on the present.

Born in 1966, my only real grasp of the post-1968 geopolitical land-scape floated in a haze of fuzzy personal memories, many of them stolen from the TV screen: a black-and-white man on a black-and-white moon, a helicopter leaving the roof of the American embassy in Saigon, the boat children who became my elementary school classmates, Nixon resigning on the new color Sony Trinitron, blood-soaked nightmares about the raid on Entebbe, Walter Cronkite with a peanut farmer from Georgia, bloated corpses lying beside buckets of cyanide-laced Kool-Aid, gas lines after bal-let class, the Ayatollah Khomeini, 444 days, Reagan's inauguration.

As for Afghanistan, the only thing I knew was that America had been angry enough at the Soviet Union for invading the place that we'd boy-cotted the 1980 Moscow Olympics, which meant that I couldn't watch my favorite gymnasts contort themselves into human pretzels. As I fancied myself a gymnast at the time, this ticked me off.

With less than a week to go before taking off for Peshawar, I knew I needed help. Lots of help, lots of information, and fast. I also needed a photo agency to represent me, an agency that, unlike Sygma, did not have someone like Pascal to send to Afghanistan. Though Sygma was distributing my Israel photos, I was not beholden to them. I was not "on staff," which in French photo agency parlance meant that I did not receive a small, monthly advance against earnings, that Sygma had less of an incentive to sell my work (hence the delayed distribution of my photos from Israel), and that I was free, in theory, to distribute my work through any agency I pleased. Of course, loyalty does count, and switching agencies is pretty much frowned upon, but I felt justified in looking elsewhere because I'd yet to earn a single franc as a result of Sygma's representation.

When I asked Chip what he thought I should do, he told me to talk to his agency, Gamma. At Gamma, he said, no one wanted to go to Afghanistan. Though many Gamma photographers had been there before, some repeatedly, not one had any interest in returning for the Soviet pullout. "Too cold and too risky, both financially and otherwise," Chip said, which probably should have raised a tiny red flag, but didn't. The only flag I saw was a shiny purple velvet one with gold tassels and embroidered letters spelling out the word OPPORTUNITY!

I made an appointment to meet with Michel, the news editor of Gamma, a bald, gleeful little man who had covered the early years of the Afghan war and who seemed thrilled to have found in me a chump willing to go.

"So, little girl," he said, "you want to go cover Afghanistan?"

"Yes. And don't call me 'little girl.' "

Little girl. What is it with these photo editors? I thought. I'd read Virginia Woolf and *The Feminine Mystique*. I'd marched in "Take Back the Night" rallies and participated in impromptu feminist consciousness-raising sessions, one of which involved sculpting Play-Doh models of our boyfriends' penises as a means of subverting their power. Proud, torch-carrying, sanctimonious to a fault, I knew a sexist remark when I heard one. Unfortunately, in Paris, especially in the macho clubhouse of photojournalism, sexist remarks were practically all I ever heard.

"Why don't you wear miniskirts more often?" a colleague once asked.

"A little makeup never hurt anyone," said another, who then stared down at my Doc Martens and added, "And what's with the clunky dyke shoes?"

And once, as I was leaning over a light table editing my *intifadah* photos from Israel, wearing a loose tank top to combat the heat from an overzealous radiator, yet another exclaimed, "Deborah, you have such lovely little breasts. You should wear tighter clothes so we can actually *see* them."

Sure. I'll get right on it.

Don't get me wrong. I'll wear a miniskirt or even some lipstick when the occasion calls for it. But when you're running around shooting pictures for a living, the occasion rarely calls for anything beyond jeans, sturdy shoes with rubber soles and climate-sensible outerwear with lots of pockets. My colleagues knew this, but they were suspicious of me, suspicious of the little girl who wanted to join their fraternity. Thus, the hazing. When I told one of them I'd bought my plane ticket to Peshawar, he actually said, without so much as a wink to lessen the sting, "Afghanistan? Shouldn't you be at home making babies?"

"No," I said, indignant, "I shouldn't."

Of this I was certain. When I left college and moved to Paris, churning out babies was the furthest thing from my mind. All of my heroes in the world of photojournalism were, or had been, childless men—photographers like Robert Capa, Gilles Peress, Jim Nachtwey—and I knew if I wanted to devote the rest of my life, like them, to traipsing around the globe in search of conflicts, a family was out of the question. Babies, I knew, required love, patience, selflessness, maternal instinct and maturity, none of which I had in any abundance. How could I nurture a child? I hadn't even begun to nurture myself. I needed to live, to learn, to observe, to create, and insofar as photography allowed me to do all four of these things, I was both smitten and satisfied.

I loved to go out and shoot in strange places, to talk to the types of people I'd never meet were it not for the excuse of the camera. I loved the heft of the black metal in my hands, the way it felt like a weapon. I loved to press the shutter, to freeze time, to turn little slices of life into rectangles rife with metaphor. I loved to collect the rectangles, like so many souvenir trinkets, to gaze at them, study them, find the one that best summarized a particular lived moment. I loved the smell of the black-and-white chemicals. Loved to dip a naked piece of white photographic paper into a bath of developer and watch the image miraculously materialize, watch life, a moment, reborn. Loved rescuing the ever-darkening image, saving it from blackness with my tongs, immersing it into the stop bath, then into the fixer, imagining all those silver crystals stopping, fixing, imagining my little rectangle living on forever.

The omnipotence of it all was overwhelming: you took chaos, threw in a camera, some film and a darkroom, and—voilà—you had order. It was like playing God. If an image looked too dark, you could just close down the aperture on the enlarger a stop or two. If the sky in a photograph was too bright, you could burn it in by cupping your hands and leaving a small hole to spill extra light wherever it was needed. If you felt there was too much empty space, you could just crop it out of the picture.

Try doing that with a baby.

Besides, I knew my limitations. I knew I loved collecting men almost as much as I loved collecting photographs. I could never choose a single photo, from all the images I'd ever shot, to hang on my wall at the expense of all others. So why should I be expected to choose a single man to share my bed for eternity?

Unfortunately, in this calculation of a desired life—a childless, adventure-filled, orgasmic photographic extravaganza—I left out a thorny variable. Namely my extra X, as in chromosome. Even though I'd come of age at the dawn of a revolution, even though my generation of girls was told by our bra-burning forebears we could do any job we pleased, choose any lifestyle we wanted, little had actually changed in terms of traditional male attitudes. Especially in places like Paris. Especially in microcosms like photojournalism. In fact, despite the great cultural strides of twentieth-century feminism, in the eyes of most of my colleagues, in the eyes even of some of my female friends, I was a freak. A little girl gone woefully astray, trying to live her life like a man.

Michel apologized for the slight. "I'm sorry," he said, "I didn't mean to call you a little girl. I just meant that Afghanistan's a scary place and a scary war, and those mujahideen are not going to want to cart around a woman. Especially a woman who looks so much like a child."

He had a point. I'm five foot two on a good day, and with my long hair constantly pulled back into a single braid down my back, I could have passed for fourteen. In my mind I was a six-foot-tall Amazon woman, swathed from head to toe in black leather. But my body, petite, impish and swathed in Lilliputian Levi's and T-shirts, betrayed me.

Surprisingly, despite the stature problem and despite the very real odds against my success, Michel agreed to let Gamma represent me. He was short, too. And, with all of his usual war photographers wimping out, kind of desperate. For the next four hours he gave me a truncated history lesson and explained the lay of the land.

Peshawar, in westernmost Pakistan, he told me, was the seat of the ousted Afghani government. It won that distinction by default. It lay just outside the border of Afghanistan at the end of the dusty Khyber Pass, which was the most direct route to the mountains encircling Kabul, the Afghani capital. There, since their invasion ten years earlier in 1979, the Soviets had set up a puppet regime. And ever since, the mujahideen—freedom fighters in a holy war who were factionalized into fifteen distinct groups, eight Sunni, seven Shiite—had been running back and forth along that road, climbing up those steep mountains and bombing the shit out of Kabul. And sometimes, for variety, out of each other. Best of all, the Americans, whom the Afghanis didn't even seem to like very much, had given these mountain boys the most exciting toys: Stinger missiles. A Stinger, Michel explained, was a portable death machine the size of an average suitcase. Worn on the shoulder, it could pluck down Soviet planes from the sky like so many clay pigeons. "Pow!" he said, firing off an invisible Stinger. "Just like that."

Michel explained that I'd have to find a group in Peshawar to take me "inside," into the interior of Afghanistan, and be my tour guide. He actually said "tour guide," as if there were going to be a big bus with blue upholstered seats and serviettes on the headrests and a polyestered man holding a microphone shouting, "And on your left folks, the remains of a thriving mountain village! And just up there on the right, dead bodies!"

"Oh, and make sure you have really good hiking shoes," urged Michel. "You'll be walking a lot, maybe for days on end. Bring a down sleeping bag, because those caves can get pretty cold at night. Bring medicine for the dysentery you'll probably get, bring as many Snickers bars as you can carry, bring toilet paper, bring a canteen and load it up with snow every morning before you hike . . ." (Tampons, I thought, don't forget tampons.) "bring a Zippo and a flashlight—one of those little Mag-Lites are best—get your shots before you go, bring a big bottle of rubbing alcohol to ward off infection in case you're wounded, and, for God's sake, *do not, under any circumstance, travel alone.*"

•

OUR TRUCK COMES TO A STOP to make way for a wandering
camel. How odd, I think. Aren't camels supposed to live in deserts? It's
thirty below and snowing. There's no way that short fur could ever keep
him warm. What's he doing here all alone? And just where is "here" anyway? He looks so lost. *Hey, camel,* I try beaming to him telepathically, *I
understand.* He plants himself in front of our truck and refuses to budge.
The driver turns off his engine and waits.

By now, just about every mujahed is sniffing around, trying to figure
out where the stench of alcohol is coming from. "My bag. Alcohol. Alcohol
broke. Sorry," I say, but the ragged men just look at me like I'm crazy. "Alcohol, you know, pee-yew! Smelly!" I'm holding my nose now, trying to
make them understand me. Hashim suddenly realizes what he's done.

"Oh, Miss Deborah. Sorry. Sorry." He gets up off the squashed backpack, unzips the side pocket and throws the offending bottle over the side
of the truck. Then, sheepishly, he hands me the soaked, crushed box of
tampons. I bring it under my burka and shine my brand-new Mag-Lite on
it to examine it. The box looks like a hydroponic garden grown amok, the
cotton swollen to at least four times its normal size. The tampons have
burst through their cardboard applicators, through their paper wrappers
and through and beyond the top of the box itself, where they droop over
the sides like soggy dead flowers. Not a single one can be saved. I turn off
my flashlight in defeat and hand the box back to Hashim. "Sorry," he says
once again, tossing the sodden mess over his shoulder, along with a few al-
cohol-soaked rolls of toilet paper. Only one roll of toilet paper has been
spared. It will be put to good use.

We left Peshawar in this truck two days ago, crossing the checkpoints
at the Afghani border with relative ease. I saw next to nothing, however,
because as usual I was stuck under the stupid burka, with only a tiny blue
mesh screen through which to view the world. Peripheral vision in this
thing is nonexistent, and the top often slips down, which makes me blind.
Not the most ideal conditions for anyone, let alone a photojournalist.

The male journalists, as usual, have it much easier. They arrive in Peshawar, grow a beard, buy their shalwar chemises (the pajamalike outfits
worn by Afghanis), their *pakuls* (cuffed wool caps), their blankets and
their army jackets. In their new clothing, with their new beards, they blend

right in with the mujahideen. I assumed I'd be able to do the same, that I could dress like a man, pass for a man like Rosalind in *As You Like It,* but I neglected to consider the facial hair problem. Or the fact that mujahideen don't come in the 108-pound, five-foot-two dwarf variety.

Since leaving Peshawar, the only time I was allowed to remove my burka was at the safe house where we spent our first night, after I was led by the arm, still under the burka, through a labyrinth of winding alleyways and up a flight of stairs. The room, where all forty-eight of us were crammed together on a bare and dirty floor to sleep, was cold and musty, with a tiny space heater in the corner and three pictures of the Ayatollah Khomeini (*444 days, Reagan's inauguration . . .*) staring down from the lime-green walls. Still, it was a room, with four walls, a ceiling, and a floor. And, relieved of my burka for those eight hours, I was happy just to look at it without a screen covering my eyes.

I have no idea where we'll sleep tonight, let alone when we'll sleep tonight, but I bet, wherever it is and whenever we get there, it won't be half as luxurious.

The camel, still not budging, starts to spit on the truck's windshield, then on us. The driver, now annoyed, turns the ignition key, perhaps to scare him, perhaps to try to drive around him, but now the motor won't turn over. He tries again. Then again. The motor is dead. The battery must be working, however, because I can still hear the manic cacophony of Islamic fundamentalist music coming from the cab section of the truck. I turn to Hashim. "What's that music?" I ask him, trying to make conversation.

"Huh?"

"Music, music!" I shout. I'm gesturing like an idiot, pretending to air guitar. "*La la la la,* you know, music!"

"Oh, music. Yes. Famous American man. Now he Muslim, go on jihad. Cat Stevens. You know him?"

I start to laugh. "Yes, I know him," I say.

How appropriate. Mr. Peace Train. On a stalled war truck.

I WASN'T ABLE to get a ticket to Peshawar on the same plane as Pascal, so I flew alone, arriving at the Pearl Continental Hotel a day after he did. The layover in Karachi lasted an excruciating fourteen hours, and I was exhausted, sweaty and jet-lagged by the time I hauled my bags through the revolving doors of the hotel. Pascal was nowhere to be found, so I grabbed a seat in the linoleum-floored, vinyl-upholstered lobby, a lobby like any other Third World hotel lobby, and waited. The plan we had hatched on the telephone back in Paris was fairly simple: since he had most of his journey paid for with assignments from various French and German magazines, and I, the ingenue just starting out, had zero in the way of assignments, I would take advantage of his free hotel room (and, it was understood, his warm body) before finding a group of mujahideen to take us inside. Then, after a brief honeymoon, after offering ourselves up to the almighty Eros, we'd saunter off together, hand in hand, into the heart of Afghanistan, to bear witness to the atrocities of war. Or something like that.

I must have dozed off in the lobby, because the next thing I knew Pascal was leaning over me, kissing my neck, handing me a steaming cup of tea, and purring his greeting, *"Bienvenue à Peshawar. Bienvenue à la guerre"*—"Welcome to Peshawar. Welcome to war." After some niceties (how was your trip fine a little long you look tired no I'm fine are you sure yes really I'm sure it's just a little jet lag I'm sure good glad to hear it yeah well), we got down to business. Sitting down next to me, notebook and pen in hand, he circled the name Abdul Haq on a piece of ruled paper and whispered, "We're in luck. I've just secured a meeting with Haq's people this afternoon. If all goes well, we should be able to go inside in a couple of days." He looked around the lobby to make sure none of the other journalists, all sporting the exact same Banana Republic vests, all running around chasing their tails and whispering to one another, all wearing expressions that screamed *I have a scoop!* even though they probably didn't, were listening to him. I was just happy I'd studied up enough to know who Abdul Haq was.

Abdul Haq was the chief commander of a group of mujahideen, called the Hezbi Islami-Khalis group—Khalis group, for short—who became infamous for dragging Dan Rather and his CBS crews around the Afghani countryside during the height of the war in the mid-eighties. Rather, dressed from head to toe in the latest rebel wear, seemed to really get off on the cowboy-at-war thing. Of course, that could also be said about every journalist in the Pearl Continental's lobby, myself included. In any case, everyone covering the story knew that Haq was smart, media savvy and had the kind of soldiers who, if they could be trusted in the mountains to guard a million-dollar ass like Dan Rather's, could probably be trusted to guard their own bargain-basement butts. Moreover, because of all that favorable CBS coverage, the U.S. had given the Khalis group many Stingers. Pascal, true to his boy nature, wanted to be with the kids with the best toys.

"Haq, huh," I said. "Good work." I said I needed a shower. Pascal, with a sly wink, said he'd like to clean me. Blushing, I picked up my heavy backpack off the floor, but before I could fling it over my right shoulder, Pascal *tsk-tsked* me and slipped it onto his own with little apparent effort. Then, with his free hand, he grabbed my camera bag, hoisted it onto the same shoulder as the backpack, and slowly wrapped his unencumbered arm around my waist, letting his fingers fall just inside the waistband of my jeans. Every hair on my neck stood at attention. *"Après toi,"* he said. After you.

The moment we walked into the hotel room our clothes were on the floor. Toward the end, toward the climax of his gyrations, he yelled out his girlfriend's name. "Élodie!" he cried, which set him back a minute, but only a minute, before he collapsed in a heap on my chest. "Sorry," he said, caressing my hair, reaching down to make amends.

"No problem," I said, and I meant it. I didn't mind playing second fiddle. In fact, I kind of preferred it. In Israel I'd had two lovers: one whose girlfriend once waited for him, sipping a coffee in the outdoor courtyard of the American Colony Hotel, while we had a quickie upstairs in my room; the other whose girlfriend was waiting for him in their shared apartment back home while we sat in his hotel bathtub rubbing fragrant oils over each other's bodies. In Paris, I seduced one conquest in the stairwell of my apartment building and another on the dance floor at Les Bains Douche, both of whom afterwards returned home to live-in lovers. In college, I practically majored in the sport.

I did draw one arbitrary moral line: no married men, never. It seemed too messy, complicated and fraught—not to mention stupid—what with those binding contracts and all. But in my little universe of arbitrary morals, the quasi-attached men, especially the ones with the wandering eyes, were fair game. Why? Because the system seemed to work. I kept my mouth shut, the girlfriends never found out, the men got off on the illicitness and adventure of the stolen moment, and I got off on the no-strings guarantees afterwards, the fact that neither party had any pretensions that what we were engaging in was anything other than sex for sex's sake. The minute a man dared to mention the *L* word, or even skirted around it by discussing some nebulous stable future together, I lost interest. I had no desire to be tied down; I'd known the pain and aching misery of actually falling in—then out—of love, and it was a place I did not want to visit again any time soon. Especially with a roving-eyed, strutting peacock like Pascal.

Pascal finished me off with dexterity and grace. Immediately afterwards he said, "I feel a little guilty."

"Sure you do," I said. *You couldn't give me five minutes to enjoy the aftershocks?*

"No, really, I do," he said, sitting up, checking his hair in the mirror across from the bed, smoothing an errant piece with his palm, lighting a cigarette. "I really do. I think I love her, my little Élodie."

Oh, please. "You think so?" I said. Pascal handed me a cigarette and, ever so gallantly, lit it.

"Yes. I mean, maybe. I mean, maybe what we're doing is wrong."

Spare me the postejaculatory self-flagellation. "Well, it's only wrong if you think it's wrong." *It's only fun until someone loses an eye.* "It all depends on your moral compass."

Pascal absently fondled my breasts. "My moral compass? What's that?"

Bonehead. "Never mind," I said. "Can we talk about this when we're dressed?"

"Sure."

Love? Who did Pascal think he was kidding? He was like me, like every other war-besotted journalist. An unapologetic hedonist. An adrenaline addict, hooked on fresh blood and the high of survival, on the headlines, the deadlines and the steamy après deadlines. He was—we all were—stuck in a state of prolonged adolescence, justifying every puerile action under the clever guise of contributing to a noble cause.

We were newswhores. Journalists. Holy and just. Upholders of the word, disseminators of the image, incapable of loving any one thing or any one person more than the story, more than ourselves.

"Why do you want to cover wars?" Pascal asked me, now lying on his back, blowing smoke rings up to the ceiling.

"I want to make an impact in public policy," I said. "I want to show the world how horrible war is, how it's not necessary, how there must be better means to achieving political ends."

The bullshit was choking me. It's not that I didn't want to make an impact on public policy or think war was horrible. It's just that by saying so I was putting the chicken before the egg. My true impetus for wanting to cover wars was, at its core, selfish. War was exciting, and I despised being bored.

THE ELDEST OF FOUR GIRLS, I grew up in Potomac, Maryland, a leafy suburb outside Washington, D.C., where we moved from our small Adelphi, Maryland, apartment in 1971 when I was four years old. There were seven models of homes in our newly constructed subdivision, all variations on the same modernist theme, with siding and doors of different hues to distinguish one house from another. Our split-level four-bedroom (dark brown siding, red door) was neither the biggest nor the smallest of the lot. From the outside, it looked a lot like the house in *The Brady Bunch*.

My parents, loving, supportive and always well meaning, had both grown up in cities—my mother in the Bronx, my father in Kansas City—and they were convinced that children needed grass, space and clean air in order to thrive. I understood the sentiment, even appreciated the reasoning behind it, but I never accepted its truth. I wanted asphalt. Access to public transportation. A quick way out. People and things to look at. Instead I got grass, lots of grass, grass whose freshly cut blades always smelled to me more like boredom than promise.

My neighborhood public elementary school, in keeping with the times, was constructed in the shape of a flower, with each petal housing different grades. There were no internal walls, no rows of desks, and each morning we'd all gather on the floor in our different "pods" to sing "Joy to the World" (the Jeremiah-was-a-bullfrog! version, not the Christmas carol) and various peace-and-love ditties by Peter, Paul and Mary.

Afterwards, the teachers would set us loose in the hexagonal-shaped room, where colorful easels, called "centers," were set up, each one describing an educational task that needed to be completed by the end of the week, such as "Draw your family" or "Write your autobiography" or "Find out which of these objects floats." I'd take some crayons, draw my father, mother, three younger sisters and me with a rainbow and sun behind us. I'd whip off my life story, remembering to include the part my dad liked to tell about how I was born with an opposable thumb. ("An opposable thumb?" the teacher's aide said. "There's no such thing.") Then, without placing a single object in the tub of water provided, I'd check off rubber duck, wood chip and ball, leaving metal washer, penny and rock blank, I'd answer a few questions about pioneers or jellyfish or whatever else we happened to be studying, and by the end of Monday, I'd be done.

In the earlier grades, I had kindly teachers who would take pity on me and on my friend Ellen, who finished all of her assignments by Monday, too. They'd drop us off in the fifth- or sixth-grade pods for an hour or two, where we'd learn about pi or long division and practice our cursive while our classmates added three apples to two pears and traced the dashed outlines of oversized letters with fat pencils. One day in second grade, Ellen and I decided to memorize fifty digits past the decimal point of pi. Just for kicks.

As I grew older, however, and as my teachers ran out of things for me to do, I had to learn to keep myself busy. Mostly, I'd wander off to the library, housed in an open rotunda in the center of the flower, but after plowing through all of Roald Dahl, all of the *Little House on the Prairie* and Pippi Longstocking books, all of Harriet the Spy and Nancy Drew and the Hardy Boys, *Little Women* and *Black Beauty* and *The Phantom Tollbooth,* all of Judy Blume and a large smattering of the *Encyclopedia Brittanica,* especially the sections on space and on my hero John Glenn, I'd pretty much depleted that source of entertainment, too.

After school, while my mother was upstairs watching TV or struggling with dinner, banging a box of frozen peas against the Formica counter, while my father, like all the other doctor/lawyer daddies in Potomac, was making his way home from his law firm in D.C., I would listen to my *Free to Be You and Me* album in the family room and fantasize about a life where I'd "run off to see the world" like Princess Atlanta, or perhaps cross prairies in my covered wagon into uncharted and dangerous territory, like Laura Ingalls Wilder. A life where I'd chance upon giant peaches and ride horses into the sunset, where I'd sport gravity-defying braids and be mischievous and sassy and witty, where I'd circle the earth in my spaceship, solve lots of mysteries, save unfortunate people from doom and grope lots of boys in darkened closets. A life where I wouldn't have to grow up and drive car pools and wear housecoats and cook meat loaf and watch *The Days of Our Lives* every day to keep up with the story.

Being a girl in the suburbs in the seventies was a tricky business. The mixed signals were everywhere. On the one hand, all the mothers I knew, all of my potential role models, were stay-at-home moms. On the other hand, we had *The Mary Tyler Moore Show*. The choice, to my young eyes, seemed obvious. Mary's life kicked my mother's life's butt.

My mom, who'd conducted at Carnegie Hall at the age of sixteen, who in high school was a virtuoso on the cello *and* on the piano, had wanted to become a doctor. But her father, himself a doctor for the Veterans Administration, told Mom he could not spend what precious little money he had on educating a daughter in the ways of medicine. So she got her master's in education, taught in an elementary school for a year, got pregnant with me, and that was it for her career. She claims she does not regret this, but I was there, and I don't buy it.

But if the signals on the home front were confusing, the signals at school were often more so. In my large public high school, the kind of high school that prided itself on sending its football team to the state championship every year but employed a guidance counselor who had to look up Harvard in the *Barron's* guide when I told him I wanted to go there, it might as well have been 1955 instead of the early eighties. To fit in, to be popular and have boyfriends and invitations to keg parties and access to the higher echelons of suburban teenage power, a girl needed to be a pretty, thin, curvaceous, blond cheerleader. While she didn't necessarily have to be dumb, she could not be smart. She had to wear makeup, lots of it, and constantly talk about her diet. She could aspire to a life as a small business owner (T-shirts, wedding invitations, Lucite napkin holders), or perhaps a dietitian, but that was only before she'd have the kids and settle down in her new Potomac house with her doctor or lawyer husband and her mink stole in the walk-in closet.

In the throes of adolescence, all I cared about was fitting in. I didn't want to spend every weekend alone, babysitting and bored. I didn't want to play Dungeons and Dragons with the pimply kids in my gifted classes. I wanted to get invited to the keg parties and kiss boys. I wanted to be normal. It became clear that I'd have to lead a double life, to hide my inner Pippi Longstocking under a lacquered Barbie mask. Since curvaceous, tall and blond were out of the question, I became a cheerleader to compensate. I bought eye shadow, eyeliner, mascara, lipstick and blush and learned how to apply them every morning before school. On the day report cards were handed out, I'd hide my *A*'s and admit only to *C*'s.

I became so adept at fitting in that I was voted homecoming queen for Christ's sake. But all the acting and hiding and pretending took their toll. I got stoned a lot, wrote bad teenage poems about plastic people who sold their souls to various devils, which I kept hidden behind my bookcase so no one would ever find them. I read Sylvia Plath, flirted with the idea of suicide. I tried to figure out whether I was crazy or whether everyone else around me was crazy, like *One Flew Over the Cuckoo's Nest*. I threw violent tantrums, once kicking an enormous hole in the wall of my bedroom. I started cheating on my jocky boyfriends, having secret, midnight trysts in my bedroom with the boy down the street, a slight, delicate-featured kid barely taller than me, a brilliant and wacky and tender boy who made me feel like I was flying but who was such an outcast in the social hierarchy that we'd ignore each other the next day in the school hallways.

Toward the end of my junior year, I sat down with my parents and told them I had to get out of Potomac. In fact, I wanted to get as far away from Potomac as I possibly could. My father had taken me on a business trip to Japan once, and I asked him if he knew anyone there, a client or even a friend of a client, who might have an extra room in their home for me. Within a week, he found one. You have to love the kind of father who finds you a free room in Tokyo and then transfers all of his frequent flyer points to you to pay for a plane ticket he could otherwise ill afford, simply because you sat him down in the kitchen one night and told him you were so *fucking bored* that if you had to spend one more summer hanging out at the neighborhood pool twirling your lifeguard whistle around your finger, you would probably kill yourself.

That summer in Japan when I was seventeen changed my life. Since my host, Mrs. Nakamura, had to shuttle back and forth between the hotel she owned in Utsunomiya and her apartment in Tokyo, since her teenage daughter spent the entire summer locked in her room studying for her college entrance exams, I luckily had a lot of time on my own. Supporting myself with money earned teaching dance to Japanese students and English to Japanese businessmen, I spent my days exploring the crowded, neon-lit streets of Tokyo, blissfully alone, and my nights with new friends, drinking, dancing to Duran Duran and making out in the bars of Roppongi. I thrived there in Japan, reveled in the daily nuisances, took enormous pride in my own self-sufficiency. Before long, I felt my divided inner and outer selves fusing slowly back together, becoming whole once again.

Anything and everything now seemed possible.

And it was. On my way back to Potomac, I had an affair with a young movie actor on a beach in Hawaii, who later that fall invited me up to New York during a press junket for his new film. I wrote an article about my Japan trip on spec for *Seventeen* and got it published, which then turned into a gig writing book reviews. I applied early to Harvard and got in. I auditioned for a film and got a small part. I cut all my hair off and fell in love—really in love—with Gabe, a well-read, semi-outcast, punk-rock drummer whose hand I proudly held while walking through the judgmental hallways of our high school. After seventeen years of feeling like a fish out of suburban water, I'd finally found the ocean.

Why war? Please. Why *not* war?

I CIRCLED PASCAL's hairless chest with my finger. "What about you, why do you want to cover wars?" I asked him.

"Same as you," he said, "you know, to make an impact on public policy . . ." He blew out three more smoke rings, a floating ellipsis he'd fill in later. Or not.

From there we moved on to the usual. Where did you grow up? Any brothers or sisters? What did you study in school? The kind of things people usually ask each other fully clothed, but I'd lived amongst the French long enough now to have embraced their ethos: fuck first, ask questions later. "What does your mom do?" I said, always curious about mothers.

Pascal smiled proudly, his eyes staring beyond me. "She was a mountain climber. I used to climb with her all the time." He stubbed out his cigarette in the glass ashtray by the bedside.

Of course she climbed mountains. Now I got it. I was no pouty-lipped, long-legged, miniskirted stunner like his girlfriend, but I reminded him of his adventurous *mère*. How Oedipal. "And now what does she do?" I handed him my cigarette to extinguish.

"Nothing. She's dead. Fell off a mountain." He whistled and made a falling motion with his hand, slamming it down on the bed for emphasis. "Just fell off." He was trying to be blasé about it all, hardened, but his blurring eyes spoke otherwise.

"Wow. I'm sorry. I had no idea," I said. Then, after an awkward pause, I added, "I imagine you don't do much climbing anymore."

"Au contraire!" he exclaimed, a little too loudly, a little too pertly. His eyes dried up and a devilish grin spread across his face. "I go all the time. Why wouldn't I? We can't live in the past, you know. I was just climbing two weeks ago." I was about to say something like "Huh?" but then Pascal started to cackle. Like a hyena. "That's funny, Deborah, huh? That I still climb?" He was shaking my shoulders now, trying to get me to laugh. I felt my neck whipping back and forth. "Funny. Ha ha ha. Don't you think it's funny?" His eyes looked possessed, psychotic. The giggling grew more manic. He sprang out of bed, howling and searching the floor for his clothing. Bending over, he thrust one leg in his jeans, then the other, too impatient to bother with the underwear.

"Stop it, Pascal!" I yelled. "You're freaking me out. It's not funny."

When I admitted to Chip that I was going to Afghanistan with Pascal the day before my trip, he'd laughed and said, "I wish you luck. He's insane." Since most war photographers are slightly off-kilter, the statement didn't alarm me. I figured it was jealousy speaking, not anything to be concerned with. Besides, I always thought that if I had to be stuck on a desert isle—or a war-torn mountain—with only one person, I'd take insane over dull any day.

But now I was starting to wonder.

Pascal glanced over his shoulder at me, his eyes frozen, empty, like ice. The tempest had run its course. He pulled his pants over his hips and turned to face me. Slowly, deliberately, and ever so confidently, he zipped up his jeans. Daring me, once again, to stare. To be hypnotized by the power of his perfectly chiseled da Vinci–man symmetry. *"S'il te plaît,* Deborah," he said, his muscles finally relaxing. *"Je plaisantais"*—"Please, Deborah. I was just kidding around." He started to laugh again, this time jovially, even lovingly. He walked over and kissed the top of my head. Then he grabbed a towel from the bathroom, wrapped it around me, and escorted me to the bathroom. "Take a shower," he said, leading me toward the tub. "And get some sleep. I'll be back in two hours or so."

"Where are you going?" I said. The towel came unhitched in front and fell to my ankles. I bent down to pick it up, suddenly embarrassed by my nudity, and wrapped it snugly around me once more.

Pascal said he was going to meet with Abdul Haq to discuss our trip. He said it would be better if he went alone, without me. When I started to protest, said that I should be there to represent myself, he smiled, cupped my face and said, "Deborah, you really do have a lot to learn." He said Muslims are peculiar about women. That we'd have a better chance of hitching a ride inside if he just told Haq that a "friend" would be coming, too, without revealing my gender. "Trust me," he said. "This is the way things are done around here."

Trust me. If any phrase in any language gives me pause, makes me suspect the exact opposite, it is this one. Why start a sentence with it, if not to point out the danger of believing whatever harebrained notion follows?

Then again, who was I to argue? This would be Pascal's third trip inside Afghanistan. I'd never been to a real war before.

THE SNOW HAS STOPPED and the sky has begun to lighten by the time the mujahideen decide to abandon our broken-down truck. We have not slept or eaten for the past twenty-four hours. Through the mesh screen covering my eyes, I can make out the jagged outline of a vast mountain range in the distance dividing earth from blue air, with only the tops of the snowy peaks illuminated by the rising sun, like electric whipped cream. Between us and the mountains lies an enormous, flat, snow-covered expanse, as yet untrod. "We walk," Hashim says, marching in place, pointing across the pristine valley to the mountains. I have no way of judging whether the mountains are near or far, an hour's walk or a day's. The only other mountains I've ever seen had chairlifts. And buses to take me to them. "Go there," he says. "To mountains. Careful mines . . ." He points to the field and makes his hands explode. "Boom," he says. Then, pointing above us, he says, "Planes . . ." Like a kid, he flies his hand through the air and makes a *vroom*-like noise between his lips. "Soviet planes. Danger."

The soldiers start divvying up the supplies, strapping random packages onto their backs, hiding their weapons under the thin brown wool blankets they wear over their shoulders both as extra layers of warmth and as portable prayer mats. Hashim removes my backpack from the truck bed and places it on his shoulders. I thank him for the gesture, glad not to have to carry it for the next few hours (days, months?) of hiking, but then Hashim lifts up the edge of my burka to grab for my camera bag, too. "No, no, it's okay," I say, pulling it back. "It's not too heavy." I may be inexperienced in the ways of war, but I'm savvy enough to know that a photojournalist, like a soldier, should avoid being separated from her weapons.

Hashim will hear nothing of it. "No pictures," he says. "Danger. Planes." He points to the sky again and then mimes a pair of binoculars over his eyes, which I assume means that somehow a Soviet pilot might see me taking pictures and realize we're not a ragged band of refugees but rather what we are, a group of mujahideen with a broken-down truck and a photojournalist in a burka along for the ride. It seems a bit overcautious, but I console myself with the thought that my batteries, the ones that power the light meters of my manual cameras and allow me to determine important stuff like f-stops and shutter speeds, have been in the cold for too long now to function anyway. "Here," says Hashim, swapping me his Kalashnikov for my Domke bag. "Take gun. Hide it."

Oh, great. I'm sure I'm breaking a cardinal commandment of journalism—*Thou shalt not carry thy subject's loaded weapons*—but I do as I'm told. I lift up the side of my burka and throw the Kalashnikov over my shoulder, which, once covered, sticks out in back like a miniature blue tent. Some of the mujahideen point at me and laugh, and I wonder if they're laughing because of the tent or because they find the sight of a girl with a gun amusing.

"I have to pee," I tell Hashim, realizing it's now or never if I'm going to deal with my little problem. As usual, Hashim assigns a mujahed to walk ahead of me to check for mines. I grab the remaining roll of toilet paper from the pocket of my backpack and follow the soldier, careful to step in his exact snow tracks as we move away from the group. After twenty yards or so, the mujahed turns his back, walks a few yards away, and lets me do my business. Before I even unbutton my jeans, I can feel the warm, gloppy blood running down my leg, soaking through my two pairs of white thermal underwear. I squat down to get started, but I forget about the Kalashnikov on my shoulder. The butt of the rifle hits the ground behind me, banging the cold metal barrel into the back of my head.

I know I should try to laugh. I know I should try to connect with the humor and irony in the situation, but somehow, with the frozen limbs, the bloody pants, our broken truck, my exploded tampons, a gun barrel at my head, the burka and the Soviet planes intent on our demise, I can't.

After urinating, I do my best to wipe up the blood sticking to the inside of my thighs, but maneuvering under the burka, even seeing anything clearly under the folds of material, is close to impossible. I remove the old tampon and, at a loss for a better means of disposal, bury it in the snow with my hands. Then I make a huge wad of toilet paper and wedge it into my bloodstained underwear, hoping it'll do the trick until I can figure out a better solution.

I button my jeans, readjust the Kalashnikov and am about to start walking back to the group when I notice the patch of snow at my feet is soiled, spotted with crimson droplets. Embarrassed, I kick some fresh powder on top to try to make the whole mess go away.

We spend the next eight hours trekking through the knee-deep snow in a single-file line, ants scurrying along as the Soviet planes circle overhead. The mountain range taunts us, never seeming to get any closer. I am exhausted and famished, on the verge of hypothermia. But my major problem is the burka. Not only is the rayon too thin to keep my head warm, the stupid thing keeps slipping down. Tripping me. Making me blind. How in God's name, or Allah's name, do Afghani women deal with these ridiculous things?

We women are cursed. Never mind the blood and the mess; that I can deal with. I'm talking about the fear of female sexuality, pure and not so simple. What is it about our bodies that scares men so, makes them take such extreme measures to put us in our places? If they're not stopping us on the streets in the supposedly enlightened parts of the world to whistle, grab their crotches, lick their tongues between opened fingers, yell obscenities or proposition us with erect bananas—I, like most women, speak from a deep well of experience here—then they're hiding us under burkas or veils in other parts of the world so that they won't be tempted to do so.

I yank the burka off my head and throw it on the ground. "No more!" I yell to Hashim, which causes all the men to stop and stare. I look around me. I know it's dangerous to be out of disguise, but under the current circumstances I could care less. Wow, I think. What freedom to see the world once again! To gaze at that beautiful, jagged, gigantic, imposing, soaring ice-capped mountain range in the distance!

"Put on," Hashim says.

"No," I say. "I won't."

"Put on," he repeats, this time more slowly.

I stand my ground. "No."

"Is dangerous," he says.

I say, "I know. So make me a man."

For a moment, the situation is tense. Hashim stares at me, at a loss for words. Some of the other mujahideen whisper to each other, point at me, gesticulate. I was told by countless mujahideen groups back in Peshawar that, as a woman, I would not be able to accompany their soldiers inside. "Women," one of them told me, "are by their very natures cursed charlatans, bent on breaking the will and sapping the strength of the soldiers of Allah." To which Pascal whispered, a little too smugly, "You see? I told you so."

But now that I'm here and Pascal's not, now that our truck has broken down and we're cold and miserable and walking through an endless minefield of snow, now that I cannot walk another inch with this idiotic rayon cloth over my head, what are they going to do? Take me back to Peshawar? Punish me for not wearing it?

And then, suddenly, an amazing thing happens. One of the soldiers walks over and hands me his *pakul* for my head. Another gives me one of his brown shoulder blankets to hide the Kalashnikov. Then, Hashim, looking slightly defeated, takes a thick cotton scarf and ties it around my neck and mouth, so no one will be able to tell that I don't have a beard. I have won. It's a small victory, but I have won.

I am, for the moment, a man. A tiny, happy, bleeding man.

We trudge farther and farther through the snow. I have no clue where we are, other than somewhere in the Hindu Kush. I try getting information from Hashim, but every time I ask, "Where are we?" he smiles politely and responds, "Afghanistan."

We finally arrive at the foothills of the mountains as the sun sets, turning the snowy tips of the smaller mountains behind us a deep orange, striating the sky above the darkened mountains in front of us into graduated shades from pink to blood red. It is the most breathtaking sight I have ever seen, and I stop for a moment to inhale the colors, convinced that they might warm my aching, frozen limbs with their fire. Up close, the mountains dwarf me, dwarf us all. It would be so easy to get lost here. To disappear.

Some of the mujahideen stop too, but not, apparently, to dwell upon the meaning of the universe and their place in it. Instead, they pass around a round metal container of green, powdery paste, a mild, teeth-rotting drug called *naswar*, which they stick in their mouths like chewing tobacco. I have no interest in trying their naswar, but I must say I am tempted by the large bags of opium I saw a few of them smoking that first night in the safe house. How pleasant it would be to stop right here, light a fire, smoke some opium and watch the red sky turn black, maybe have some great stoner thoughts about being a cell on a giant's thumbnail, or a quark in a Milky Way dust storm.

After another pee stop, we fill our canteens with snow and march on and up. We have not heard a plane for over an hour now. The silence is profound, broken only by the wind and by the rhythm of our crunching footsteps. "Soon there," Hashim says. "Very soon."

By nightfall, we finally reach a cave. It's a large cage, a furnished cave, actually, with a potbellied stove, a couple of heroic-looking framed portraits of various Islamic men hung, somehow, from the stone wall, some kerosene lamps, a black metal pot, a tin tray with a whole stack of glass cups for tea, a few stacks of tin bowls, a wooden box of tin spoons and a large gun rack to hold all the Kalashnikovs. The mujahideen step inside, lay down their brown blankets on the cold earth, face Mecca, and for the fourth time today begin to pray. *"Bismillah al-rahman al-rahim"*—"In the name of the God, the beneficent, the merciful . . ." Knees bend, hands palm in palm, worry beads dangling, bodies up, bodies down, bodies prostrated to Allah, blessed be He.

Before leaving Peshawar, Hashim had asked me if I were a Christian. When I told him I was a Jew, his face tensed and he said it would be best if I did not admit this to any of the other mujahideen. "They no like Jew," he said.

"Yeah, well, get in line," I said, but when he looked at me quizzically, I said, "No problem. Our secret."

Then, as an extra precautionary measure, he insisted on teaching me the first line of the Koran along with the *kalima*—the profession of faith—suggesting I mouth the words along with the mujahideen when they pray. *"La ilaha il-Allah Muhammad al-rasul Allah . . ."*—"There is no god but Allah, and Muhammad is his prophet . . ."—the men continue, and I dutifully move my mouth in unison. Apparently, if you can recite that one line from the kalima, you can be considered a Muslim. A snap, as conversions go. Unfortunately, I find that every time the mujahideen pray, it triggers the Hebrew tune "He Nay Ma Tov" to pop into my head, which competes with my mouth's ability to recite the Islamic prayers. Probably some ancient Hebraic defense mechanism wired into my genetic code.

Another band of mujahideen—same Shiite group, the Harakat-I-Islami—have stopped here, too, for the night. The have a fire going underneath the metal pot, and four of them are sitting around it, stirring its greasy, glutinous contents with makeshift spoons, pausing periodically to puff on their Winstons. "What is it?" I ask Hashim.

"Fat," he says. "From mutton."

I feign excitement. "Oh," I say. "Great."

It must be either from this vat or from the tea water that I will contract the amoebic dysentery that will dog me for the next few months. As blissfully unaware of the single-celled creatures swimming around my food as they are of me, I slurp up the steaming fat with the rest of the men sitting cramped together in our cave, our new home, dipping in freshly baked nan and drinking glass after glass of sugary tea, feeling the warm liquids slide down my esophagus and into my cold, empty stomach. Life is good, I think. I'm not frozen, I have shelter, bread and a bowl full of warm fat. I can handle this.

After dinner, the men spread out their brown blankets, and I unroll my very expensive light blue French down sleeping bag, tested in the cold of the Alps, and prepare for slumber. Some of the men huddle together for warmth. Little puffs of steam emerge from our mouths. If I'm a bit concerned about being the only woman in a small cave full of men, I try not to show it. Besides, these are Islamic warriors, most with wives and families back in Peshawar; were they to commit adultery with me, their prescribed penalty would be death. This is a comforting thought.

One of the mujahideen tunes his radio to the Pushto version of the BBC, and though I can't understand a word of this evening's report, the familiar regal horns that usher in the hourly news is unexpectedly soothing, like a lullaby.

The voice from the radio begins. Suddenly, some of the men sit bolt upright. Then more. A few men start to speak angrily, gesticulating wildly. Two are laughing. Soon all the mujahideen are sitting up. Uh, guys, what's going on? I strain to understand anything being said, and suddenly I catch a familiar refrain. "*Blah, blah, blah,* Salman Rushdie, *blah, blah, blah, blah, blah, blah,* Salman Rushdie, *blah, blah,* Rushdie, *blah, blah, blah.*" I know Salman Rushdie is a writer, but why is a book review leading the top of the BBC?

I tug on Hashim's jacket, but he shoves me away. "Shh," he says, "must listen." Then, after a minute or so, he says, "Ah, Miss Deborah. It's book. Book. Salman Rushdie, he write very bad book."

So no one will buy it, I think. What's the big deal?

A lively discussion is now erupting all over the cave. The men grab their Kalashnikovs. What the hell is going on?

"Sorry," I say. "I don't understand."

"Ah, Miss Deborah. Salman Rushdie write bad book. Bad for Allah. Not nice to Allah. Bad, bad, bad to Allah. We Muslim. Must kill him." And with that, Hashim and his band of crazy warriors of Islam run out of the cave into the cold darkness, where they proceed to shoot off hundreds of rounds of ammunition into the starry night sky, yelling, *"Allah akbar! Allah akbar!"*—"God is great! God is great!"—each vowing to kill Salman Rushdie should the unfortunate writer stroll through our cave in our nameless mountain somewhere in Afghanistan. I follow them outside, but now Hashim tells me they're yelling, "Down with America! Down with America!" and I start second-guessing my decision to be out here.

Amid the frenzied delirium, I try explaining to Hashim that Salman Rushdie is either British or Indian, depending on your cultural bent, but he's certainly not American, and that in any case, weren't we Americans funding this war of theirs anyway? We donate Stingers to your jihad, I remarked, but a writer—an Anglo-Indian writer, at that—insults Allah and now you want to kill Americans? Am I missing something here? The noise of the bullets is deafening. I feel a little ill. I make my way back into the cave, and suddenly I'm barfing semidigested mutton fat all over my fancy blue sleeping bag.

PASCAL AND I SPENT the week after our arrival in Peshawar in suspended anticipation of our trip. Hedging our bets, we hired a driver to take us around the city in search of other rebel contacts in case the Khalis trip fell through.

Not getting lost in Peshawar, let alone finding the scattered houses used by the mujahideen as their headquarters, was no easy feat. Peshawar, a warm and mild place even in the winter, seemed not so much a city as it did an outgrowth, a chaotic, crowded, litter-strewn jumble, a haphazard frontier town to its core. Its narrow, dusty roads, many unpaved and unmarked, were overrun with cars, colorful rickshaws and horse-drawn tongas and bordered on either side by squat, sherbet-hued buildings with Juliet balconies. The ground floors of these buildings housed tiny open-air shops and four-table restaurants, always crowded, always busy. Pedestrians, a variegated mix of clean-shaven Pakistanis, bearded Afghanis in their shalwar chemises—many of whom were amputees on crutches—as well as the random flock of Afghan women, walking in tight burka bouquets like boxes of crayons sprung to life, shared the bustling sidewalks with street vendors selling warm nan and various kebabs, whose steamy smoke mixed with the smell of burning trash and car exhaust to give Peshawar its distinct aroma: polluted mesquite, if I had to pin it down.

Once we reached the arid, flat outskirts of the city, where most of the mujahideen headquarters were located, the air was cleaner but more pungent, which was not surprising considering that at dawn, in certain parts of town, entire extended Afghani families lined up together to squat over the nearest ditch for their morning constitutionals.

It usually took our driver about half a dozen tries to find the correct building housing our mujahideen contacts, after which we had to convince the bored security guards to let us through the gate.

In deference to the soldiers, I kept my head covered under a veil during these visits, as I'd been told to do, but even so the mujahideen would often insist that I wait in an outdoor courtyard or on the floor of a tiled hallway while Pascal conversed, drank tea with and charmed the shalwars off the groups' leaders.

"Ça va?"—"Everything okay?"—he'd say with a smile when he'd emerge from the smoky room.

"Oui," I'd lie. "Ça va."

The truth was that everything was not okay. During those long waits in the courtyards and hallways, smoking cigarettes and drinking tea by myself, I had way too much time to reflect and worry. I didn't like having to depend on one person for so much: for contacts with the rebel groups, for my lodging, for sex, for comfort, for companionship.

Pascal had been acting irrationally lately, one minute playing the adorable clown in the middle of a busy intersection, pretending to direct traffic, smiling and blowing kisses at me and making everyone laugh, the next minute losing his temper because I'd left one of my shoes on the bed. One minute skipping hand in hand with me through the colorful bazaars of Peshawar, buying me an army jacket and my blue burka and blushing

PESHAWAR, PAKISTAN, 1989

as he handed them to me in a crumpled pink plastic bag. The next minute having a tantrum because he missed an important phone call.

Then there was the day he drove me to the squalid Kachagari refugee camp so I could photograph the war widows there. It was the only place, he said, where he was sure I'd be more welcome as a female photographer than as a male. "I know you've been having a hard time," he said. "It'll be good for you." When we got there, since Islamic law forbade him from photographing the women's faces, he helped me by distracting the hordes of curious children. He gave them ballpoint pens and peanuts. He bent over and tenderly wiped a smudge off a little boy's face. He danced with the children in a circle, sang songs and held hands with them right there in the midst of makeshift tents and open pits of human feces, made them giggle and soar like children should giggle and soar.

But on the way home in the car, he realized he'd lost one of his notebooks. He started screaming, accusing me of leaving it somewhere. "Where the fuck did you put it?" he bellowed.

"I didn't touch your notebook," I said, trying to remain calm. I'd learned that with Pascal, it was best to remain calm.

When we got back to the hotel, he turned our room upside down looking for his missing notes and in his swirling frenzy wound up shoving me so hard I fell to the ground, hitting my head on the nightstand on the way down.

That night, after apologizing profusely, after making love to me with such tender contrition I thought he might cry, he told me, once again, that he felt guilty about having sex with me, that he loved Élodie, that I should get my own goddamned hotel room.

It was becoming a nightly pattern.

"But I can't!" I'd tell him. "You knew that from the start."

"I know, but I feel stuck now!" he'd yell.

"Oh, yeah?" I'd yell back. "Well, you should've thought of that before you invited me to come here with you, because so do I!"

I *was* stuck. Never mind that with every visit to these mujahideen groups I realized just how dependent I was on Pascal to get me inside. Never mind that with every one of his mood swings I trusted him less and less and was fearful of letting him out of my sight, lest he should try to make arrangements to go inside that wouldn't include me. The simple fact was that I did not have enough money to cover more than two or three nights in the Pearl Continental (all the cheaper motel rooms in Peshawar were booked solid), which would have left me with nothing for food, transport or emergencies in the long days, perhaps weeks of waiting to follow. And the last thing I wanted to do was to have to stoop to asking my parents to wire money. Never mind that I knew it would stretch them financially— with three more daughters either in or about to enter college, they were stretched just about as thin as a family could get—my pride simply precluded it. I valued my independence and my freedom and my privacy and my new sense of myself as a self-sufficient professional far too dearly to make that call.

Five minutes after one of our altercations, and you could time a watch by it, Pascal would calm down and apologize: I'm sorry I yelled at you. I'm sorry I accused you. I'm sorry I pushed you. I'm sorry I don't love you.

It's okay, it's okay, it's okay, it's okay, I'd say. I never expected you to be a saint. And I certainly never expected you to fall in love with me. I could never fall in love with you either. I only expected you to help me. To keep me warm at night. To take me to war. That's all.

"Come on," he'd say, taking my hand, "let's go to the American Club."

The American Club was the only place in Peshawar allowed to serve alcohol, so you could be sure that any CIA spook, journalist or aid worker you needed to speak to would be there at night. It was at the American Club where I befriended one of the only other women covering Afghanistan, a *New York Times* stringer named Donatella, who took me under her wing, gave me an entire notebook's worth of contact names and numbers and told me not to trust anyone. *Anyone.* Not the spooks, not the mujahideen, not that guy Kurt over there, not the bartenders, not those two aid workers sitting in the corner and for God's sake, not the French journalists. Especially that pretty-boy frog I'd been shacking up with.

"You mean Pascal?" I asked Donatella, knowing full well who and what she meant.

"Keep your eye on him," she said.

"Oh, he's okay." I feigned confidence. "I trust him. I mean, he invited me here. We're going inside together." Of course, after a week of spinning our wheels in Peshawar, I was starting to doubt we'd ever see the war, ever get inside. That's why all the other journalists sitting around us were so drunk. Waiting took its toll.

When I told Donatella that Pascal was pretty sure we'd be going inside with Abdul Haq's group any day now, she looked at me skeptically. "Haq doesn't like women," she said. Donatella was the first woman Abdul Haq had allowed to accompany him on his most recent raid inside Afghanistan, but Haq knew Donatella's words in *The New York Times* would be read by presidents and policy makers. Even so, it had taken her a lot of cajoling to procure a seat with the Khalis brigade. The more she explained to me, the more ludicrous it seemed that I'd ever have a chance of hitching a ride into Kabul with Khalis, with or without Pascal's help. Because unlike Donatella's words, which filled column after published column, my as-yet-unshot photos were highly unlikely to ever see the light of day.

Most of the other photographers covering Afghanistan had at least five or six assignments from various international publications—from *Paris Match* or *Der Spiegel* or *Il Venerdi* or *The Independent*—regardless of whether or not they actually saw a day of war. Their day rates would be paid, their film reimbursed. Pascal had at least seven magazines waiting for whatever images of Afghani soldiers at war he might produce. My one piddly conditional assignment from *U.S. News & World Report*, which I only got because I happened to have lunch at the American Club one day with their correspondent Emily MacFarquhar, who took pity on me because I'd gone to college with her daughter Larissa, was practically a joke.

The pending assignment had been arranged back in the States not through Gamma, the photo agency I was supposed to be working for, but rather through Contact, another photo agency that had been courting my services. I met the president of Contact, Bob Pledge, when I was a senior at college; my black-and-white photo thesis had been nominated for a prize in the W. Eugene Smith Humanitarian Photography Award, and Bob had been one of the judges.

Most photojournalists worked with these agencies in a not-so-mutually-beneficial relationship that initially benefited the agency much more than the photographer. The photographer basically had to front the money for his or, in my case, her trip. Sometimes the agency threw in the film, sometimes it didn't. Some agencies split expenses with the photographers, others didn't. Once a photographer decided to jump on a plane, to jump on a story, the agency was then supposed to be in charge of finding assignments from magazines like *Time* or *Newsweek* that paid measly "day rates" of $350 at the time of my trip to Afghanistan, a range which had not budged since the early eighties. The photographer had to then split his fee with the agency, along with equally dividing the earnings for individual photos used in the magazines, if any.

What little money there was in photojournalism rested in archive sales after the fact, with the average photojournalist earning, at that time, somewhere between five to thirty thousand dollars a year from such sales along with assignment money if he was lucky. So while a photographer working steadily for ten years might have a lean year or two, for temporary want of a war or a flood or a famine or two, he could theoretically live off the money from archive sales during the down times, especially as his archive grew in size and scope. However, more often than not, a fallow year meant missed mortgage payments, delayed alimony payments, increased credit card debt. World peace could really kill your cash flow.

Gamma was a bigger agency, with a convenient office in Paris (at that time, Contact only had an office in New York), and with their vast international network of photo distribution, I'd be sure to earn more money with my pictures in their archives. But Contact was more prestigious, smaller. Annie Leibovitz was a member; so was David Burnett.

Ultimately, however, I placed a call from our hotel room to Jeffrey, Contact's assignment editor in New York, to let him know I'd work for Contact instead of Gamma during my time in Afghanistan, not because of Leibovitz or the prestige or Bob, but because Pascal, when he found out I'd signed on with Gamma, became so enraged he knocked over a lamp. When he calmed down, he let me know in no uncertain terms that if I were working for his agency Sygma's direct rival, there'd be no way we could go inside Afghanistan together. No way. Not possible. And I had no intention of traveling alone.

When I called Michel at Gamma to tell him of my decision, he was furious. But when I explained that it was because of Pascal, he suddenly softened. Grew paternal, even. "Pascal? From Sygma?" he said. "*Putain*, Deborah . . ." (There's that word again, I thought. Whore.) ". . . be careful."

"Just be careful," Donatella was saying, "I don't want to see you get hurt." She slugged down the rest of her beer and asked me if I wanted anything from the bar.

"Another beer," I said. I handed her some money.

She pushed my hand away. "It's on me."

When she stood up, I stared over the length of the bar at Pascal. He was chatting up the head spook, sitting directly under a concentrated cone of amber light, glowing. Smoking a cigarette whose fiery embers flew through the air with every exaggerated flail of his hands. Bombs. He's making bomb motions with his arms and laughing with the spook, I thought to myself. I knew, because I'd seen those exploding arms before, the couple of times I'd heard him tell his Beirut stories. "*Mon dieu*," he'd say, laughing, "You should have seen those bombs!"

Mon dieu, indeed, I thought, continuing to stare, feeling my heart race despite my head. People should not be allowed to be born that beautiful. They get away with too much. Beauty is truth? That last couplet always bothered me. In art, in an urn, maybe, but in people, no way. In fact, sometimes I think physical beauty may be the biggest scam ever played upon mankind.

Pascal finished recounting his tales and then came sauntering over to my table. He was dressed in his uniform of choice. Levi's. Paraboots. A photographer's vest. And underneath the vest, a clean, pressed blue button-down shirt, opened at the collar to reveal a red bandanna tied around his neck. In our hotel room he had a whole stack of these blue shirts, all pretty much the same. And six more red bandannas. You'd think I would have seen through this. I mean, who packs seven neck scarves to cover a war? He presented me with a Kahlua and cream just as Donatella returned with my beer. "That's okay," I said, grabbing a drink in each hand, "I'll take both."

"Hello, Miss Donatella, how are you?" he purred. When Pascal spoke English, he sounded like Inspector Clouseau. No *h* sounds. It came out as, "Eh-lo, mees Doe-natella, ow ahr yew?"

"Just lovely, Pascal, 'ow are you?" She smiled. "Deborah tells me you're taking her inside. With Haq, of all people. Impressive."

"Yes," he said, lighting another cigarette to avoid her dubious stare.

We soon had a crowd around our big wooden table, a rabid pack of cowboy journalists, smoking cigarette after cigarette, all of us drinking ourselves into a stupor. Even though I was still a novice, I was starting to realize that this is what war journalists do. You go out in the morning, make contacts, or not, try to work, or not, dodge a bullet or two, or not. Then you run back to the bar and join the others so you can get drunk and brag, like Pascal, about that bomb in Beirut or, like the grizzled Italian cameraman, about the Tonton Macoute in Haiti who wanted to adorn his hut with your severed head, or, like the BBC documentary producer, about how you personally saved an entire Bangladeshi family from drowning during last monsoon season. All the while you're stubbing butt after butt into the communal ashtray with precision and dramatic purpose, as if daring God to strike you down. And if you hang around with the same journalists in the same godforsaken city long enough, you get to hear the same war stories again and again, the bombs growing bigger and more deadly with each retelling, the black humor becoming darker and more cynical until every single word is drained of meaning.

Sometime around midnight, I was dully staring over at a dart game in the back corner of the bar when I realized I recognized one of the players. His face looked vaguely familiar, but it was covered with a beard and attached to an emaciated body, and I couldn't, for the life of me, figure out where I might have seen that face or Giocametti body before. But he caught me staring at him, put down his darts, and ran over. "Deborah!" he shouted, embracing me. "What the hell are you doing here?"

The voice gave him away. "My God, Robert, is that you?" Already thin to begin with, Robert appeared to have lost nearly thirty pounds, and this together with his unkempt beard made him look a bit like what I imagined

Jesus must have looked like, if he'd been hung from the cross in a frayed Brooks Brothers shirt and old khakis. Robert and I had been good friends in college—and once lovers during a giddy, drunken weekend at a friend's lake house in New Hampshire—and it was so incongruous seeing him there, in that strange bar, in that strange city so far from Cambridge, Massachusetts, that I thought I was having an alcohol-induced hallucination.

Robert told me he'd decided to move to Peshawar after graduation and that he'd been writing freelance articles on the war for the London *Times*, as well as teaching English and math to nine- and ten-year-old Afghani boys, the future generation of mujahideen. "You know, 'If I give Ali three Stingers and Mustafa takes two, how many Stingers will Ali have left?' Stuff like that." He laughed, keenly attuned, as always, to the absurdities of life. When he caught me studying his emaciated stomach, he explained that he'd had a few bouts with dysentery. "Nasty little buggers, those amoebas," he said. He eyed Pascal, trying to form an opinion. "And who's this?"

Pascal stuck out his hand to shake Robert's with dramatic flourish and purpose. "Pascal. *Agence Sygma. Bonjour.*" When Pascal introduced himself like that it made me cringe. Turning to me, still speaking in French, he said, *"C'est ton ancien petit copain, n'est-ce pas?"*—"He's your old boyfriend, isn't he?" His voice was laced with arsenic.

Robert responded, in perfect French, *"Pas exactement."*—"Not exactly." The two men stared at each other as men and lions are prone to do. After a pause Robert added, also in perfect French, "Never assume that all of us stupid Americans can only speak English." He smiled. *"N'est-ce pas?"* Pascal threw a proprietary glance my way and then excused himself to go join another table of drunk journalists recounting their never-ending war stories. Over the din of the bar I could hear the BBC guy shouting, "Liberia? Now that's a pig fuck if ever I've seen one."

Robert took Pascal's vacated seat. "Well, he seems like a perfectly nice asshole," he said. We spent the next half hour gossiping, and then Robert and his housemate Steve, one of the many conservative activists who'd flocked to Peshawar to watch the mujahideen kick some commie ass, brought down the house with their guitar and harmonica version of the old Chuck Berry song "Maybelline." Only in this version, the title female's name had been switched to Gulbuddin, so the song came out as *"Oh, Gulbuddin, why can't you be true? Oh, Gulbuddin, why can't you be true? . . ."* Rumor had it that Gulbuddin Hekmatyar, rebel leader of the Hezbi Islami-

Hekmatyar group, liked to kill journalists. Since most of the people hanging out at the American Club that evening had nightmares about stuff like that, they laughed and sang along in a raucous, drunken chorus. Years later, after the Soviets were long gone and the notes from Robert's song had long since faded, Gulbuddin Hekmatyar would become the president of Afghanistan.

Sometime after midnight, the party moved to Robert's house, which offered a welcome change from the dreary Pearl Continental. Because Robert was a resident, the spacious house he shared with Steve, various other Western roommates and their pet hawk, Zia al Hawk (named after the former president of Pakistan, who that summer had died when the plane he was flying on blew up), felt homey, lived in. And as a large group of us began to smoke opium on the intricately woven Afghani rugs in the living room, it felt downright womblike.

Robert's roommates, some of whom smoked with us, others who slept through our revelry, were a motley crew. Lisa, a conservative like Steve, was a freelance writer for the *Washington Times* and the Asian *Wall Street Journal*. Bill, a liberal, produced for CNN. Sparkle, who lived up to her name, was Bill's wife and spent much of the day with her typewriter. Joe shot pictures for the Associated Press. Steve smoked a lot of opium, wrote an article here and there, told a lot of jokes and basically kept the house running smoothly. (Lisa would go on to write Dan Quayle's *Murphy Brown* speech, Sparkle would go on to divorce Bill and write detective novels, Steve would continue his humanitarian fieldwork in war-torn countries, Robert would get his Ph.D. from Oxford and Joe's body would be found approximately a year later, for reasons not entirely clear, at the bottom of a swimming pool in Thailand.)

There were other faces, other stories assembled that night in that smoky living room, but as the opium started to take effect, as the disparate tales of searching and self-discovery blended one into the other, everything became fuzzy and pink, like cotton candy. With Pascal passed out on the floor, Robert crawled over to me, eyes half mast, and said he often thought about that night we'd spent together in New Hampshire, how it was nice. And good and true. And what I saw in this impertinent—he pointed to Pascal—bandanna-wearing shit, he'd never understand.

"He's taking me inside," I said, repeating the mantra. "We're going inside together."

Robert lay his head in my lap. "Oh, I get it," he said. "So you're using each other."

I digested the words. "If you want to look at it that way, yes." I could have elaborated. I could have told Robert that sex with Pascal was like listening to Bach's Double Concerto, only better. Or explained that the only thing I really cared about was getting inside that war. Or warned him that I had no overly pressing need for things nice and good and true. Like love. Or him. Or admitted that the night after our tender tryst in New Hampshire, the one he remembered with such fondness, I jumped into bed with one of his best friends while he was passed out in another room. But Robert closed his eyes, fell asleep and the moment, thankfully, was lost.

I looked around the room and realized I was the only one left awake. I took Robert's head in my hands, lifted it off my knees, and gently laid it on the carpet. He didn't stir. Then I woke up my crazy French lover with a kiss and a shove to the ribs, and the two of us slipped out into the cool night, the human detritus of the evening sprawled haphazardly all over the floor behind us.

The next day, finally, we had a breakthrough. As Pascal and I lay in bed, nursing twin hangovers, the phone rang. Pascal answered, as usual. I wasn't allowed to answer the phone in case Élodie called. It was Abdul Haq's people. They said they were all set to take us inside the following day. Pascal sprang out of bed and started dancing naked around the room. "See, Deborah, I told you everything would work out okay." He lifted me up and tangoed me across the floor.

To celebrate, we took advantage of the Pearl Continental's private sauna for our one last taste of civilization and cleanliness. We sat there together, quiet and calm, watching the steam envelop each other's bodies. I breathed in the heavy damp air, trying to purify my lungs from the previous night's debauchery, all the while staring at Pascal's lean, muscular torso, simultaneously cursing and savoring its perfection, its power.

Tomorrow I will see a war, I thought. I wonder what that means?

After the sauna, Pascal and I went back to our room, made love and fell asleep. Just before dinner, he decided to take a shower, and that's when everything went downhill. While he was off scrubbing himself, the phone rang. I knew I wasn't supposed to answer it, but I was worried that it might have been Haq's people trying to reach us with further instructions for our trip inside. The phone rang again. I didn't know what to do. I yelled to Pascal, but he couldn't hear me, and then the phone rang a third time and I decided I had to pick it up. "Hello?" I said into the receiver.

"*Uh, bonjour.*" The voice was female, melodious. "*Qui êtes-vous?*"—"Who are you?"—she asked. It was the voice that I remembered so distinctly from the dinner party at Pascal's apartment in Paris.

"Oh, I'm, uh, a friend of Pascal's. Uh, a journalist. We were just going over some notes together, you know, contact names and such. . . ." I stumbled over my words, uncomfortable with lying. I'm a bad liar.

Pascal emerged from the shower, one towel slung around his waist, another with which he massaged the water out of his wet, black hair. He saw me on the phone. His face visibly reddened.

"Who's that?" he barked. "Who's on the phone?"

My hands started to shake. I struggled to breathe. "Uh, it's Élodie." Then, with the receiver pressed into my palm lest she should hear, I whispered to Pascal, "I told her we were just going over some notes. That I'm just a journalist friend—"

He yanked the phone from me, turned on his ever-so-charming demeanor and continued the lie where I left off. "*Salut, ma biche!* No, she's just a colleague. Yes, yes, you have met her. Right, at our dinner party. Yes, Chip's girlfriend. The American girl. Sure, I'll say hi. I miss you, too, my darling." He told her he'd be going inside the next day, that she shouldn't expect a phone call from him for another few weeks, maybe even a month or so. Though his voice was calm, even fluffy while speaking to Élodie, as I stood there by the side of the bed his eyes stabbed me with their daggers. "Right, then. Yes, I promise to call as soon as I'm out. Yes, I'll be careful. Okay, I love you, too. Bye."

Pascal hung up the phone. Then he slammed the receiver down onto the cradle over and over and over. Slam! "What the fuck were you thinking!" Slam! "Didn't I tell you never, ever, *ever* to pick up the phone!" Slam! Slam! "*Putain!* What the fuck were you thinking!" Slam! Slam! Slam! Suddenly, instead of slamming the receiver into the phone, he was now bashing it into my head. Slam! Slam! Slam! Slam! "*Idiot! Qu'est-ce que tu pensais?*" I began to cry, and not just from the physical pain. Pascal threw the phone down on the floor, then, rethinking the matter, picked it up and hurled it at my stomach, the force hurling me onto the bed. I couldn't breathe. As I lay there, he yanked my jeans off, screaming like a lunatic, and then I was underneath him, naked from the waist down, hyperventilating.

Not this again, I thought. Please, God, not this again.

"You don't want to do that," I said, and maybe the words snapped him out of his tempest, or maybe he thought too much of himself to follow through, or whatever it was, I'll never know; Hurricane Pascal stopped blowing, and I was left lying on the bed, my body badly battered but inviolate.

There'd been a time I was not so lucky.

AIDAN INTRODUCED HIMSELF to me on the eve of my graduation from Harvard. We were at a party, both slightly drunk, flirting a bit. He seemed perfectly nice, if pompous in that way Harvard boys can get, but I was so exhausted by the pregraduation festivities, I wasn't really in the mood to take it any further. Nevertheless, he had a car, and I was far from my room and on crutches. Earlier that day I had taken mushrooms with a few of my roommates and had convinced myself I could fly—if only I could build up enough speed and throw my arms out just so—in the middle of the Boston Common. Which, of course, I couldn't.

Aidan offered to drive me and my sprained ankle home. My apartment was on his way, he said, and besides, he'd heard about my photography thesis and really wanted to see it.

The thesis was called "Shooting Back," and it was a series of photos of men who had accosted me in various red-light districts up and down the Eastern seaboard. New York's Forty-second Street. Boston's Combat Zone. South Philly. The whole project evolved as a sort of radical form of self-therapy after I'd fallen victim to a number of armed robberies (two) and assaults (four). It was the equivalent of an acrophobe tackling Mount Everest, or an agoraphobe facing down the mall at Christmas: I was a bad-guy-o-phobe, hanging out in the belly of the beast.

I'd troll the seedy streets outside the strip clubs and the porno shops and wait for the inevitable comment, which ran the gamut from "Hey, baby, wanna get it on?" to "Suck my dick, bitch." To every proposition I would quickly and confidently reply, "No, thank you, but I *would* like to shoot your photo." This retort and the presence of my camera changed the entire dynamic of the encounter. My clunky old Nikkormat became my weapon, turning hunter into prey, and as I held my wide-angle 28-millimeter lens mere inches from these men's faces, distorting their images, I felt the universe tipping for a moment in my favor.

BOSTON, 1987

NEW YORK, 1987

NEW YORK, 1987

Aidan parked his car and helped me down the stairs to my basement apartment. Then he followed me into my bedroom, where I had gone to fetch the thesis. The photos were enclosed within a heavy, black sixteen-by-twenty-inch cloth-covered cardboard box, which, because of my crutches, was too unwieldy for me to carry into the living room. I handed the box to Aidan. "Let's take this into the other room," I said, but he ignored me. Instead, he laid the prints down on my bed, flipping through each of the thirty photos one by one, emitting a "Wow" or a "Cool" at regular intervals while I made a point of yawning loudly.

When he finally reached the last photo in the series—a flasher, happily exposing his penis to my camera—Aidan turned to me and said, "I bet you liked it when that guy did that." I wasn't sure I had heard him correctly, but when I said "What?" and he repeated it, this time louder and more suggestively, with a knowing smirk and jumping eyebrows, I didn't even have time to ask him if he was joking or out of his mind before he'd thrown me onto the bed.

He started kissing me. I kissed him back, more out of drunken inertia and resignation than anything else. He tasted like gin. I was desperate for sleep. The kisses grew more aggressive, sloppy, like being bit instead of kissed, and when I felt the hardness of his groin rubbing forcefully, almost

BOSTON, 1987

angrily against my thigh, I pulled away, said I was tired, thanked him for the ride home, suggested he leave. That's when everything got weird. Frustrated by my change of heart and by a couple of unyielding buttons, he ripped open my blouse. Then he held my arms up behind me, stared at my exposed chest. "Please," I said, "I don't want to do this. Let's not do this. I'm really tired." He laughed. My sprained ankle was throbbing, and I distinctly remember the crutches standing there, propped up against the far corner of the room, next to my camera, taunting me with their inaccessibility. Then there was this irrational thought: My roommate's mother is sound asleep in the next room, and if I yell, I might wake her. I thought of kicking him in the balls, but couldn't figure out how to do it with the bum ankle and my good leg pinned underneath him.

My body went numb at the moment of penetration, froze. As Aidan pounded away I tried pretending that my torso was somebody else's torso altogether, tried to step outside myself and watch with detached disinterest from above. So this is it, I thought. This is the ugly realm beyond the borders of consensus, what all the politics, the no-means-no's, the campus date-rape crisis centers are all about. It was the day before graduation, and I had to go put myself in the embarrassing position of becoming just another statistical cliché.

Rape. Even the word sounded aggressive, like an onomatopoeia. Rape, rape, rape, rape, rape, rape, rape. I held on to my tears, let them build up behind my eyes until I felt they would explode. I did not want to give Aidan the satisfaction of seeing a single one.

I tried visualizing how nice the water would feel when I could finally get to a shower. I tried visualizing anything other than what was happening between my legs. Ice cream, trees, a beach. But my mind kept crashing back into my body.

I started to blame myself. It's your fault, I thought. You should never have drunk. You should never have flirted. You should never have accepted the ride, showed him your photographs, taken the goddamned pictures in the first place. You should never have kissed him back, you idiot. You should never have been born a girl. *Fuck you, Aidan, this is not fair.*

"Please," I said, once again. "Please stop."

Aidan kept at it, pounding harder and faster. Rape rape rape rape rape rape rape . . . rape . . . a final whimper . . . rape.

It was over. Aidan was passed out cold on the bed, lying in a small puddle of his own semen.

I pictured my parents, sleeping in their hotel room, waiting eagerly for the first notes of "Pomp and Circumstance" to usher their eldest child into Harvard Yard, where her diploma and various academic prizes awaited her. How could I tell them about what had just happened to me?

For the first time in my life, I felt a distinct role reversal, as if I now had to shield my mother and father from an ugliness I could barely pronounce. I tried to picture myself, dressed in my cap and gown with my diploma tucked under my arm, saying the words to them: *Mom, Dad, I was raped.* No, I thought. I'll tell them later, after graduation. In a couple of weeks. Maybe in a couple of years. Or maybe never.

My body had just been entered against its will. It didn't seem fair that the man responsible for such an intrusion should be able to wreak any more havoc in my life. Like ruining my graduation day. Like permanently desecrating the psyches of the two people I loved most, the two people who'd always taught me to appreciate the beauty of sex, the two people who had, through the same penetrative act turned on its tender, loving, procreative head, made me.

"Get up!" I shouted into Aidan's ear. "Get up right now, you asshole!" Aidan lay there in a stupor with his arm around me, unmoving. After freeing myself, I took a long shower and spent the rest of the night on the floor of my bedroom, staring out the window, sitting in a shaft of moonlight, hugging my knees and rocking back and forth like an autistic child. Watching the sun rise. Watching the sky turn gray. Weeping as the raindrops collected on the windowpane.

When Aidan finally woke up, he stumbled out of bed, said, "Fuck, it's raining," dressed, and wrote his name and phone number on a yellow Post-it note, which he stuck to the tiny gray screen of my Macintosh. "Give me a call sometime," he said with a wink, sauntering out as if nothing unusual had happened. As if he'd not just put another tiny, irreparable crack in the lens through which I saw life.

"GET OUT," PASCAL SAID, his voice now controlled and calm. He adjusted the towel around his waist. "Get out of here right now." He told me he would hold me personally responsible if Élodie left him.

I was thinking, It takes two to tango, asshole, but I didn't even dignify his threat with a reply. Instead, I put my jeans back on and packed my things silently and in great haste, throwing socks and underwear and pants and toothpaste and batteries and shoes and T-shirts and sweaters and film all together in the backpack in a jumbled mess. My Tampax box wouldn't fit into the main compartment, so I shoved it in the side pocket, next to the bottle of rubbing alcohol. Pascal stood with his arms crossed and his back against the wall of our hotel room, staring at me and breathing through flared nostrils. "Where are you going?" he asked.

"I'll stay at Robert's tonight," I said. What a relief it was to finally have an out.

"Yeah, go fuck him for a change," said Pascal. "He looks like he needs it."

I stopped packing and stared back at him, incredulous. "Fuck you," I said.

As I walked out of the room, I turned to Pascal and told him that just because he'd beaten the crap out of me with a telephone receiver, just because I was furious at him, just because he was a cheater and a liar and an arrogant son of a bitch with a cold heart and a drawer full of ironed bandannas did not mean I would forgo my one and only chance to cover the war. We'd spent ten long days arranging our trip with the most reputable group of mujahideen, I said, and I refused to start over from scratch. Besides, I needed him to get inside, and he knew it. "It's purely logistical," I said. "Business."

"Right. Business," he said. "Be here at nine A.M. tomorrow morning. And don't be late." Before I could shut the door, however, Pascal, looking suddenly remorseful, placed his hands on my cheeks and bent over to kiss the top of my head, in the exact spot he'd just bruised with the telephone receiver.

"Ouch," I said, pulling away. "It hurts." I was trying not to cry.

"Oh, Deborah," he said, now hugging me as if nothing had happened, wiping the tear that had fallen down my cheek despite my valiant efforts to keep it in. "I'm sorry the way things turned out. It'll be good for us to spend a night apart."

He waited for a response, but I said nothing.

"Tu sais que je t'aime"—"You do know I love you," he said. "In my own way."

Love? I thought. Jesus fucking Christ. That's the problem with the French. Even their language is deceptive. Je t'aime can mean either "I like you" or "I love you." That's a very wide chasm for one little phrase to straddle. "Sure," I said, sticking with English, and not hugging him back.

"Nine A.M.," he said, as he watched me walk down the hallway. "Don't be late."

I called over my shoulder. "I won't."

To save money, I hitched a ride on a tonga to Robert's house instead of taking a taxi, but the clip-clop vibration of the horse and cart, normally so soothing to me, only made my head hurt more. By the time I arrived, covered in a light coating of dust whipped up by the horse's hooves, the two largest bumps on my head were throbbing.

"You okay?" Robert said as he let me inside, with a look of sympathy implying he assumed otherwise. I'd called him from the lobby of the hotel to tell him I was coming, explaining that Pascal and I had had a tiff. He was kind enough not to ask me to elaborate.

I looked around the living room, at the warm-toned rugs and couches, at the comfortably worn chairs, at the glowing electric heater in the corner. "I am now," I said. I eyed the guitar propped up in the corner. "Please, Robert, play me something beautiful."

"Something beautiful, huh?" he said. He grabbed the guitar, started tuning it. "Let me see what I can do."

Robert has always been a genius with a guitar, and that evening he strummed a bit of Dylan, some Grateful Dead, and the dulcet notes and chords filled my head, calmed me. Beauty may not be truth, I thought, but it's certainly a good salve. Especially with Robert around to administer it.

Growing up in a house full of girls, I'd always dreamed of having an older brother like Robert. Someone to protect me, to adore me, to teach me the ropes of that alien species with their smelly socks and strange protrusions. My friend Sandy had two older brothers at home when we were growing up, and I used to go over to her house just to watch them, to study their habits like an anthropologist. I made mental notes. They collected beer cans and read *Mad* magazines. They enjoyed torturing us with choke holds and noogies. They threw tennis balls at our butts and chased us willy-nilly through the neighborhood. They played The Who at ear-splitting decibels—"Pinball Wizard," "Tommy Can You Hear Me"—and were always in a constant state of pinball motion themselves, tripping over furniture, their dirty socks half on, half off, their knees always scabbed and always bouncing, even while seated. They were fascinating yet terrifying; I could not figure them out. But I always knew that if any of the neighborhood bullies dared to drop frogs down our shorts or run us over with their bikes, if they called us names or made fun of our budding breasts, Sandy's brothers would come running to our defense. I felt safe at her house, protected.

That night, as Robert showed me how to play the chords for "The House of the Rising Sun" on the guitar, as he carefully taught me when to strum and when to pick the strings one by one, he gave me a small taste of how my long-lost brother might have acted, had I come to him with two bruises on my head and a heart filled with anger and confusion. "*Oh, mother, tell your children,"* we sang, loudly, as if our very lives depended upon it, *"not to dooooooo what I have done . . ."*

That night, to keep things clear between us, I slept in my sleeping bag on Robert's floor. "You can stay here for as long as you like," he said. "Sparkle and Bill are leaving tomorrow, so you can have their room."

I told him that wouldn't be necessary. "I'm going inside tomorrow," I said. "But thanks anyway."

The next morning, I called Pascal at the hotel at 7 A.M. to make sure everything was still on. The clerk at the front desk looked up his extension. "Room 801? Yes, he checked out over an hour ago. Sorry." I asked her if she was sure. She asked me if he had black hair, a green army parka, a red bandanna and nice teeth. I said yes. She said she was sure.

The bastard had gone in without me. I slammed down the phone. "Fuck him!" I said. "Fuck fuck fuck him!" I cursed and slammed some more.

And then I thought, Okay. Fine. I'll go in by myself if I have to.

For the next week, I began afresh, visiting one group of mujahideen after the other, drinking one glass of sugary tea after another. I was snubbed, insulted, told to wait outside, made to step off their property, given the runaround, made to beg and fed lies until finally, almost a full week after Pascal's departure, the Harakat-I-Islami group told me to meet them at their headquarters at 6 A.M. the next morning to go inside.

"Are you insane?" Robert yelled, when I told him of my plans. "They're Iran-funded Shiites! They're in bed with the Ayatollah!" (*444 days, Reagan's inauguration . . .*) We were standing on the sidelines of a *buzkashi* game, watching a headless goat being dragged over a dusty field by a bunch of agitated Afghani men on horseback. Buzkashi—literally "goat grabbing"—is played kind of like polo, except instead of scoring goals with balls and mallets, the object of the game is to drag a dead goat with your bare hands from one end of the field to the other. A goal is scored when the goat is dropped in the middle of a circle, called the *halal* circle, the "kosher/pure" circle, as opposed to the *haram* or "unkosher/impure" circle on the other side of the field.

Buzkashi is supposed to be a team sport, with two teams facing off against each other, unified in their goals. But because each point scored earns cash prizes for the individual who scored it, the match usually devolves into a vicious free-for-all, with every man trying to grab the goat for himself. Journalists who'd spent any time covering Afghanistan usually jumped on buzkashi as the perfect metaphor for the internecine conflicts between groups of mujahideen, who were all supposed to be driving out the Soviets together instead of devoting a large part of their energy to killing one another, keeping their rival groups from grabbing the desired "goat": the future governance of Afghanistan.

"I don't care if they're giving the Ayatollah nightly blow jobs," I said. "They're the only group who's agreed to take me, the war's about to end and I'm tired of all the jokes at my expense—'Where's your boyfriend? Wasn't he supposed to take you inside?' Fuck Pascal. I'm going."

Robert looked at me and shook his head. "Debs, swallow your ego for one second and reconsider. It's not a good idea. They're an unknown entity. They're Shiites. If anything happens to you, the embassy has no leverage. They won't be able to help you."

"So don't tell them I'm going," I said.

A giant roar of applause surged out from the audience as the headless goat was thrust inside the "pure" circle. The victorious player, standing up in his stirrups, clasped his hands above his head in triumph. The rest of the players milled about on their horses, looking slightly miffed. "Men," I said, with a tone of disgust. "Halal circles, haram circles, good, bad, Madonnas, whores, goats, penises, it's all the same."

Robert started to laugh. "I think you're losing it." He tried his best all day to convince me not to go; he even tried to switch around his class schedules so that he could accompany me inside. But in the end, I was a stubborn mule, going inside like an ass, coming out riding on another.

I FINALLY ASCERTAIN THAT this new and equally frozen cave where we have now holed up for the past few days is somewhere north of the Sanglakh Valley, in a ridge of mountains circling the capital city of Kabul, just south of the city. Though the Soviets are set to retreat any day now, they leave their parting gifts of aerial bombs all around us. We hear them falling and exploding in the night. During the day, I go out with reconnaissance troops to check out the immense craters, but there's very little to photograph. A hole is a hole is a hole.

The only hole that both fascinates and repels me here is the deep and narrow one dug into the ground just outside our cave, the one I have to squat over behind a flimsy, filthy curtain whenever the amoebas send me running. There's something uniquely humbling about having to face—and defecate over—an enormous, frozen drip castle of other people's feces ten times a day every day. After a while, as my dysentery worsens, it starts to feel like my only home.

The mujahideen spend the greater part of their days cleaning out their Kalashnikovs. I've shot six rolls of this already. Mohammed cleaning his gun. Mustafa cleaning his gun. Ali cleaning his gun. Mohammed and Mustafa, together, cleaning Ali's gun.

SANGLAKH VALLEY, AFGHANISTAN, 1989

I myself have become quite adept at handling the Kalashnikovs. Some days, when there's nothing better to do, the mujahideen set up a couple of cans on distant rocks and challenge one another to games of marksmanship. The rules of the game are simple. Two people play, and whoever hits the most cans first wins. I play a lot. And, though my shoulder is getting progressively more bruised from the gun's kick, I hardly ever lose. (Thanks in part to years of summer camp riflery classes, a lifetime of perfect vision, and extremely steady hands, which allow me to shoot photographs in low light at slow shutter speeds.) At first the mujahideen thought it was funny, my prowess with a gun, but as my victories mounted, they stopped letting me play as often. Which is probably just as well, considering the fact that I've been having dreams where the tin cans turn into people after I pull the trigger, after it's too late to warn them to get off the goddamned rocks. Also, there's the whole virility thing. Men get angry when they lose to a woman.

And then they get even.

SANGLAKH VALLEY, AFGHANISTAN, 1989

One day during morning exercises, I am shooting pictures of a couple of the soldiers crawling on their bellies through the snow under a barbed-wire obstacle course when one of the mujahideen, whom I'd just vanquished the previous day in a shoot-the-can match, pulls me by the arm and drags me away from the group. He mimes for me to take a picture.

I shrug, throw out my hands palms up. Of what? We're in the middle of a narrow valley, with mountains jutting up on either side of us. In front of me, where he's pointing, there's nothing but snow and the cloudless horizon.

He puts out his hand. *Stay.* Then he mimes taking a picture again. Then he pulses his palm five times. *Wait. You'll see.* He walks away.

I crouch in the snow, my camera to my eye, waiting for whatever it is the mujahed wants me to photograph. He runs behind me, yells something in Pushto to one of his pals and in an instant, with a deafening boom, the ground just yards in front of me explodes, radiating snow and ash up and out. I fall to the ground, hold my hands over my head and, with the explosion echoing inside my chest, I start to scream. I'm choking on ash. My pulse is racing. My hands and body are shaking. I yell, "What the fuck was that?" but it comes out as high-pitched gibberish.

All of the mujahideen leave their morning exercises and come running over, laughing hysterically and pointing at me. Then I notice the green box with the T-handle: fucking string-detonated mine. What assholes! The mujahed who had dragged me to this spot takes a small, cracked hand mirror from his pocket and shoves it in my face. A moment clearly rehearsed. With his other hand, he takes his palm and starts rubbing the surface of his own face and making a sour look. Then, laughing once again, he says, "Dirty," which is the first and only English word I've ever heard out of his mouth. I peer into the mirror. My face is black with ash, with only two narrow, tear-stained streaks of grayish-pink skin. Some of the men are now convulsing with laughter, unable to control themselves.

"Yeah, very funny!" I yell, my nose now running, the tears now flowing steadily, my body still shaking uncontrollably from the jolt. "That was some joke! Ha ha ha." But the anger in my voice only makes the mujahideen laugh harder.

That night, back at the cave, Hashim tells me he thinks it's best if I do not compete in the shooting matches anymore. I thank him for the advice. Then I unfurl my brown blanket, lay it on the dirt floor in a corner as far away from the others as I can possibly get. I unroll my now filthy sleeping bag, slip inside, pull off my ash-covered, blood-encrusted jeans, and put them under my head as a pillow. Soon, the men are snoring. I'm wide awake, fantasizing about the smell of Bounce. I try to force myself to sleep. I am so lonely here, I think. So fucking lonely. And with the diarrhea and the cold and the dirt and the stench and the snow and the boredom and the bombs and the hazing and that ever-expanding pile of shit in the hole outside our cave—my only real measure of time—I don't know how much longer I can take it. At some point that enormous pile of human excrement is going to get so tall it'll burst out of the ground. And then what? *Then what?*

Another week passes, and now we are marching through the snow on a two-hour hike to check out a nearby village that was recently bombed, although by whom it is unclear. Hashim tells me he thinks Gulbuddin Hekmatyar's men might have done it in retaliation for some perceived wrong or another. As we near the village, colored flags stick out of the snow, marking the graves of the dead. The village itself is nothing more than a few haphazardly placed mud-colored walls, their torn, jagged edges reaching to the sky, useless. The villagers, about fifty or so people, mostly women and children, have all taken refuge in two rooms whose walls were left miraculously intact but whose destroyed roof looks to have been quickly reconstructed out of sheets of corrugated metal and a translucent green tarp. In one room, a room I imagine used to be someone's kitchen, a few men sit around a stove on the dirt floor, drinking tea. In the women's quarters, a larger room that was probably once a living room, the older women are seated on the floor, huddled next to one another under blankets, their backs against the walls. The younger ones flit about, caring as best they can for the children, many of whom, despite the cold, are barefoot.

Since the mujahideen are convinced there are Soviet-funded spies in every village, and because they think that as an American (read "noncommunist") journalist, my life might be in danger, Hashim lies to the villagers. He tells them I am a doctor with Médecins Sans Frontières, a stalwart group of medical professionals who travel to war-torn areas and offer their much needed services.

"You can't do that!" I say, when Hashim tells me what he's said.

Hashim looks bemused. "Yes, I can." In Hashim's world, dissension is not allowed.

There are two major problems with this lie. First and foremost, I'm not a doctor. So I can't help the boy with the open, gaping wound, or the women pointing to their babies' bottoms covered with diarrhea, or the young girl with a dirty old eye patch gesturing for a new one. But like flies swarming around a grain of sugar, they surround and engulf me with their pleas for help. "I'm an impostor!" I want to yell, shaking my head, overcome by a mixture of guilt at our ruse and pity for those who believe it. "Really, an impostor!" But Hashim shoots me a look that says, Don't you dare. Then he takes my camera bag away.

"Hey, give that back to me," I say, now thoroughly annoyed with Hashim's paranoia.

"No, Miss Deborah, no pictures. Many spies. You doctor. Be doctor."

Which brings us to problem number two with the fake doctor scenario. To be perfectly crude, I have finally hit pay dirt as far as documentary photography goes. Images of suffering and pain jump out from every corner of the room, taunting me to capture them. This is the real face of war. A few dexterous clicks of the camera, and these people would be plastered all over *U.S. News & World Report.* Or at the very least they might peer out from a quaint, $250 quarter-page photo somewhere in the middle of the magazine, which will not necessarily save their wretched lives or reimburse my trip, but will let everyone back home know the internecine war in Afghanistan is still raging, despite the Soviet retreat; that the story is not as simple as Reagan would have had us believe. But because I'm supposedly a doctor, because Hashim can't imagine a scenario in which a doctor might take a few souvenir photos, because Hashim is stronger than me and will not give me back my camera bag, I can't shoot a single frame. It's like a bad O. Henry plot.

The women with the diarrhea-encrusted infants are now making wild hand gestures, putting their fingers to their mouths as if they were eating small morsels of food. I turn to Hashim. "Do they want food?" I ask. I tally up my stash in my head. I still have ten Snickers bars left, which I have begun to ration very strictly between cigarettes. A third for breakfast, a third for lunch, a third for dinner. I also have half a box of Tic-Tacs, but they don't do much to calm my appetite. I feel hungry all the time, and this on top of the dysentery has started to take its toll. I am quite literally wasting away, my fetid Levi's now hanging on my increasingly bony frame in defiance of gravity. Though I feel badly for the villagers, and though I'm usually the first one to share my food with others, there's no way I'd ever share my Snickers bars with these people today. Hunger, I freely admit, has transformed me.

"No," laughs Hashim. "They want medicine. For babies. Poo poo no good. Bad poo poo."

"It's called diarrhea, Hashim. Di-a-rrhea," I say the word slowly so he can learn it, "and I have no medicine for baby diarrhea. I have Flagyl for adult diarrhea, but I can't give it to babies. Too strong. I don't know the dosage." Hashim looks like he understands half of what I'm saying. Christ. I don't want to give these babies a medicine that, for all I know, might kill them. But the women are now desperate. There's a doctor in their midst, and they are not going to let her go back where she came from until she gives them diarrhea medicine for their ailing babies. So I do the best I can: I give each of the women two Tic-Tacs. I tell them to dissolve it in some water, give it to their babies. And then I pray for a miracle.

We leave the village a few hours before nightfall and head back to our cave. An hour or so into our snowy march, we stop to pee. As usual, the men wait for me to be led away by one of the mujahideen before they will relieve themselves on the side of the road. If it were my choice, we'd all urinate together, one big happy family. Call me crazy, but I don't like having to trudge twenty to thirty yards through a snow-covered minefield whenever nature calls. It seems unduly risky and stupid, and it makes me feel like a burden to boot. But I do understand the laws of Islam. These men get upset if I so much as forget to cover my lap with a blanket when I'm sitting Indian-style in our cave, as if the sight of my jeans-covered crotch, the mere intimation of a vagina, might cripple them.

As my mujahed guide and I walk away, I make sure, as usual, to step exactly into the snow tracks he's marked for me with his feet. We've worked out a system: I walk to the very last track in the snow, he turns around and walks a few paces back over his already trodden path and waits with his back toward me for me to finish. But on this particular day, neither of us makes it that far. As if in slow motion, I watch the ground directly underneath the soldier erupt, a sonic boom ripping through my body. The explosive energy of the detonated mine throws me to the ground, where I lay stunned and screaming. I look over at the dark blood slowly seeping into the snow where the mujahed now lies, his right leg severed in half. Suddenly, as the maimed man quietly begins to weep, I can control my bladder no longer. The warm liquid gushes out of my body.

I sense only a minor pain in my right hand. A piece of shrapnel the size and shape of a small guitar pick has lodged itself into the weblike skin between my thumb and index finger. I yank it out, and the wound begins to bleed. But feeling my legs just to be sure, I realize I'm fine. Whole. I'm now sitting up in the snow, shivering. My urine-soaked jeans are starting to freeze and stick to my thighs, but I'm so happy to be alive I barely notice the discomfort. I stand up and walk carefully over to the soldier, the crunch of my boots through crimson snow drowned out by the man's wails. *"Allah akbar, Allah akbar . . ."* he cries, writhing in pain. I gently stroke his hair. I tell him I'm sorry, over and over again.

The other mujahideen have now come cautiously running to his aid, stepping in the tracks he's already laid, circling around him, screaming at one another in Pushto. But the chaos is orderly. Rote. I realize that these men, these soldiers of Allah, must be used to so much blood, so much missing flesh and bone. I step back through my own tracks to give them room to work.

I know I should be working, too. Shooting pictures of this. But I feel so guilty about the whole thing, I can't do it, cannot even fathom doing it. A man gets his leg blown off taking me to pee, and then I'm supposed to shove a lens in his face and shoot? No way. Maybe I'm not made for this job.

The men fashion a makeshift stretcher from two sticks and some cloth. Then, the same soldier who'd played the practical joke on me just one week earlier approaches me with his own piece of cloth. He rips it in half, tying the first piece tightly around my injured hand. With the second piece, he moistens it in the snow and tenderly wipes the ashes off my face. "Dirty," he says once again. This time he isn't laughing.

The men take turns, four at a time, carrying the injured soldier back through the narrow, snow-covered valley to our cave. It takes us a little over an hour to get there, during which time the man's screams subside to yelps and finally to silence. He's alive but in shock, and Hashim tells me they'll be transporting him to the nearest medical outpost by donkey.

"A donkey?" I say. It suddenly occurs to me that I have to find a donkey myself. I must have a donkey. A donkey! A donkey! I think, My cameras for a donkey! Enough of this war, I want to go home. I've been stuck in these mountains for nearly a month, I've taken mediocre pictures of a lot of nothing, I haven't showered once and now I'm covered in urine on top of menstrual blood on top of layers and layers of sweat and dirt. My Snickers bars are almost gone, I have probably lost nearly twenty pounds, my bouts of diarrhea are becoming more and more severe and, frankly, Hashim has been very unclear about when his troops might go back to Peshawar.

Two Dutch doctors, a married couple working for Médecins Sans Frontières, do a clean amputation just above the knee of the mujahed, saving his life moments after we arrive—yes, by donkey—at their makeshift medical facility in Paghmon, a province in eastern Afghanistan. I wait outside with the other mujahideen, and when the doctors step out to tell us everything is okay, they take one look at me and start to laugh. "What the hell are you doing here by yourself?" the man asks.

"It's a long story," I say, and leave it at that. The doctors clean and bandage my hand and give me some medicine for the amoebas. And then, those two angels sent down from wherever angels are sent down from tell me they will be leaving for Peshawar by truck in a few hours, and wouldn't I like to accompany them? "Yes," I say. "Oh, yes."

IT IS THREE DAYS and many miles later. The doctors drop me off at Robert's house in their car, which was waiting for them at the border, and when I walk inside Steve is in the living room, drinking a beer and chatting with someone who looks eerily like conservative pundit P. J. O'Rourke. "Hi, Deborah!" says Steve. "Welcome back. Do you know P. J. O'Rourke?" Introductions are made—from afar, lest my fumes overwhelm them—niceties exchanged, but the whole scene feels surreal, like a hallucination. "What happened to your hand?" Steve asks, noticing the bandages.

"Oh, it's nothing," I say. "Just a cut." I don't have the strength to tell the story right now—*You see, a man was taking me to relieve myself and got his leg blown off* . . . Actually, I can't imagine a time I will ever be able to tell that story. Teetering just this side of sanity, I turn to P.J. "So," I say, "what are you here to write about?"

"I'm not sure. Maybe traffic," he says, with a roguish smile.

"Oh," I say. "Traffic. That's nice." I am suddenly overwhelmed by the same feeling I used to get whenever I was tripping on acid and simultaneously trying to hold a conversation with anyone who wasn't. I realize I have to escape. I excuse myself to go take a shower.

When I get up to my room, there's a message scrawled on a piece of paper, in Robert's handwriting, sitting on my bed. I pick it up and read it. *Call Pascal,* the note says. *He's back. Pearl Continental Hotel, Room 509. And Deb, don't forget, he's Satan.*

I run downstairs and pick up the phone to dial. Pascal answers. "Oh, Deborah, my darling. How are you? How was your trip?"

Fine, honey, and yours? Did I mention that not a day went by in those icy mountains when I didn't berate myself for ever trusting you? "That was some move you pulled," I say, not answering his question. "Abdul Haq had never said he'd let me in with you, did he? I was never really slated to go, was I?" I catch a glimpse of myself in the mirror. The bones are jutting out of my cheeks.

Pascal makes some lame excuses, says he was sure he told me 6 A.M., not 9 A.M., and maybe I just heard him wrong, transposed the number in my head. "Fuck you," I say. There's nothing else, at this point, I can say. But before I can politely hang up, Pascal starts grilling me about my trip.

"I heard you got inside. With the Shiites. Where were you? What did you photograph? Did you see any battles? Any dead people? Tell me, tell me what you saw."

"What? Nervous I saw better stuff than you?" I say, knowing full well this is exactly why he's interrogating me. "Well, you can rest easy. I saw shit." I tell him about the nighttime mortar, about our endless reconnaissance trips, about the destroyed village I wasn't allowed to photograph. I tell him about the rocket-propelled grenade launchers the mujahideen fired off into an empty hillside, about how I shot only a few pictures of the staged spectacle just to make them happy but then had to pretend to take an entire roll just so they would stop. I tell him about my donkey ride, about the doctors who got me out.

I do not tell Pascal about the exploding mine or the maimed soldier. I don't want to give him the ammunition—to berate me for being a lousy photojournalist, to allow him to justify leaving me behind. In fact, so embarrassed am I by the nature of my injury and by the fact that I did not have the courage to shoot when I know I should have, when *Photomagazine* asks me to submit my Afghanistan diary for publication along with my photos, I will rewrite two of the entries before handing it in, blaming the piece of shrapnel in my hand on that first explosion, the one where the mujahideen laughed at my ash-covered face.

"What about you?" I say. "Get anything good?"

"Oh, Deborah, I saw the war. The real war!" These are the words that will forever ring in my ear whenever I think of Pascal: *"J'ai vu la guerre, la vraie guerre!"*

His voice starts to crescendo. He's clearly enjoying himself. He tells me he was in Jalalabad. That there'd been a huge firefight while the Soviet troops were giving up their positions. That it was horrible. Horrible. That he took such great pictures. Amazing pictures. That the pictures were so good, he transported the film immediately to the airport in Islamabad to send it off with a passenger flying that very day to Paris. (So that's how you get the pictures back.) That *Stern* was going to give him ten double pages. *Paris Match* wanted to give him six. He made a bundle, he says, and wouldn't I like to go out and celebrate with him with a bottle of Veuve Clicquot at the American Club?

I'd rather rub broken glass into my corneas. "So nice of you to ask," I say, "but it's not going to work out tonight." I tell him I just got back, that I'm really tired, that maybe we could have lunch tomorrow. But I have no intention of ever seeing Pascal again.

"*C'est dommage,*" he says. "I'm leaving tomorrow on the first flight to Karachi . . ." *And you wanted to get laid one last time before heading back home? My heart bleeds for you, cowboy.* ". . . I guess I'll see you back in Paris, then."

Not if I can help it. "Yeah, sure, back in Paris," I say. I fret over running into him at future news events, photo exhibits, dinner parties. But my worrying is in vain. Less than a year after our trip to Afghanistan, Pascal will quit photojournalism, marry Élodie and start a family. And our paths will never cross again.

I hang up the phone and start searching for some soap and shampoo, realizing I'd left my backpack in the front hallway by the living room. I wave hi to P.J. and Steve again, and as I pass by the kitchen, I spot Martin, a British journalist who'd also gone inside with Abdul Haq's men. He's sitting at our large communal table, the site of many a lively discussion, drinking a beer and reading a month-old copy of *Time,* his legs propped up on another chair. He takes one look at me, holds his nose, and chuckles. "Just get back from inside then, did you?" he asks, burping. "We got back a few days ago."

"I know," I say. "I was just on the phone with Pascal. I hear you guys saw some pretty hairy stuff." He looks like he's not exactly sure what I'm talking about, so I elaborate. "You know, Jalalabad. The firefighting, the fierce battles . . . Pascal said it was pretty outrageous."

"That joker!" Martin laughs. "He's incorrigible. We saw zippo, baby, zilch." He tells me that Pascal got so frustrated by the lack of action, he made the mujahideen fire off their rocket launchers just so he could get some pictures. That he made one of the soldiers crouch down and hold his ears as the thing exploded. "Excellent visual stuff, but no real bloody fucking war, if you know what I mean. I couldn't even file a decent story."

Of course. It all makes perfect sense, actually. Pascal lied to Élodie. He lied to me. Several times. He probably lied about those bombs in Beirut, for all I know. *Mon dieu,* you should have seen those bombs, he always said, laughing. You should have seen those bombs. And now his pictures of Afghanistan, appearing in beautiful, glossy, double-paged splendor in magazines in every kiosk in every city, are lying to the world at large.

I find my soap and shampoo, head to the bathroom, and peel off layer upon fetid layer of soiled clothing. Later, I will burn them in a pile of trash, but for right now, I stand in the hot shower, soaping myself over and over and over again, scrubbing the blood, the urine, the silt, the ash, the shame, the grime and the war from my body. Beneath me, the standing water is black. I empty the tub and start all over again.

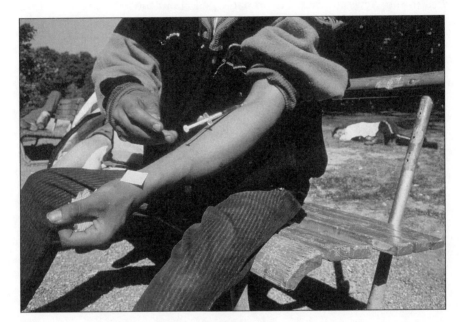

ZURICH, SWITZERLAND, 1989

THE PHOTOGRAPHER IS PACING BACK AND FORTH, shaking his head, staring up at the bombed-out house and then back down at his cameras. He stops, crosses his arms and kicks the tip of his steel-toed boot into the pavement twice. Then he runs his fingers through his chin-length black hair and starts to laugh. *"C'est de la merde!"*—"This is bullshit!"—he says, speaking to no one in particular. After a minute or so, he sighs, fishes a roll of film out of the pocket of his black leather jacket, one of those biker numbers with lots of diagonal zippers and secret compartments and pointy lapels, and shoots off a few frames anyway.

I, too, have been pacing in front of the house here on this quaint Dutch street, shooting a few random pictures here and there, but I'm not laughing anymore. When I first arrived half an hour ago, panting and out of breath from having practically sprinted from the Arnhem train station, I was hoping to see the kinds of things I'd read about in the wires this morning: vigilante mobs reclaiming a drug-infested neighborhood, the still-smoldering ash of the heroin den they'd loaded up with dynamite and exploded, throngs of supportive neighbors carrying antidrug signs, junkies walking around jonesing and looking confused, local policemen trying to keep the peace. The random moments of pure chaos all photojournalists crave.

Instead, I saw what my rakish colleague now finds so amusing: a slightly singed town house with its windows boarded up. A pathetic hand-lettered sign strung between two lampposts and written, alas, in Dutch: KLARENDAL DRUGS VRIJ! (What the hell does *that* mean?) A quiet, middle-class neighborhood of modest attached homes, empty save for the presence of us press people: two television camera crews shooting stand-ups, a couple of journalists interviewing a kid on his bike and half-heartedly jotting down notes and me, standing idly, stubbing out a cigarette with the ball of my foot, watching the TV and print reporters create stories out of nothing and worrying about how I'm going to make enough money shooting a boarded-up house with no back story in Holland, a place nobody cares about anyway, to cover my expenses.

I walk over to the photographer. *"Tu as raison,"* I say—"You're right"—*"c'est vraiment de la merde."*

He looks me up and down. His eyes move from my cameras to my face, spending equal time on each. I mirror his inspection, noticing the following: a Nikon F2 (good body) with a 20-millimeter lens (tremendous width and depth of field but distorts reality), broad shoulders (good body), a motor drive on the F2 (noisy and unnecessary), laughing eyes (brown), a Nikon FM2 (acceptable) with a 180-millimeter lens (nice piece of equipment, long but easy to manipulate), black jeans (snug.) He also has a Leica (odd, since I wouldn't have pegged him as the serious type), a black Domke camera bag (practical, well padded) and a voluptuous pair of lips (red, also well padded).

"Pierre," he says in a thick Parisian accent, holding his hand out to shake mine. His dimples are deep, winsome and, like the boyish grin that carves them, at odds with the rest of his attire.

I introduce myself and watch a flash of recognition cross Pierre's face. It has been almost a year since my foray into Afghanistan, a year during which I was offered an exhibit of my work at a photojournalism festival. A year filled with dozens of magazine and newspaper assignments and long, liquid lunches with kindly photo editors who were willing to take a chance on a rookie. A year when I was published and profiled, flatteringly, in the two trade glossies all French photographers read, *Photomagazine* and *PHOTO.* A year in which I turned twenty-three and suddenly realized that my hard work was starting to pay off, if not exactly monetarily then psychologically. I'm no Sebastiao Salgado or Joseph Koudelka—not at all—but in the small, incestuous world of photojournalism, I'm generating a small burst of heat. And yes, it feels nice.

"From Gamma?" Pierre asks.

"Yeah," I nod, trying my best to remain nonchalant. "From Gamma."

Gamma, even after I screwed them over by jumping ship to Contact while in Afghanistan, nevertheless offered me a staff position with their agency when I returned to Paris. They promised to pay for half of all my expenses, to develop, edit, store, distribute and sell my film, to advance me money against future sales and to feed me as many appropriate assignments as they saw fit. In return, I would have to participate in *permanence*—weekend duty (which sometimes, unfortunately, meant a bit of paparazzi shooting, which I hated), I would have to sell my pictures only through Gamma, even if the assignment had come through my own personal connections and, within reason, I would have to jump on any plane, train, car, bus, boat, motorcycle or scooter the agency saw fit for me to jump on at any given moment. Since I'd decided to stay in Paris and not move back to the States, since Contact was in New York and was not offering me a similar deal, I accepted Gamma's offer and apologized to Michel for my lapse in good judgment with regard to Pascal. "Don't worry," he said, "we all do stupid things sometimes."

When Michel was later fired, for reasons I never understood, Henri— nicknamed L'ours, "the Bear"—took over his job as news editor and promptly decided that, besides wars and fast-breaking news, which are the assignments most of the Gamma photographers covet, I would be useful in covering the drug addict and derelict beat, which no one really wanted. It was Henri who, in his inimitable brusque, ursine manner, shoved me out the door of the agency this morning and told me to buy a train ticket to Holland and find the junkies and the vigilante neighbors and the dynamited drug den in Arnhem *vite vite vite*, even as I protested that the story seemed iffy and trivial and would most likely be finished by the time I got there.

Pierre's smile widens. "I've heard all about you," he says. "The crazy American girl. I heard about your exhibit in Perpignan. I've seen your pictures all over the place—that heroin park in Switzerland, the Afghan war diary in *Photomagazine*. You do wars and drugs, right?"

"Right," I say, "that's me." A pigeonhole, even. Please, stroke my ego some more.

"Cool," he says, in English with a French accent. The French, especially the cool ones in Perfecto jackets, love the word "cool." Pierre stares down at the Leica hanging from my neck, a graduation present from my parents, and then picks it up to fondle it. "An M6. Cool."

"The coolest," I say.

He takes a narrow manila envelope with the word "Sipa" splashed across it out of his camera bag, sticks his one roll of film inside and, blushing, licks the seal with a playful flutter of his tongue.

"Sipa, huh?" I say.

"Yeah, been with them for a little while now." He shoves the envelope back in his camera bag, a nuisance to be dealt with later. "So," says Pierre. "You want to go to a bar with me and smoke some hash?"

I smile. "Sure," I say, "I'd like that."

PHOTOGRAPHERS ALWAYS SNIFF one another out. Most of the time it's just guys checking out other guys, however, so they don't notice things like voluptuous lips. (As a group, photojournalists are pretty much as heterosexual as they come.) But most photographers, like good anthropologists, will take notice of their competitors' stuff—everything from camera equipment to clothing to even small details like film envelopes—as a means of determining each other's standing in the socio-professional pecking order.

I became a photojournalist during the late eighties, the last days of the manual camera. Before the Canon EOS was introduced in 1991, no one had yet come up with an auto-focus camera that actually auto-focused. Besides, auto focus was for wimps. So having a Nikon F2, F3 or FM2 signified both a technical proficiency with manual cameras as well as a seriousness and commitment to photojournalism. Even cooler was a black Nikon camera body with a few well-placed dents and scratches on it. It said to the others, I'm a rugged person, and if these dented, scratched cameras could speak, oh, the stories they could tell. Olympus or Minolta owners, on the other hand, were strictly second-tier—local photographers, beginners, maybe even amateurs.

If your cameras had motor drives, that could mean a number of different things: 1) you covered a lot of press conferences; 2) you did a little sports coverage or fashion work on the side; 3) you liked the authentic-sounding noise it made; or 4) you lacked the confidence to leave it at home. For me, the whole issue was moot. Motor drives weigh a lot. I never owned one because it was all I could do to carry what little equipment I was already carrying without breaking my back.

I did have that Leica, however. It was an M6, the kind with the built-in light meter. Owning a Leica M-series camera put you in a whole other league. The Leica was the Porsche of the camera world; it was small, light, exquisitely crafted, mechanically perfect and very, very expensive. It was the "it" camera for the "concerned" photographer—a loose definition for a photographer who cares deeply for his subjects, who spends years and years shooting a single, thematically unified story on subjects like prisons, sweatshops or anything remotely related to Ethiopia. With a Leica slung casually over your shoulder—always with the lens facing in toward your rib cage to protect it, otherwise you'd be pegged immediately as an amateur—you could always pretend to be a concerned photographer, whether or not you'd ever stepped foot in Ethiopia.

Inside the Leica you kept a roll of Tri-X 400 ASA black-and-white film. This was for your very important "personal" work. By the end of the Vietnam War, color film had become de rigueur in the world of magazine photo publishing. While *Life* still did accept and always would accept black-and-white photo-essays, if you wanted to have your pictures published in *Time* or *Newsweek* or in any of the other newsmagazines around the world, you almost always had to shoot in color unless you were specifically assigned otherwise. But color lacked subtlety. It was crass. So the *artiste* photojournalists, channeling their inner Cartier-Bressons, all started carrying at least one camera body (preferably the Leica) with black-and-white film wherever they went. That way, they could work on loftier, noncommercial images while being financed to shoot vulgar color ones for the magazines. Some of the more self-righteous photographers shot only in black and white, but they were either unfazed by a life of poverty or, like Cartier-Bresson, they'd been born into wealth.

The type of shoes and jackets you wore were important, too, if only to identify your country of origin. Most of the Paris-based photographers wore a French brand of leather shoe called Paraboots, which were smart-looking as well as rugged. I bought myself a pair of sturdy black ones that I loved, even though on me they just looked big and clunky. As for outerwear, anything in black or tan with large pockets was acceptable. The

British photographers had footwear and outerwear that, in typical British fashion, divided them into their respective classes. The working-class guys tended to wear Doc Martens or Clarks, while their Oxbridge-educated colleagues favored the more expensive Timberlands, imported from America, or a well-worn pair of Church's for less strenuous terrain like 10 Downing Street. The guys with the Doc Martens could wear any type of cool jacket imaginable, while the Oxbridge guys wore one jacket and one jacket only: a green Barbour, the kind usually worn with a pair of green Wellies during duck-hunting season back home. The Americans—along with the Japanese, who were always trying to be just like the Americans— liked any jacket and/or vest manufactured by Banana Republic, which they wore with either Timberlands or with sneakers, the latter for which they were teased mercilessly by the French. The Germans had ugly jackets with decals and boxy, utilitarian shoes made by companies like Birkenstock, and the Soviets, if they ever made it out of their country, wore nylon windbreakers and those hideous gray fake-leather loafers from the central Soviet shoe factory.

A photographer's pants, on the other hand, told you nothing. Everyone, to a person, wore Levi's.

Now, the manila film envelopes that you stuck in the back pocket of your Domke camera bag were the truest anthropological talismans of all. The envelopes were fairly sturdy, long and narrow—about ten inches long and four inches wide—with the opening on the short end. The guys with the Olympuses usually had either blank envelopes or no envelopes at all. The guys with the beat-up Nikons usually had envelopes bearing the names of one of the three big agencies—Gamma, Sipa or Sygma—in big black letters, or they had the coveted ones with the red letters that spelled out the words *Time, Life* or *Newsweek*. These belonged to the photographers on assignment and, more important, on expense accounts. It was their unwritten duty to buy philanthropic rounds of drinks for their less fortunate colleagues shooting on spec. But the mother of all envelopes was the one bearing the name of a photo agency called Magnum. A Magnum envelope in your Domke bag was, for all intents and purposes, the photojournalism equivalent of a field marshal's epaulets. Never mind that the cooperative agency's finances were in shambles—most "concerned" photographers are too busy being concerned to earn any money—and that every photographer who joined Magnum started to think of himself as a latter-day Leica-toting Spinoza ("I am not a journalist," one of them once told me, pronouncing the word "journalist" with the same disgust one reserves for words like "bowel movement." "I am a visual philosopher.") Magnum was the holy grail.

Magnum was founded in 1947 by four photojournalists: Robert Capa, George Roger, David Seymour (aka "Chim") and Henri Cartier-Bresson. It was the first and, for a while, the only cooperative photo agency, and it created a new precedent in the business of photojournalism by providing its photographers with the right to retain sole copyright over their images. Until that point, copyright was retained either by the magazine or by an agency itself; if an image was reprinted, the photographer never saw a penny of resale profits. Other agencies were soon created using Magnum's business model, but none other required such an intimidating initiation process. You can't just join Magnum by setting up a meeting with an editor and showing a portfolio. Like a candidate for a secret club, a photographer has to be nominated by a current Magnum member to set the election process in motion. After that, there are numerous portfolio reviews, a vote by members, and years of tangential association before the title of "Member" is bestowed upon the lucky few.

Gilles Peress, Magnum photographer, taught at Harvard as a visiting professor during my junior year when I was just beginning to study photography. I wasn't in his class, but I sat in on a lecture he gave and was immediately seduced by the intensity of his speech and the in-your-face nature of his photography. Gilles is a black-and-white purist, and his pictures are like little two-dimensional jails; once you're inside, there's no escape. In his pictures from the Iranian revolution—my favorite photos of all time—faces pop up from the bottom of frames, arms fly out, hands fly in, eyes stare out with the intensity of bombs about to explode. "A good photographer is never afraid of death," he said to the assembled students. "He seeks it out, he gets close enough to smell it. He lives every single one of his days as if it were his last. Otherwise, his pictures are shit." I remember writing in my notes "SEEK OUT DEATH/OTHERWISE SHIT" in capital letters and underlining it.

Though up to that point I had never shot anything other than snapshots on my Instamatic camera, I'd always appreciated good photographs. My childhood piano teacher had a book filled with old pictures from *Life* magazine in her waiting room, and I would pore over it every Monday after school as I waited for my sister to finish her lesson. I'd be sitting there, wracked by guilt over having not practiced my scales or "*Für Elise*," and I'd take one look at those thalidomide babies or Riboud's flower child or the starving kids in Africa with the distended bellies and feel okay. I hated the piano lessons, but I loved that book.

My favorite, the one I would always turn to first, was that Pulitzer Prize–winning Nick Ut napalm bomb shot of the naked Vietnamese girl screaming in pain as she runs down a road toward the camera. I could stare at that picture forever, my eyes moving from dead center—the naked girl with her arms stretched limply on either side of her—to the clothed, wailing boy in the immediate foreground, to the other children running with the girl, to the soldiers very casually strolling behind them (as if this kind of fiery apocalypse were all in a day's work), to the ominous smoke behind them all and then back to the naked, crying girl, all the while awed at the absolute perfection of the image. I remember thinking at the time that most photojournalists probably work their entire lives and never take a picture like that, a picture truly worth a thousand words, if not more.

A prescient thought, in retrospect. But it never stopped me from trying.

When I got to college and started shooting pictures myself, my appetite for the medium was insatiable. I shot at least eight and sometimes fifteen rolls of film a day. I went to the library and to bookstores to pore over the photography books. I memorized every image in Robert Frank's *The Americans* and marveled how they echoed the words of my favorite book at the time, Kerouac's *On the Road*. I devoured Walter Benjamin's *Art in the Age of Mechanical Reproduction*, Roland Barthes's *Camera Lucida*, Cartier-Bresson's *The Decisive Moment*, Susan Sontag's *On Photography*, old *Aperture* magazines, anything by Vicki Goldberg and everything I could get my hands on that chronicled the life and career of Diane Arbus. "Push yourselves," my professor Christopher James told our class. "Take pictures that challenge you, that challenge the way you see the world and the way the world sees you." As this was a photography class at Harvard—a roomful of valedictorian geeks with cameras—half of them took Christopher's advice as a call to shoot naked self-portraits. I took it as an excuse to shoot strippers.

I couldn't believe it was that simple. I couldn't believe that just hanging a camera around my neck gave me carte blanche to see any sordid thing I wanted to see. Like Arbus, I'd always wanted to slog through the grimy underbelly of life, to visit strip clubs, sex clubs, heroin dens, to see the kind of places where life was as raw and on the edge as it could get, but before studying photography I'd never been able to figure out how to do so without becoming a stripper or pervert or drug addict myself. And then I walked into the Pussycat Lounge with my dad's old Nikkormat around my neck, said, "I'm a photographer," and voilà, the gates magically opened.

Okay, well, not so magically. First I had to fight off the Pussycat Lounge owner, who suggested I have sex with him and then said, "With that tight little ass, you should be up on stage with the rest of the girls." I politely declined both propositions and then struck a deal with him: I'd bring him and his girls free eight-by-ten photos every week if he would keep his paws off of me and let me shoot in peace. "Fine with me," he said, "but I'm not the only one you're gonna have to convince."

He was right. The strippers themselves—and who could blame them, really?—were extremely distrustful. My first day of shooting, they put me through the wringer. They made me get stoned with them. Then they passed me a rolled-up hundred-dollar bill and a mirror with three lines of cocaine on it and forced me to snort all three in rapid succession right then and there. I was a casual user of both drugs, so that part of the hazing didn't faze me, but then, just as the high kicked in, they sat me in a chair in front of the mirror and watched as one of the girls smeared makeup all over my normally unpainted face. "So," the stripper said, applying (and quite forcefully so) scarlet lipstick above my upper lip, then all the way down to my chin, "now do you feel good enough to fuck?" Now *that* was truly disturbing.

But, hey, that was all part of the fun, too: the perversion, the naughtiness. Never mind that spending my afternoons at the Pussycat Lounge shooting pictures of naked women and (sometimes) getting high was the perfect antidote to quiet mornings spent in Harvard lecture halls scribbling notes and making valiant if mostly failed attempts to wrap my brain around the tenets of Lacan and Derrida. The Pussycat Lounge was everything I'd hoped it would be—raunchy, dirty, vulgar and lewd. And the strippers? Right out of central casting.

There was Boom-Boom, with her enormous sagging breasts and her sadomasochist handcuff shtick. She was studying to be an accountant. There was Sally, who fake-masturbated on stage. She claimed to be an heiress, which, judging by her poise, Brahmin accent and mink coat, could have been true. There was Venus, the coke fiend/stoner strumpet. She was young, dimpled and totally fucked up—Shirley Temple after a gang rape. She stripped on stage to the song "I Know What Boys Like" while sucking on a giant lollipop. Then there was Steve with the Aerosmith haircut and skin-tight black T-shirts, whose job at the club I could never figure out. As far as I could tell, he was paid to hang out backstage, stare at the girls, bring them drugs and every once in a while, when the mood struck his fancy, to stand in front of the mirror with his jeans around his knees and jerk himself off in front of all of us. I took a not-so good picture of this one day, but all these years it's stayed, unprinted, a tiny postage-stamp image on my contact sheets.

Not that I was fundamentally opposed to the idea of public masturbation or to shooting pictures of it. In fact, my favorite photo from my forays into the Pussycat basement was of Sally touching herself, shot from the neck down. My professor Christopher told me the fact that she was headless made a much stronger image—it signified the universal stripper rather than the individual stripper. I was more than happy to take credit for the artistic forethought, but the truth of the matter was that when I saw Sally sticking her fingers in her vagina, for perhaps the third time that day,

BOSTON, 1986

I was so inept with the camera that after I found focus and calibrated the proper f-stop, I forgot all about proper framing and clumsily chopped off her head.

One day, while I was printing up a copy of this picture, Gilles, the visiting Magnum photographer, stopped me in the long corridor just outside the darkroom. "Your naked girls are very good," he said. "Derivative, of course, because Arbus did it first and better, and then Susan Meiselas after that, but yours are good, too." His French accent was thick, and he spoke with a conspiratorial air. He kept looking over his shoulders to make sure no one was listening, even though it was late at night and the hallway behind him was empty.

I had been wondering when he was finally going to speak to me. I'd noticed him staring at my work for weeks as I'd walk in and out of the darkroom with wet trays filled with stripper photos, but he never said a word. When I'd run into him in other parts of the campus, he would acknowledge our unacquainted acquaintance with a silent and perfunctory nod.

"Thanks," I said. "Arbus is my newest hero. She's now right up there with Sylvia Plath and Virginia Woolf." These were actually my heroes at the time, and I meant it both as an opening to a philosophical debate— Discuss: Why did all of my heroes commit suicide?—and as a morbid joke, but Gilles didn't laugh.

He invited me into his office for a chat. We talked for what seemed like an hour but what could have been only five minutes or so. You could never tell with Gilles. He was so intense, so full of passion for his art, it was exhausting just being in his presence. He told me all about Magnum, about his work. I was concentrating on the gray streaks in his hair, trying to avoid the searing blast of his eyes, when out of the blue he offered me a job as a summer intern in the agency's New York office. I was surprised. Since I wasn't one of his students and since he'd never before deigned to speak to me, I had not realized to what extent he'd been paying attention to my pictures. I thanked him, said I'd try to work out some sort of summer lodging in Manhattan and that I'd get back to him. When I turned around to head back into the darkroom he stopped me. "Arbus killed herself, you know," he said, as if he were letting me in on a big secret. "They said she saw too much. Went insane."

Hence my Plath/Woolf joke, I thought, but never mind. "I know," I said. "So what?"

"So watch yourself," said Gilles. "I don't want to have to clean up any messes."

The Magnum internship that summer was unpaid, so I had to work the dinner shift four nights a week as a waitress at the New Fuji Sushi and Steak House to make ends meet. But I would have been just as happy to pay Gilles to let me sit there in the Magnum office and sort through those photos. There they were, right in my hands, my favorite images since the dawn of photography. Cartier-Bresson's man jumping over a puddle, Robert Capa's dying Spanish soldier, Joseph Koudelka's 1968 Czech uprising, Sebastiao Salgado's antlike gold mine workers, Gilles's own masterful work during the Iranian revolution.

My job at Magnum was hardly mentally taxing. I was to open up all the return packages of slides and prints, make sure nothing was missing and then pass the pictures on to Doug, whose job it was to file them back into the archives. Doug had tattoos, a crucifix earring, spiked hair, a beat-up Nikon and leather pants, and every morning he'd swagger into the office cradling his motorcycle helmet under his armpit. He sat immediately to my right, close enough to touch, which was convenient both for our filing system and for lobbing pheromones back and forth at each other. We'd spend hours together, staring at the stockpile of famous images scattered on the surface of our shared desk, trying to figure out what distinguished a brilliant photo from an ordinary one and trying to carefully avoid the magnetic field that had formed between us. Then one day, right after we agreed that Cartier-Bresson kicked butt over every other photographer who'd ever lived, he showed up for work carrying two helmets under his armpits: "We could go down to Coney Island, take pictures of freaks, eat some hot dogs. Whaddya say?"

I'd had few propositions in my life more tempting than that. A boyfriend in high school used to drive me around on his older brother's motorcycle, and nothing I'd ever experienced up to that point had ever come close to delivering the same thrill. I loved everything about it: slicing through the wind, leaning into each sharp turn, bodies and machine as one—arms embracing leather, legs hugging metal—while the sweet ambrosia of gasoline and aftershave filled my lungs.

"Sure," I replied. "Love to."

Doug and I rode down to Coney Island, took pictures of freaks, ate some hot dogs. We wiped the sauerkraut off each other's cheeks and kissed. Then he drove me on that motorcycle back into Manhattan, where, drunk with only the pleasure of our journey, we made out some more.

"YOU HAVE A MOTORCYCLE BACK in Paris?" I ask Pierre, taking a hit off a hash cigarette he's just rolled. We've been sitting in a café a couple of blocks from the bombed house in Arnhem for well over an hour now. You have to hand it to the Dutch and their laissez-faire legal system. Marijuana is not legal, nor is it illegal. So at many cafés, along with a menu for pastries and coffee, you can also ask for the hash menu. It's nice to be able to say, Hmm, let's see . . . I'll have a croissant, an espresso and a quarter ounce of Jamaican gold. And if you don't mind, I'll just sit here all afternoon getting stoned.

"How did you know I have a motorcycle?" Pierre asks.

I eye his jacket. "Just a hunch," I say.

"I see," he says. Then he leans forward, as if to tell me a secret, and smiles seductively. "But, I must tell you, it is not a Harley. It is only a Honda."

"A Honda? Well, in that case, forget it." I stand up from the table and pretend to walk away.

"No, wait, Deborah," Pierre says, laughing and chasing me through the café. Like Pascal, he pronounces my name in three syllables, with the French *accent aigu* over the *e. Dé-bo-rah.* It sounds so much better than plain old *Deb-ra.* Unlike Pascal, however, he doesn't raise one of his eyebrows when he says it. And his laughter is genuine.

"Where are you going? Let me come with you," Pierre says, momentarily grabbing my hand then self-consciously letting it drop.

"I'm going to go find some junkies," I say, paying the café bill in full and heading out the door. Pierre tries to split the tab, but I shove his hand out of the way. "I'm not going to let this trip be a total waste of time and money." If the pictures of the boarded-up house aren't going to sell, which I'm sure they won't, I figure I can at least shoot some useful stock images. The royalty checks from pictures I shot a few months earlier of heroin addicts in Switzerland have been rolling in unabated, allowing me to pay my rent every month, keeping my dreams alive.

But even better than the money I've earned from them, my junkie pictures have suddenly turned me into a "concerned" photographer in the

eyes of some of my colleagues. When Patrick Zachmann, a Magnum photographer, saw an exhibit of them included in my show at the first annual
Perpignan photojournalism festival, he showed up at my hotel room and
approached me about joining his agency. When he spoke the words out
loud—"Have you ever considered joining Magnum?"—I found it difficult
to breathe. Have I ever considered it? I thought. It's the only thing I've ever
wanted since the day I picked up a camera.

"Sure, I've considered it," I said.

Patrick told me I had exactly one year until the next Magnum election.
He urged me to build up my portfolio, shoot more drug stories, more
wars, more everything. He told me I had an eye, a vision, and he said he
was fairly certain I had what it takes to be a "concerned" photographer.

I blushed at the compliment, but I wasn't convinced. Concerned photographer? What exactly did that mean? I once read that Nick Ut, after
shooting his famous photo, took that naked, napalm-covered Vietnamese
girl to the hospital himself, saving her life. I liked to think I would have
done the same thing in his position, but I couldn't really say for sure.

During the weeklong festival in Perpignan, I was interviewed by a
number of French radio, television and newspaper journalists. They all
wanted to know why I did it, why I ventured into the types of places and situations I chose to photograph. Unfortunately, my French was not yet up to
par, and it just seemed easier to answer *"Oui"* to their complicated questions. "Is it because you see drug addiction as a scourge to our cities, but
yet you sympathize with the addicts?"

"Oui."

"Are you absolutely horrified by the destruction wrought upon the
Afghani people by the Soviet Union?"

"Oui."

"Do you choose to shoot horrific places and situations to make us uncomfortable, to alert us to the wretched injustices of the world?"

"Oui."

It wasn't that I was lying. I did see drug addiction as a scourge, I did
sympathize with the addicts, I was horrified by what I saw in Afghanistan
and I did like making people feel uncomfortable with my pictures. But that
wasn't the main reason why I did it. I did it because those things—drugs,
wars, whatever—were there. I did it because I was curious, because I was
young and I was hopeful, because it was exciting, because I enjoyed it, be-

cause I wanted to, because sometimes I felt like I *had* to, because I figured if we all have just one life to live, I might as well fill mine with interesting stuff. Adventures.

I did it because I was searching for myself amidst the mayhem.

The only way I could describe this impulse to people who claimed not to understand it was to equate it to the one thing we humans all understand: sex. As with arousal, where the pulse pounds at the thrill, anticipation, and yes, even the danger of exploring a new body, a new mind, each new story I covered fulfilled a pressing inner need to feel that same ardor, to inhale the world and all it had to offer, regardless of the risk from self-exposure.

Photography was my transformative phone booth. With a couple of cameras hung around my neck, I was no longer the tiny, mild-mannered homecoming queen from suburban Potomac. I was a superhero, a leaper of small land mines in a single bound; invincible. I was, now don't laugh . . . *Shutterbabe!*

But was I a concerned photographer? Let's just say I had my doubts.

Walking out of the café I turn to Pierre. "Will you be joining me?" I ask him.

Pierre looks confused, but he follows me anyway. "How are you going to find junkies? How do you even know what they look like?" he asks, walking briskly to keep up with me. I have short legs, but I've always been a speed walker. A compensation thing, I'm sure.

"Don't worry," I tell Pierre. "Like I said, I'm usually pretty good at finding them."

While we were getting stoned, I told Pierre about the junkie I found in the Paris Métro, the one I followed into one of those self-cleaning public street toilets just off the Place de la République. He needed his fix, so he paid his two francs, the door slid open, we slid inside, and for the next twenty minutes I stood on the immaculately clean toilet seat shooting photos of him getting high. An odd arrangement, yes, and kind of stupid in retrospect, but the guy seemed happy enough just to have the company. Anyway, I needed more drug pictures for my Magnum application, and I had nothing better to do that evening either.

Pierre, in turn, told me that this trip to Arnhem would be his first foray into a story involving real live human beings. Pierre had joined the Sipa photo agency on the strength of his animal pictures. He'd spent a couple of months in Morocco with a falcon breeder, and he traveled all over Canada shooting pictures of wolves.

As he spoke, I couldn't help but think that it takes a certain type of disposition to sit all day long in the snow, patiently waiting for wolves. And quite another to follow a junkie into an enclosed public *pissoir*.

Ah, the variety of the human animal.

We must have lost track of time in the hash café because it's getting dark by the time we head out. After a couple of loops around the neighborhood, I suggest we get some sleep and try again tomorrow. Besides, we're too stoned to keep looking. As it is, we barely find our way back to the train station to reclaim our bags. And now we still have to find a place to spend the night.

Pierre offers to carry my overnight bag while we look for lodging, and this time I accept his assistance. The two hotels across the street from the station are all booked, but the concierge at the second one gives us a tip on another, which we find and check into. Our rooms are clean and cheap: perfectly acceptable. Sure, there's no CNN, the bathroom is minuscule, the carpet is worn and the bedspread is made out of something really scratchy and synthetic, but that's okay. Those things are all incidental. Out of the four possible permutations of the two most important attributes, cost and cleanliness—1) dirty and cheap, 2) clean and expensive, 3) dirty and expensive or 4) clean and cheap—we've hit the jackpot.

I've always found it helpful to keep my requirements for satisfaction to a minimum: fewer basic needs equals greater contentment; the fewer variables you concern yourself with, the less chance you have for disappointment. In fact, when you look at the pure math, it's amazing to see to what degree the odds start stacking up against you as the number of variables increases.

(The equation, should you have some spare time, is fairly simple: $n^2 - n + 2 = x$, where n stands for the number of variables and x equals the number of possible outcomes. Two variables give you four possible outcomes; three give you eight; four give you fourteen, etc.)

Here's the rub. These elementary laws of probability apply to love as well. In fact, when you look at the math, when you think about all the variables each of us requires in our ideal of a mate, it's nothing short of a miracle that two people might find each other amidst the morass of humanity and actually *fall in love*. The heart might be fooled for a short while (lust clouds the mind), but numbers never lie. Statistically speaking, true love is extremely rare.

At the age of twenty-three, though I've had many boyfriends and lovers, many of whom I've loved, I've only been *in* love—the kind of love where you can project into the future and see yourselves growing old to-gether, the kind of love that makes walking feel like floating, smiling feel like bursting, touching feel like free falling—exactly twice.

Both relationships, one in high school, the other in college, ended in tears. Gabe and I were never the same after the abortion. And Matthew, at some point, although I was never sure exactly when, simply stopped loving me back. Or maybe he never really loved me at all.

And so I content myself with fewer variables. I make do with the less messy, less entangled, less heartbreaking act of loving without being in love. What can I say? I love men, all varieties. Men are like books, to be read or skimmed, studied or forgotten, enjoyed for the moment or di-gested in a forever kind of way. A few go back on the shelf and gather dust, others I might pull out now and again to reread a passage or two or three or fifteen. What I mean is that they can't all be *Anna Karenina,* but that doesn't mean I can't enjoy them just the same. I love talking to men and listening to their life stories. I love smelling them and holding them and making love to them, because, really, this is the most pure, metaphysical form of communication I know. I love their idiosyncrasies—this one likes his thighs caressed on the inside, not the outside; that one fixes me a plate of scrambled eggs after each assignation; this one is haunted by dreams of nuclear holocaust; that one has a thing about Dylan Thomas and earlobes. And just as each book I read changes me in some small, or perhaps large way, each man I bed, to be perfectly hyperbolic, makes me feel that much more attuned to the transcendence and bounty and beauty of life.

And so when, a few minutes after arriving in my clean and cheap hotel room, Pierre knocks on the door and asks me if he can borrow some soap, even though he hasn't read a book since high school, even though he be-lieves dogs are smarter than people and that the greatest philosopher of all time is Jim Morrison and that astrology is a more reliable science than, say, physics, I invite him inside. Pierre is kind. And attractive. He makes me laugh. What more do I need?

Later in bed, after an extremely satisfying romp, Pierre is kissing his way down the length of my right arm, muttering, *"Merci,"* after each kiss, when he suddenly stops. "What's this?" he asks, running his fingers along a faint white scar.

"It's a long story," I say.

"So tell me," he says. He clutches my naked body close to his and nuzzles the back of my head. I feel like a security blanket, only better.

FOUR MONTHS EARLIER, in the spring of 1989, the Swiss government decided to set up a free needle exchange program in the Platzpitz, a verdant park in the center of Zurich. The idea was to curb the spread of AIDS, but the result was a rollicking heroin circus. The park—bordered on one side by a river, on the other side by chocolate boutiques, watch stores, banks and quaint cobbled streets sprouting well-dressed Swiss matrons pushing prams full of blond babies—had suddenly become a netherworld of ravaged bodies slumped into little puddles of heroin-dazed goo. Virtually every junkie in Europe had heard about the Platzpitz, and they had all come to stay.

But no one was getting any good pictures of the place. All of the European magazines were planning their own needle park stories, but none of the photographers sent out to shoot the Platzpitz were coming back with anything worth publishing. A few Italian war photographers had staked themselves out with a couple of telephoto lenses in the window of a museum that bordered the park, but covering the heroin beat is not like covering a war. Bombs still look like bombs when they're shot from a relatively safe distance. Not so with junkies. To properly shoot junkies, you have to interact with them, make yourself vulnerable. You have to crawl out of the trenches far enough to actually shoot the details—the lighters under powder-filled spoons, the bubbling liquid, the needles stuck in arms, the syringes filled with blood, the ravaged skin, the tightly wound tourniquets, the haunted stares of the walking dead.

I'd never shot pictures of heroin addicts before. In fact, I was all set to go to Beijing to shoot what I thought would be boring student demonstrations in Tiananmen Square when Henri called me into his office. "Cancel your flight to China," he said gruffly. Henri said everything gruffly. That's because, true to his nickname, he was a grizzly bear stuck in the body of a man. He was an ex–war photographer, prone to spontaneous angry outbursts, and way too bulky and restless for his desk chair. I was afraid of him.

"Why?" I asked.

Henri was standing up behind his desk as usual. He almost never sat. "You're going to Zurich," he barked. "Alexi and Georges came back with shit, so now it's your turn." Alexi and Georges were two of the golden boys of Gamma, and if they'd come back empty-handed, I wasn't sure why Henri thought I could do any better. But Henri had what he said was a foolproof plan—he wanted me to lie. He told me that all of the photographers who'd tried to take pictures of the Platzpitz had been roughed up by the drug dealers who'd set up shop there. A couple of cameras had been smashed. The dealers knew they had a good thing going with the free needle-exchange program in the Platzpitz. With a centralized market, low overhead, plenty of grass and park benches for their clients to collapse upon, and relatively little hassle from the Swiss police, they weren't about to let bad publicity from some magazine photos ruin their fun.

Henri thought if I went undercover, I could get some pictures. He told me to go only with my Leica (which, to the untrained eye, looks like a cheap toy camera) and a few dozen rolls of film in a fanny pack around my waist—no camera bag, no photographer's vest, no press pass, no outward sign whatsoever of my pedigree as a journalist. He told me to wear shorts, a colorful T-shirt and sneakers so that I'd look as much like a silly American tourist as possible. If anyone were to ask, I was to say I was a photography student from America on vacation. I wasn't sure the plan would work, but I warmed to the idea of going undercover in a T-shirt. For once in my life, the fact that I was five-two, female and young would not be a liability or a physical disadvantage or a curse to be hidden under an electric-blue burka.

"You better come back with some pictures," Henri said. *"Sinon, je te casse la gueule!"*—which, directly translated, means "Or else I'll break your face."

Two hours later, I was on a train to Zurich. Not one of the magazines was willing to ante up any assignment money; they'd all been burned when other photographers they'd sent had come back without any pictures. Henri told me I'd just have to split the expenses of my trip with Gamma. Since I had only about 200 francs ($40) in the bank at the time,

I had to take an advance of 1,000 francs ($200) from the agency, which I would then have to pay back with any future sales of my photographs. Because I had no idea if there would be any future sales or even any photographs to sell, I was determined to keep my expenses down.

But unlike Afghanistan, where for weeks I could sleep in smelly caves for free and never have to pay a hotel bill, Switzerland was not—and never has been, at least as far as I know—a country at war. And lodging in Zurich was somewhere between expensive and outrageous. I ended up finding a cheap rooming house about half a mile away from the Platzpitz in a pretty unsavory part of town. As I was filling out the registration card at the front desk, I felt slightly queasy.

The rooming house was filled with recent Third World immigrants, all male—Nigerians, Sri Lankans, Indians and the like. I couldn't tell if they were awaiting processing or if they all lived there or what. I never asked. The hallways smelled like a mix of armpit sweat and onions, a scent regenerated at every mealtime when the men would crouch in small groups in the corridors to cook their rice and meat dishes on portable hot plates. They were preparing dinner when I arrived. To get to my room, I had to step over seven hot plates, fifty men mid-meal and two guys passed out sleeping. The few whose eyes I caught looked at me as if I were either an alien or dessert.

About fifteen minutes after I'd started to unpack, one of the Nigerians knocked on my door to hand me an extra key to my bedroom. He told me he'd been friends with the last man who'd stayed there, and he'd forgotten to return the key to him. I thanked him and, glancing around the room with its peeling wallpaper and stained bedsheets, wondered just how many other keys to my room were currently in circulation.

The next morning I took precautions. When I went out to shoot, heading to the Platzpitz on foot, I stuffed my fanny pack with all of my valuables—film, the advance from Gamma, my wallet and passport. As Henri suggested, I dressed like the prototypical American tourist, with the sneakers and the green tank top and the garish floral shorts. I also took a small piece of black gaffer's tape and covered the word "Leica" on my camera, which is etched in white letters just above and to the left of the lens. That way it would be less likely to be stolen or peg me—like the press pass I'd deliberately left back in Paris—as a journalist. I'd seen other photographers do the same thing with their cameras, but I'd always thought of it as a pretentious affectation until now.

It was a warm spring day. As I approached the Platzpitz, I noticed the lace of new leaves that had formed a canopy over the grass. It dappled the light, made everything glow. From a few blocks away, the park—filled with people, burgeoning with activity and life—looked like a Georges Seurat painting. But as I got closer, the impressionist mirage disappeared. This was no "L'Après Midi Sur L'Herbe." It was Danté's *Inferno*. Syringes and emaciated bodies littered the landscape. Boyfriends were shooting up girlfriends. This one's teeth held tight the rubber tourniquet around the arm of that one. One raggedy guy was looking for a free vein in his ankle, having exhausted the rest of the veins on the surface of his body. A woman screamed, trying to thwart the flow of blood down her arm. Next to her, drool spilled and crusted around the mouth of a man passed out like a blissful zombie on the grass.

In the center of the park, in a carefully constructed circle surrounding an empty gazebo, the dealers had set up brightly colored wooden folding tables that they manned as if they were selling apple pies at a county fair. But instead of baked goods, these tables were filled with everything the discerning junkie could possibly want—metal spoons, lighters, syringes, cotton balls, individually wrapped alcohol swabs, rubber tubing and, of course, little bags and foil packs of powdered heroin. The only thing missing were the needles, and these were being dispensed for free by government-paid doctors and nurses in a converted bus about twenty yards away. The line of bodies snaking around the friendly green bus was long.

I was anxious to get started, but I didn't know where to begin. So I sat on a bench with my *Herald Tribune,* pretending to read. Over the blurred zigzagged edge of the newspaper, I could see a teenage boy throwing up on the grass. Henri had told me that most of the kids in the park were from solid, middle-class families. I wondered what the boy's mother thought about her junkie son. For that matter, what would my mom think of me sitting here? Before I'd left Paris, I'd called her to tell her I'd be going to Zurich—"Yeah, Ma, it's sort of a medical story"—and she'd let out a sigh of relief. "At least it's not Afghanistan," she'd said, believing I'd turned a wise corner in my career.

I spotted a junkie couple making out. They were standing in the center of the park in the empty gazebo, oblivious to the needles and the powder and the tourniquets and the hundred or so other ravaged bodies in the

Platzpitz, all orbiting around them like planets in Galaxy Chaos. It would have been a good photo, but I was still not ready to shoot. I needed a plan. And if I sat there too long pretending to read that stupid newspaper, someone was going to wonder why a young, healthy-looking American tourist would choose to read her morning paper right there, on that particular bench, so close to the embers of hell. I reread the word "Tiananmen" on the front-page headline for what must have been the thirty-eighth time. I thought about Alexi and Georges and the Italians staked out in the museum and the smashed cameras.

Back in college, during my Pussycat Lounge days, I learned that the best way to inculcate oneself into a group is by befriending a single member of that group. This is not a profound or new or even very interesting concept, but it seemed so to me back then. I was surprised and pleased when I saw that once I'd made friends with Boom-Boom, the other strippers milling about backstage had no problem letting me shoot them, too.

Sitting there at the edge of the Platzpitz, I knew I needed another Boom-Boom, and I needed one fast. Ten minutes or so later, when I nervously glanced up from my newspaper, he was there. "What are you looking for?" the man asked in English, after failing to elicit a response using German. "Works? Powder? I've got everything you need." He was short and reed thin with an enormous white splint running the length of his left forearm. His black wavy hair was dirty and matted to his head, grown to shoulder length not by design but by neglect. He looked Sri Lankan, like the men in my hotel, although he could have just as easily been of aboriginal descent. Up and down his unsplinted arm were the telltale tracks, along with a couple of nasty-looking abscesses.

I swallowed hard, ready to lie. "No, thanks," I said, "I'm a student. Majoring in photography." I felt bad about lying, but then the man told me his name was Tom Jones, which made me feel better. Besides, it had only been a year since my graduation from college; I still felt like a student. "Tom" said he'd been living in Amsterdam until one of his friends told him about the Platzpitz. So he came for a visit and never left. When I asked him where he was living now that he was in Zurich, he mentioned a number of places he was able to crash with friends for free, including my hotel. Oh great, I thought, I wonder if he has a key to my room, too.

"What happened to your arm?" I asked.

"Abscesses," he said. "Infections. Shit like that."

About an hour later, my new junkie friend let me shoot pictures of him shooting up next to the gazebo. He crouched and cooked and then stuck a needle into a vein on his left arm just above the top of the giant splint. The couple who'd been making out were now getting ready for their next fix. They watched me shooting Tom. "She's a student," he told them. "It's okay." Then the couple let me shoot them shooting up. I took a close-up of the man's blood squirting back into the syringe, where it mixed with the boiled heroin just before being pushed back into his veins. I took a nice picture of the couple collapsed in a blissed-out heap on top of each other with the museum in the background. Soon, everyone was letting me shoot them shooting up. "It's okay. She's a student. She's a friend of Sunil's,"

ZURICH, SWITZERLAND, 1989

ZURICH, SWITZERLAND, 1989

they all told each other. Sunil? So that was his real name. They shot, I shot, it was a big shooting orgy that lovely spring day in the Platzpitz. And by sunset, I was as high from my pictures as they were from the smack.

I knew the photos were good. I finished off eight rolls of film that first day, and I should have just jumped on the late train to Paris and left it at that. But I was greedy. I wanted more. It was dark when I turned to walk back to the rooming house, and Tom/Sunil—ever the gallant new friend—insisted on accompanying me back there. I told him I'd be okay, but he insisted. Just before we reached the rooming house, I thought about all the copies of my key floating about and, lying once more, told him I was staying in an apartment. "It's right there," I said, pointing to a building at random.

"Right there," he repeated, staring at the building and looking slightly hurt. "Okay, well, I'll see you tomorrow," he said, turning to leave.

"Yeah, see you tomorrow," I said. I walked in the direction of the building, tried the front door in vain, and then waited a few minutes before turning around to head toward the rooming house. When I looked over my shoulder to make sure Sunil wasn't watching, he was. He paused there, illuminated by a few errant rays of a street light, and stared at me with his arms crossed. Our eyes locked for a brief moment, but he quickly looked away. Then he turned around, retreated into the darkness and headed back in the direction of the Platzpitz.

The rooming house was in full swing. The men were drunk, the cigarette smoke filled the hallways, and the voices and laughter ricocheted off the water-stained walls. I tried to drown out the noise, but I couldn't do anything about the smell of mildew and old sweat on the sheets.

The next day in the park, I couldn't find Sunil, but I saw a few familiar faces from the day before and started shooting anyway. This was a bad mistake. I was barely ten pictures into my first roll of film, shooting a close-up of a lighter under a spoon, when a dealer from one of the manned tables ran over and grabbed my camera strap angrily. He yelled something in German, but the only word I understood was "journalist."

"I'm a student!" I said, pushing him away from me. "Leave me alone." But underneath, my heart was pounding furiously. A few of the junkies gathered around us in a circle. They weren't taking sides.

"Ah, a student," he said, mocking me. "Vell, go study some-veer else." His German accent was thick, which gave the whole encounter a surreal edge to it. I can't help it. Whenever I hear a German accent, I automatically think *Nazi*. The dealer pushed me, and the junkie circle around us widened and grew accordingly. Then he grabbed me by the shoulder and whispered in my ear, "Get out of here before I kill you."

"Leave me alone," I said, but when I saw him take out a switchblade from his pocket, I ran.

I ran as fast as I could out of the park. I ran north, toward the chocolate stores and the banks and the cable cars, past the bodies and the bloody needles and the vomit. When I reached the perimeter of the park, I lost myself in the crowds of people and wound my way through the unfamiliar streets of Zurich back to my hotel room.

The rooming house was in its usual state of curried commotion when I got there. As I made my way to my room, the Nigerian who'd stopped by my room with the extra key on that first night approached me in the hallway.

"Your friend was here," he said. "Mr. Tom Jones."

"He was?" I said, startled. I immediately thought about Sunil, standing there last night under the streetlamp, watching me. I was such an idiot, letting him walk me home. "What did he say?"

"He said you had something for him. I told him you'd gone out for the day."

"Shit."

I ran down the hallway to my room. The door was unlocked. I was certain I'd see Sunil inside, waiting for me. But when I turned the knob and pushed it open, what I saw sent a jolt through my body. Every drawer in the room was flung open. Socks and T-shirts and underwear and shorts were strewn haphazardly over the floor. A chair lay on its side. The mattress was pushed halfway off its box spring, the mildewed sheets peeled back in a rumpled heap. And there, rummaging through my suitcase, and there, bent over my dresser drawers, were two junkies from the Platzpitz. When they saw me they froze. I froze. We stood there for a split-second eternity, face-to-face, saying nothing. I stopped breathing. One of the men, pale, ugly and squinty-eyed with a tired, pockmarked face and long brown hair, tapped the side of his thigh with his fingers nervously. The other man had scraggly, dirty blond hair and train-tracked arms; he stared straight ahead, bug-eyed. He was looking for an out.

Every synapse in my body was firing. My first rational thought was that Sunil must have brought them here. But where was he? And why were they still here? To steal money? To look for my film? Did the dealer who threatened me in the Platzpitz put them up to this? Did he promise them money or drugs for my film? If I ran, would they catch me? I thought about jumping out the window. The room was on the second floor, but the eaves of the building would make it easy to climb down.

My feet, in their bouncy white Reebok sneakers, felt like lead.

And then, the frozen tableau exploded. The blond was the first to move. He slid over to the door and slammed it shut, placing the one chair in the room under the doorknob for good measure. "Hold her!" he yelled to the ugly one, wielding a switchblade and walking toward me. As the ugly one held me from behind, my eyes followed only the knife. Was it the dealer's knife? It looked similar: small, with a green-marbled handle. It could have been. Or was the handle on the dealer's knife blue? I couldn't remember. The blond grabbed my long braid and held the knife to my throat, his hand shaking, his eyes filled with not so much anger as fear.

The ugly one now stepped in front of me, holding my wrists tightly together. I was outmuscled, and I knew it. In my mind I could picture the grisly scene—a severed throat, the blood, an ambulance. I started to cry, and I begged for my life. "Please don't, please don't, please don't . . ."

Suddenly, the blond removed the knife from my neck and sliced it into my forearm. It was the kind of cut you'd make on the skin of an orange you wanted to peel—deep enough to be effective, but shallow enough not to pierce the sweet, juicy fruit below. I screamed.

"Leave," said the blond. "Next time we kill you." But the threat, like the knifing, seemed like an afterthought.

My body was too filled with adrenaline to feel much pain. Exposed to the air, the wound pulsated and stung, but no more than a giant paper cut. When I saw the blood drops falling off my bent elbow, the room started to spin. As I sank to the floor, clutching my arm, the two men ran out the window. I could hear them yelling German to each other as their feet scrambled over the eaves.

I ran to the bathroom, cleaned the wound with some soap, and held a washcloth tightly around my forearm to stop the bleeding, crying hysterically all the while. I searched the room for a tissue to blow my nose, but had to sit down on the bed before I could find one because I was hyperventilating too hard to stand any longer. Worried that I might pass out, I grabbed an old paper bag out of the trash can and breathed into it, trying to relax my lungs with each breath drawn—in-and-out, in and out, in . . . and . . . out . . .

I barely remember the next hour. Somehow, I mustered the strength to gather the strewn clothes in a pile on the bed, I packed, I paid my bill, I procured some gauze and tape from a first aid kit they kept at the front desk ("I cut it on a fence," I told the clerk, who couldn't care less), I bought a box of chocolates, I smoked a cigarette and I sprung for a taxi to the train station. I contemplated calling the police but then quickly rejected the idea outright. When you've been the victim of as many crimes as I have, you learn the sad truth: few criminals ever get caught, despite the best efforts of the police and victims. Besides, I had no desire to spend another nanosecond in Zurich if I could possibly help it, and getting the Swiss police involved would probably mean at least another overnight stay, if not two or three.

When I got to the train station, I called Marion. Marion was one of my editors at Gamma, but she was also my best friend. As she picked up the

phone, I could hear the magazine pages rustling in the background. I pictured her there at her desk, smoking a cigarette and perusing the latest
Paris Match in the same way all photo editors do, by flipping the pages
back and forth between the photographs and the photo credits at the front
of the magazine to see who'd shot what. People in the photo world have little use for text.

"Hi," I said, my voice quivering. I was standing in the train station,
holding on to the pay phone booth for support.

"Hello, there!" she replied, her voice as chipper as always. "Have you
seen the new *Match?* Langevin's pictures from Beijing are unbelievable."
She went on to say something about tanks and crushed bicycles in Tiananmen Square, but I couldn't process the information.

I cut her off. "Marion, listen, I was stabbed. I'm on my way back to
Paris."

"What?" she asked, her voice incredulous.

"I was stabbed," I repeated, louder and slower. "Some guys ransacked
my hotel room and I caught them and they had a knife and they cut my
arm and—"

"Oh, shit," said Marion, now cutting me off. "Are you okay? Where are
you? Are you in the hospital? What the hell happened?"

"I'm fine. I'm at the train station. It's not deep. Just bloody. I'll explain
everything when I get back."

"Come home," said Marion. "Just come home."

The overnight train from Switzerland to Paris was scheduled to arrive
in the Gare de Lyon at dawn. I should have slept, but instead I spent the
night staring at the two-inch gash in my arm. The bleeding stopped before
I even got on the train, but the scab was not strong. When I removed the
gauze pad to change it, I noticed that if I pulled the skin around the wound
outward, I could still get the blood to ooze out. I never put on a new dressing. I kept hoping that some stranger would see the laceration and the
blood, ask me what had happened and offer me a shoulder to cry on. *Help
me, help me,* I'd say. *I have a bizarre job, I just spent two days hanging out
with heroin addicts, my room was ransacked, I was stabbed, my arm hurts
and I'm so, so lonely.*

There, there, the stranger would respond, pitying my woes. *Everything
will be all right.*

But no one on the train noticed my blood. It was late at night, and all of the potential saviors in my compartment were either reading about the massacre in China or sound asleep.

The train pulled into the station in Paris, and I took the Métro to the Châtelet–Les Halles stop, a short walk from my apartment. I figured I'd stop home, get some sleep, then take the films over to Gamma for processing. Normally, I would have gone straight to the agency, but with Tiananmen gobbling up the headlines, I knew no one would be looking to publish my pictures for at least a week or so. Besides, I was exhausted.

But when I finally arrived at the front door of my building on the rue St. Denis, it didn't feel like home. The section of the rue St. Denis I lived on, with its ancient cobblestones underfoot and its neon signs overhead, was just off the Place du Châtelet in Les Halles. Les Halles—which means "the halls," from its former incarnation as the city's central food market— is a bustling tourist area in the center of Paris, just to the north of the Seine on the Right Bank. Like many of the older, cobbled streets in Paris that are closed off to cars, the rue St. Denis is what the French call a *rue pietonne*, which roughly translates as a "street for walkers." This struck me as funny, considering the history of St. Denis as one of the major Parisian thoroughfares for prostitutes.

The first day I moved into my little eight-by-ten apartment on the rue St. Denis, I was spooked half the night picturing the faces of the hundreds of women who must have lain on tattered sheets in the very room I now occupied, staring out the very same windows, watching the very same shadows on the very same walls, trying to separate mind from body.

The rue St. Denis apartment was the third place I'd lived since arriving in Paris less than a year earlier. As with many decisions in my life, I had decided to move to Paris on a whim. Annie and Phyllida, two of my girlfriends from college, hatched the idea of a post-graduation Parisian adventure at the end of our senior year, and I, enchanted by *A Moveable Feast, Breathless* and—yes, I admit it—Madeline, figured the land of Cartier-Bresson and Magnum would be as good a place as any to start my photojournalism career.

Our first apartment was two blocks from the Tuileries. Phyllida's boyfriend, Ben, found it a week before she, Annie and I arrived. "It's in a beautiful neighborhood," Phyllida called me to say, on the eve of my flight, "but it's small." I had never been to Europe, and I was so excited to move to Paris, I didn't care what the apartment looked like or where it was located. When I arrived, however, I realized Phyllida's choice of descriptive words—"beautiful" and "small"—were both slight understatements. My first glimpse of the city was the one I saw as I rose out of the Tuileries Métro stop; to my right was the rue de Rivoli with its arched arcade walkways, to my left was the Jardin de Tuileries, straight ahead was the swirling Place de la Concorde and behind me was the Louvre. *Beautiful?* I couldn't think of a proper word to describe such beauty.

The apartment was another story. It was a tiny one-bedroom, and we were four people. Phyllida and her boyfriend took the bedroom. Annie was given the couch in the living room. And for the next six months, except when I was working in Israel or Afghanistan, I slept in the closet.

Parisian home number two was the pullout couch in my colleague Hubert's living room on the rue Vieille du Temple. This was an improvement over the closet, but barely.

So as I stood there at dawn in front of apartment number three on the rue St. Denis, a tired vagabond with a camera bag on one shoulder, an overnight bag on the other, and a two-inch freshly coagulated scab running down my arm, it suddenly occurred to me that despite the house keys in my pocket, I was not home. The streets of Les Halles were all but deserted save for the green men with their brooms and their trash cans and their giant dog poop vacuums, and the bread guys delivering their brown bouquets of morning baguettes to Café Costes on the corner.

"Come home," Marion had urged me on the phone. Luckily, she lived nearby.

I walked across the street, turned half a block north up the Boulevard Sébastopol and punched in "B394" on the keypad outside Marion's building. The door clicked open, I let myself in, and I walked up the six flights of stairs to her apartment. She answered the door in her pajamas. The sun had just started to stream through her window, and the combination of the pajamas and the light brought tears to my eyes.

I handed her the box of chocolates, the little ones with the pictures of the Alps and pastoral Swiss villages and church spires as wrappers. "These are for you," I said, smiling.

"Ooh, Swiss chocolate. Yum! Let me see your arm." She grabbed my hand and stared at the wound above it. "Ooh! Lovely. Let's get you cleaned up, shall we?" Marion was my only French friend who spoke to me in English. She was schooled in proper British diction, and when she said things like "lovely" or "shall we," she sounded a lot like Mary Poppins. One day when we were talking about her boyfriend, I taught her the phrase "little shit." She liked it a lot, using it often and correctly.

I fell asleep on Marion's bed, a new bandage on my arm. When I woke up, she had a baguette, butter, raspberry jam and fresh coffee laid out on the table. Just like home.

"STABBED? SHIT."

"Yeah, shit," I say to Pierre.

He pauses to think about it for a moment, weighing and measuring his words. And then, sympathetically and without a hint of irony, he says, "The planets were probably really out of alignment that day."

"The planets . . ." I say, pausing as if I were really pondering the possibility. "Yes, the planets. You're probably right." I kiss him maternally on the nose.

He runs his thumb over my scar back and forth, trying to erase it. Exhausted, I fall asleep with my head in the crook of his neck. With his free hand, he strokes my hair. A few hours later, I wake up in a cold sweat. In my dream, sweet, sexy, goofy, wolf-loving, leather-clad Pierre had held a knife to my throat and decapitated me.

The next day, we head out on foot back to the bombed-out house. Besides some additional police tape, it looks the same. Pierre wants to head back to Paris, but I convince him to look for junkies with me one more time. And this time, we find one.

He has mocha skin, overgrown black facial hair, a long, aquiline nose, sunken eyes. He could be twenty. Or forty. With junkies, you can never tell. We spot him two blocks from the bombed house, pacing aimlessly in front of a billboard seeking donations to end hunger. Though the junkie must be well over six feet tall, he looks far less robust than the image of the starving African kid looming larger than life behind him. It's a mild autumn day, but the man's shoulders are hunched, as if to ward off the coldest of winter winds, and his hands are shoved deep inside the pockets of his loose, filthy jeans.

I tell Pierre to let me do the talking, and he just stands there in his black leather jacket and muscles smiling. *"Qu'est-ce que tu vas faire?"* He laughs. "You are just going to go up to him and say, 'Hello, my name is Deborah and I'd like to take a picture of you shooting heroin'?"

"Yes," I say, "that's exactly what I'm going to do."

Pierre looks at the ground, kicks his steel-toed boot into the sidewalk, and shakes his head in bemused disbelief. But when I walk away, he obediently follows me down the block to meet the junkie. Up close, I notice that the man's hands are not in his pockets to protect them from the cold. Rather, he is absentmindedly and quite vigorously scratching his thighs.

The man starts to walk away, but I call out to him. "Hi," I say, "don't leave. We want to talk to you." I tell him we are photographers. That we've been sent to cover the house bombing. That we'd like to shoot pictures of him, if he wouldn't mind. His eyes dart back and forth from Pierre to me suspiciously, examining the camera equipment, the clothing, the press pass I wear in a clear plastic pocket in my photographer's vest. Then he speaks.

"It was a nice house, that house they blew up," he says in English with some sort of an Arabic accent I'm unable to place. "A nice house." His arms across his chest, he's now scratching each elbow simultaneously. After a few minutes of polite conversation—what's your name? (Ahmed), where are you from? (Egypt), how long have you lived here in Holland? (five years), are you addicted to heroin? (yes), for how long? (five years), can we take pictures of you shooting up (if you pay me)—we've struck up a deal. Since giving Ahmed plain old cash would be construed as journalistically unethical, Pierre and I are to buy him a container of orange juice, some yogurt and a loaf of bread. In exchange, we can shoot pictures of him doing heroin.

I can tell that Pierre, who's nodding his head in agreement with the plan, hasn't understood a word. *"Tu as compris?"*—"Did you understand?"—I ask him.

"Pas du tout." Not at all.

"It's simple," I tell him. "Ahmed needs some groceries. We'll buy them for him and, in exchange, he'll shoot up for us." As the words leave my mouth—or rather, because they leave my mouth—I'm immediately struck by their callousness. So is Pierre. For the first time in the two days since I've known him, his smile fades.

"Oh, I get it," he says. "This isn't journalism. It's a transaction."

Well, yes, I think, sort of. Ahmed needs food and maybe he even needs a little company. I need a picture. Perhaps "barter" is a better word. "Call it whatever you like," I say to Pierre, "but it's still journalism. Look, if you want to go back to your wolves and your falcons, go back. I can't afford not to shoot these pictures."

Pierre looks at me. He looks at Ahmed. He looks back at me. And then, in his heavily accented, almost nonexistent English, he says to Ahmed, "Okay, zen, ve go?"

"Yes," says Ahmed. "We go."

Pierre shoots me a look of pained resignation.

We buy the yogurt and the bread and the juice at a nearby store; Pierre mimes his offer to carry the plastic bag, but Ahmed just waves his arms no and says, "I'm okay." His thigh-scratching has become intense, he bites his bottom lip, and he leans forward—braced against that nonexistent wind—on a mission to reach his syringe. I look over at Pierre. He suddenly looks tiny in that big, black jacket with its shiny zippers and oversized lapels.

As we trot along, trying to keep up with Ahmed, I attempt to load my Leica with a roll of color film. But to load a Leica you ideally need three hands: one hand to hold the camera, the other to load the film and a third to hold the removable metallic underside of the camera. As usual, I put the thin, cold piece of metal between my teeth, but while I'm simultaneously running and trying to ease the plastic tail of the film into the tiny slats of the camera's spool, my teeth lose their grip on the metal and it falls with a clang on the sidewalk. When I bend down to pick it up, I catch a glimpse of the scar on my arm.

The sight of it unhinges me, as it often does, and I'm flooded by images I've worked hard to suppress. They come to me like slides in a rapidly spinning carousel, projected in the dark of my mind. I see Zurich, the clothes on the floor, the startled men, the blood-soaked washcloth. I see the junkie in the public toilet in Paris. He had half a lemon with him. What did he need the lemon for? Was it to clean the needle or boil the heroin? I can't remember. I see Steve at the Pussycat Lounge, staring at himself in the mirror and ejaculating into his palm, and I see him wiping his hand on his Led Zeppelin T-shirt afterwards. I see the mujahed and the mine and the way the flesh hanging from his knee looked fake and the diarrhea on the infants and the grateful smiles of their mothers as they thanked me for the Tic-Tacs. I see the flasher in the Combat Zone and Venus and her lollipop and Sunil and the couple passed out in front of the museum and the dust in Ramallah and the Palestinian boy who showed me the round scar on his calf the size of a rubber bullet and the mujahideen who fired off their Kalashnikovs into the frigid night air yelling, "Down with America!"

Call it the curse of the photographer. Unlike the memories of my childhood—fuzzy around the edges, suffused more with movement and smell and sound than with the rigidity of graphic lines and shapes—most of the memories I have since becoming a photographer are four-sided and flat. When you learn to properly frame an image in the viewfinder of a camera, you start to frame and catalog everything you see, whether you photograph it or not. And suddenly, memory has the shape of a rectangle. The vastness of a forest becomes twelve trees with a rock balancing out the foreground. A person becomes a close-up of the crow's-feet around his eyes. A war becomes red blood in white snow. Sometimes I feel like my brain has become nothing more than an overstuffed spiral notebook full of negatives, printed at will in a disorganized flurry by the tiniest provocation.

We arrive at what appears to be a perfectly normal-looking attached house in the middle of a perfectly normal-looking block. There is a separate entrance to a basement apartment. We walk down the small, steep flight of stairs, and before we even turn the corner into the room, a noxious but unidentifiable stench blasts our nostrils.

The room is fairly dark, illuminated by one bare bulb and the few slivers of daylight that creep in from two small windows. "That's Gunther," Ahmed says, pointing to a blond man passed out amidst half-eaten food cartons, crumpled newspapers, extinguished cigarette butts, metal spoons, old scraps of paper and foil and a small puddle of what looks to be his own urine. The leather belt that was used as a tourniquet around his arm is loose now, his face calm and strangely angelic. Ahmed puts his groceries on a makeshift milk-carton table and clears a spot for Pierre and me on the floor in front of his bare mattress. "Sorry about the smell. The toilet hasn't worked in weeks," he says, with no more regret in his voice than a Park Avenue hostess making excuses for the sawdust her contractors left behind. In a small, tidy heap, at the bottom of the stairs in the far left corner of the landing, is a pile of human excrement.

Pierre offers me a cigarette and I take it gladly. Then he offers one to Ahmed, who waves it away while reaching into his pocket, from which he excavates a small treasure wrapped in silver foil. I take one drag from the cigarette, but then I spot the powdered heroin in Ahmed's hand, and I immediately stub it out. I grab my Leica. I stop thinking about the fact that we're in a trash-filled drug den and start concentrating on the immediate task at hand. Suddenly, I am no longer an American girl chatting with an Egyptian junkie in his shit-filled basement. Suddenly, space loses its third dimension, time breaks down into the fractions of a second and motion—frozen for eternity in a viewfinder—ceases. I am a machine, a mere mechanical extension of my camera.

This should be shot in black and white, I think to myself, but my camera is loaded with 400 ASA Ektachrome color film instead; Gamma won't be able to sell it if I shoot in black and white. I briefly contemplate using a flash, but decide to try to use the ambient light—a mixture of daylight and tungsten—instead. The mixed light will give the picture a reddish hue, but I figure this is preferable to the flash, which would just flatten the image, leaving it devoid of contour, emotion. Then I notice that with a wide-open aperture, I can barely get by with an eighth of a second shutter speed, so I fret over the flash once more but now Ahmed has started to boil the heroin in a spoon and I'm stuck. Okay, no flash. I'll just push the film to 800. That'll give me a fifteenth of a second, and I'll be okay. The image will be grainy, blurred by any small movements Ahmed might make, but it's the best option I have. Pierre follows my lead and keeps his flash in his camera bag. But then he looks into his viewfinder at the light meter and turns to me, dumbfounded. "Uh, Deborah, there's no light," he says.

"No flash," I say. "You'll ruin my pictures if we shoot at the same time."

"What pictures?" he asks, almost in a whisper. "We won't have any pictures at this speed." Pierre is used to shooting his wolves in the blinding snow and his falcons in the desert sun; in that kind of light, even at 1/500th of a second, he could have all the depth of field he'd ever need.

"Push to eight hundred," I say, slightly annoyed.

He looks through his viewfinder once more. "I can't shoot at a fifteenth!"

"Just do it!" I snap.

Pierre senses my annoyance and stops talking.

Close-up of spoon and lighter. Snap. Close-up of tourniquet around arm. Snap. Close-up of needle entering skin. Snap. Close-up of blood entering syringe. Snap. Horizontal medium shot of Ahmed's torso, his bent elbow in the center of the frame. Snap. Vertical shot of same. Much better. Snap. A few more medium shots from different angles. Snap. Snap. Snap. Wide shot of Ahmed passed out on his mattress with the brown stains and Gunther passed out in the background and the food containers and newspapers and the cigarette butts and far, far off at the edge of the frame the pile of shit at the bottom of the stairs. Snap.

With Ahmed passed out, Pierre hands me another cigarette and lights one for himself. These we smoke, all the way down to the filter, in silence. Pierre extinguishes his in the swill at the bottom of an old beer bottle, and then, with a sudden manic surge of energy, he jumps up. He takes the grocery bag, empties its contents onto the table, and starts to fill the bag with trash from around the room. He throws away cigarette butts and milk containers and empty Coke cans and beer bottles and old pieces of cotton and the paper wrapping from the alcohol swabs and some week-old rice and a chicken bone and some crumpled-up paper and a plastic fork with one tine

ARNHEM, HOLLAND, 1989

missing and a broken needle and even a few dust bunnies from the corners of the room. I grab the bag from him and hold it open. In goes a shard of foil. In goes a gum wrapper. In goes half of a lemon, its fragrant juice squeezed out long ago. But when Pierre reaches the excrement, he stops short. "I can't do it," he says. He looks as if he's about to cry.

"I'll do it," I say. I lay down our garbage bag and pick up an empty one off the floor. With my hand covered by the plastic, like I'd seen dog owners do in Central Park the summer I worked for Magnum, I scoop up the pile and shove it in the garbage. I can feel myself gagging, but I stop just short of throwing up. I take the now full bag, tie the two plastic handles together, and place the entire enclosed mess at the bottom of the stairs.

"The room's still dirty," says Pierre. Tears fill his pleading eyes.

"I know," I say, "it's a mess." But you can't help every fucked-up person in the world, I think. You can't help every junkie, every starving African kid, every screaming, frightened Vietnamese girl covered in napalm who happens to cross your path. It's just not possible.

Shutterbabe? Shudder, babe.

On the back of one of my Gamma envelopes, I scribble a note to Ahmed: *Dear Ahmed, Thanks for helping us. Take care of yourself. Love, Deborah and Pierre.* With a piece of gaffer's tape, I stick it on the unopened orange juice container. I figure if he ever needs to reach me, he can call the agency phone number written on the envelope. But I know he'll never call. I motion for Pierre to come, and he grabs the garbage bag on the way up the stairs. On our way back to the hotel, we throw it out in a public trash can. Later, riding on a nearly empty train back to Paris, we decide to leave the window of our compartment wide open despite the snap of autumn.

Pierre will be so traumatized by what he has seen today that he will not be able to pick up his camera for an entire week. Then he will go back to Canada to be with his wolves.

I will file the rectangular memories in a sturdy drawer in my brain, go back to my tiny apartment on the rue St. Denis, sleep for an entire day, and then I'll call Patrick Zachmann and tell him I don't want to apply to Magnum. I'll tell him it's because I'm not ready, but I won't tell him it's because I know I'll never be ready. I will edit the slides from Arnhem and hand over the good ones to the agency. The pictures will definitely not be worth a thousand words, but they'll merit at least eight: "This is Ahmed shooting up. It is sad." Over the next year, Gamma will sell that picture of Ahmed enough times for me to pay off my expenses from the trip. The photographs of the bombed-out house, the ones I was sent to shoot, will never earn me so much as a single franc.

When Pierre comes back from his Canadian wolf expedition, he will take me on a long ride around Paris on his Honda. We will become friends, lovers, whatever you want to call it, and we will spend many bliss-ful nights together whenever either one of us gets too lonely. We will never talk about Ahmed or his basement or the garbage bag. And the scar on my arm, while it will never fully disappear, will fade into an almost impercep-tible line.

PART TWO

STOP

MANA POOLS NATIONAL PARK, ZIMBABWE, 1989

JULIAN

MR. NDUKU BRUSHES A SPECK OF LINT off his gray polyester suit. "I'm sorry," he says, sitting on the edge of his metal desk, "but it will not be possible for you to do this story." Mr. Nduku is a mid-level bureaucrat in the Harare press office here in Zimbabwe, where I've come to cover a semicovert jungle war fought, curiously enough, in the name of rhinoceros conservation. A few days ago, he sent me a confirmation fax through the Zimbabwean consulate in Paris, granting me permission to cover the war—dubbed Operation Stronghold—and promising to arrange my transport into the jungle, where the antipoaching team has its headquarters.

"What do you mean?" I say. "I have your confirmation fax right here." I start to rifle through my papers, but Mr. Nduku stands up and motions me to stop, his chubby palms patting down the air. He's almost exactly my height, but at least four times as round, with extra folds of dark brown skin protruding out of his collar, as if he were being choked. Behind him, hung with yellowed Scotch tape on the cinderblock wall, is a ripped and fading tourism poster with a cartoon rhino standing on a map of Zimbabwe. In big black letters it says ZIMBABWE IS RHINO COUNTRY.

"Please," he says, now placing his hand on my upper arm and smiling, "there's no need to show it to me. I wrote the fax myself. I know what it says." The smile is disingenuous. Taunting, even.

"Well, then, what exactly do you *need*?" I ask, pulling my arm away brusquely. I'm used to corrupt officials by now, and I know the language of bribery. I ask them what they "need" and they tell me how "happy" it would make them to acquire this bottle of Johnnie Walker Red or that carton of Marlboros or, even better, that pair of size-ten Nike sneakers with the aerodynamically enhanced arch supports. A smart journalist carries around such presents just in case, especially in less developed countries. In fact, many news organizations have budgets for these kinds of soft payoffs, sending their producers and their cameramen, their writers and their photographers off into the world with enormous sacks of ABC News baseball hats or NBC News key chains or *Newsweek* lapel pins or *Time* magazine ballpoint pens. Gamma doesn't have the money for this sort of extravagance, so I carry around a couple of Zippo lighters I've bought in various airport duty-free shops just in case the "need" should arise.

But as I stare into Nduku's eyes, trying to read him, I suddenly understand that a fancy lighter won't cut it this time. I can see it in the way his gaze is just slightly askance, in the asymmetry of his smile, in the sideways cock of his head. It's that interrogatory look: the same look the flasher gave me in the Combat Zone, the same look Aidan had that night before graduation. It's the same look I've seen many times before—the one where the facial muscles are controlled by sinew connected to the groin.

"What do I *need*?" he asks, his smile widening. "Come to dinner with me tonight, and I can show you."

"Excuse me?" I say, playing dumb. Wishing this weren't happening.

"I said," he says, now grabbing my hands and rubbing my left palm with his thumb, "that I can show you what I need if you come home with me tonight." He brushes his body against my thigh. He is aroused.

I yank my fingers out of Mr. Nduku's sweaty palms and take two giant steps back, bumping into a chair as I do. "I'm sorry, Mr. Nduku," I say, "but *that* will not be possible."

There are few things more abhorrent than having your hands touched by a stranger with a hard-on, especially one whose approval or services or interview or photograph you require in order to do your job. During one of my trips to Israel, I was interviewing and photographing Moshe—a white-bearded, octogenarian, ultra-Orthodox rabbi transplanted from Brooklyn—about his belief in the Messiah and his friendship with Yasir Arafat when, in the middle of our discussion, he turned off my tape recorder and grabbed my hands together in his coarse, bony grip. This would not have alarmed me so much were it not for the fact that ultra-Orthodox Jewish men are not supposed to look a woman in the eyes, let alone touch her hands. Then there was the whole issue of venue: because Moshe was not allowed to be seen even talking to a woman in public, he'd insisted we conduct the interview in my hotel room. But just as I was about to say something along the lines of "Excuse me, Rabbi, but what exactly do you think you're doing?" he pushed me down on the bed and stuck his tongue in my mouth. That was more abhorrent, but not by much.

(And yes, if you were wondering, I beat the crap out of him afterwards. Would have thrown him down a flight of stairs had a horrified bystander not intervened.)

GOING TO ZIMBABWE to shoot Operation Stronghold was Xavier's idea. Xavier was the editor at the helm of one of the more profitable departments at Gamma, called simply *"magazine."* It took me a long time to figure out that *"magazine"* meant "feature stories," and that within the Gamma hierarchy, doing *magazine* instead of spot news accorded one more status. It meant you were more of an artist, less of a cowboy, that you were well established in your career. Before I understood this distinction, whenever another photographer would ask me, *"Tu fais du magazine ou du news?"*—"Do you do features or spot news?"—I thought I was being asked if I worked for magazines or newspapers, to which I'd always reply, *"Les deux,"* meaning "Both." This never ceased to impress, because first of all I was very young and second, normally only the best photographers from each agency were given the plum feature assignments.

I was also surprised to learn that shooting *magazine* paid well. Unlike news stories, where expenses are split between the photographer and the agency, feature assignments from a magazine like *Géo* included all expenses paid up front plus (at the time) approximately 10,000 francs ($1,800) a week in assignment fees. When Sylvie, the photo editor of *Géo,* one day called to tell me she wanted me to spend two and a half weeks traversing the globe shooting a round-the-world treasure hunt—for which she would pay my expenses plus 20,000 francs—I couldn't believe my good fortune.

The downside of feature assignments, however—particularly in the case of the slick, right-wing *Figaro* magazine—is that the photos the magazines expected often required the use of expensive and cumbersome light kits and the blurring of fact with fiction. Feature photographs are often set up in a fashion the French call *photo montée,* a phrase derived from the verb *monter,* which has about twenty-three various definitions, ranging from "to mount" to "to edit," but which in this formulation means "to stage."

For example, let's say I had a feature assignment to shoot hookah-smoking in Cairo. Instead of going to a hookah bar and just shooting the scene as it exists, I would move people and tables and hookahs around to my liking. I'd sit two Egyptians at a table on one side, and two Western tourists at a table on the other, and I'd make sure to put them on some sort of balcony overlooking the sparkling city below at precisely the hour of dusk. I'd bounce a Balcar or perhaps a Dyna-Lite or a Norman flash onto the ceiling for better illumination, and I'd direct another freestanding flash muted by a soft box onto my subjects, making sure to balance my exposure time and aperture to record both my subjects and the fading light in the background.

I thought photo montée was bullshit. It was advertising, not photojournalism, and it rankled my purist sensibilities. Besides, who wants to lug four large metal cases of flash equipment around wherever you go? To me it didn't make sense. Even worse, the growing popularity of photo montée was just enough of a slippery slope for photographers like Pascal to create a battle, shoot it and pass it off as photojournalism without a second thought.

"*Tu sais comment ça se fait, la photo montée?*"—"Do you know how to do staged photos?"—Xavier asked me one day. I was sitting at a long conference table in the photographers lounge at Gamma, going through two foot-high piles of slide sleeves filled with various photos I'd shot over the past month, throwing out the bad ones, organizing the good ones. It was one of those tasks that, like bill paying, could become completely overwhelming if left to fester for more than a month or so.

"*Non,*" I replied, not even looking up. "*Et je n'ai pas envie d'apprendre*"—"And I have no desire to learn." Xavier was the one who'd made the "you have such lovely breasts" comment when I first arrived at Gamma. So I didn't mind being rude to him. Besides, he was yet another ex-photographer turned photo editor, probably once roguish and charming, but now potbellied, balding and bored. He gave me the creeps. "Why do you ask?"

"Oh, nothing," he said. He told me he had a feature story that needed to be shot, "some bizarre little war down in Zimbabwe," he said, but that if I didn't want to learn photo montée, I shouldn't worry my pretty little head over it, because he could just have one of the other English-speaking Gamma photographers shoot it instead.

My response time was short: three seconds, maybe four. A feature story (easy cash) about a war (adventure) in Zimbabwe (faraway place I'd never been to)? "When do you want me to go?"

"Viens dans mon bureau, mon petit chou," he said—"Step inside my office, my little cabbage." Then he winked at me. I self-consciously crossed my arms over my chest and stood up to follow him. But then with a bow and a wave of his arm he said, *"Après toi,"* positioning himself behind me for the short walk down the narrow corridor to his office. As we made our way down the hall, I heard a grunting noise behind me followed by *"Quel jolie cul!"*—"What a pretty ass!"

I stopped in my tracks and turned around to face him. "Hey, fuck you, Xavier," I said, unable to stop the words from escaping. "Just stop it already. You know, where I come from, words like that are called sexual harassment."

Xavier laughed, mimicking my admonition in a high-pitched, American-accented falsetto. (*"Va te faire foutre, Xavier . . ."*) Then, with yet another wink, he said, "Yes, but this is not America, my little cabbage." I wasn't fluent enough in the idioms of the French language to tell him to take his little cabbage and stuff it.

Once inside his office, where I made sure to keep the door open, Xavier explained the situation to me. Because rhino horns were becoming extremely rare, and because one of the things for which rhino horn powder was valued in the Far East was its alleged ability to act as an aphrodisiac, the illegal poaching of rhinoceroses had become a big business in Zimbabwe—big enough that the poverty-stricken Zambian poachers were sneaking across the Zambezi River into Zimbabwe and killing not only rhinos but also the game wardens who tried to stop them from doing so. It was, Xavier explained, somewhat akin to the war the American DEA was waging in the Colombian foothills.

To save the rhinos and the game wardens who guarded them, the government of Zimbabwe decided to institute a shoot-to-kill policy against any poacher caught red-handed with a rhino horn. Xavier wanted me to go down to Africa, to the Zambezi River Valley, where the antipoaching squads had set up a base camp, and do a *magazine*-style photo-essay on the soldiers fighting there. He gave me a contact at the Zimbabwean consulate in Paris, told me to arrange everything quickly before someone from Sygma or Sipa beat me to the story and then, gesturing skyward with his hands, looking soulfully into the distance, he told me of his vision of how the photos should look. "Well lit," he said. "A little blast of Balcar, maybe some fill light or a gold reflector. Pose the soldiers with their guns, make them look menacing and scary."

I'd been told that Xavier was a mediocre photographer in his time. The fact that he wanted me to lug cases of freestanding flashes to go cover a war gave me pause. "Xavier," I said, "have you ever covered a war?"

"No. Why?"

"Okay, well, here's the thing. It's not the kind of story that lends itself to photo montée." I told him I preferred to work with natural light, especially when it involved traipsing through the jungle with armed men.

He asked me rhetorically if I'd ever shot *magazine* before, and when I said no, he looked at me smugly and said if I wanted to sell the story I should consider bringing a light kit.

"What do you mean *if* I want to sell the story? There's no assignment yet?" I asked. So much for easy cash.

"No, not yet," he said, twirling a pen like a propeller on the knuckle of his thumb. He told me not to worry. That Gamma would front the money. "You can pay us back half when we've sold the story to *Fig* mag, which I'm sure will happen when they see how well lit the photos are going to be, huh?"

Unfortunately, I wasn't so sure *Fig* mag—short for *Figaro* magazine— would buy my rhino story, even if it was well lit. *Figaro* liked stories about French cheese makers, French wine makers, French aristocracy and French actors. They didn't like stories about non-French people, unless the articles were about Algerian immigrants wreaking havoc in the suburbs of Paris or the text accompanied a photo-essay mocking British eccentrics. A war on rhino conservation in Zimbabwe had three strikes against it, as far as selling it to *Figaro*: 1) war, 2) rhinos and 3) black people. Because my finances were, as usual, on shaky ground, this was worrisome.

Working as an agency photographer was like indentured servitude. You could become so indebted to the agency, especially when a story you'd spent a lot of money on didn't sell, that you'd have to keep working just to prevent the debt from escalating. With spot news photos, the risk was lessened by the fact that, because the news would make headlines for a few weeks or so, there was a much better chance that a few pictures would sell. Maybe not to *Time* or to *Newsweek,* and maybe not immediately, but to some magazine somewhere sometime. But with feature stories done on spec, photographers risked accumulating thousands upon thousands of dollars of debt if no one cared about the story they'd just spent two months shooting on, say, circuses in Cyprus or midwives in Malta.

My round-trip ticket to Zimbabwe alone would cost me around 6,000 francs (approximately $1,000). But it sounded like an interesting story, and I was just about due for a new adventure. I was also due for a new stamp in my passport. Because I was living in Paris on a tourist visa, I had to leave the country at least every three months or face the possibility of deportation. And besides, whether I sold the story or not, I figured I could always just shoot a lot of stock pictures of elephants. You can never have enough elephant pictures in your archives. I decided the financial risk was worth it.

"Okay, Xavier, I'll go, but I'll do it my way," I said.

Xavier was staring at my breasts again. "And what way would that be, my little cabbage?"

"No Balcars, no reflectors," I said. "And I'm not your fucking cabbage."

"*Comme tu veux,*" Xavier said dismissively. "It's your money." He was cleaning his fingernail with a corner of a plastic slide sheet as I turned to leave. "Oh," he said, stopping me mid-stride, "and don't forget to shoot a photo of a dead poacher. There's no story, my little cabbage, without a dead poacher."

I LEAVE MR. NDUKU'S OFFICE pissed off and worried. While Xavier was concerned that I might fail to return with pictures of a slain poacher, I don't think he ever imagined that I'd come back empty-handed. What a joke. The one man who can get me inside a war where men are killing other men over a mythical aphrodisiac won't let me go unless I sleep with him. Since that's out of the question, I now have no escort, no contact name, no way of knowing where the war is being fought, let alone how to get there. The Zambezi River Valley is a big place; you don't just take a bus there and shout, "Hey, anyone seen a war around here?"

When I call Xavier from my hotel in Harare to tell him of my predicament, he doesn't seem concerned. "What's the problem?" he says. "If Nduku's the gatekeeper, then you better be nice to him."

Oh, sure, I think. Easy for you to say, you old lech. "That doesn't sound like a solution to me," I say. I slam down the phone and call back the Gamma switchboard. This time I ask for Marion.

"Oh, sweetie, I'm so sorry," she says. She tells me to cut my losses and fly home.

I hang up the phone and go down to the bar for a drink, hoping to calm myself down enough to come up with a less drastic solution than giving up. The weather is warm and sunny, so I decide to sit outside on the patio, drink my beer, read the *Herald Trib* and figure out my next move. As I'm reading a story on Lech Walesa, the midday African sun beating down, I overhear two journalists at the next table discussing a recent clash in Mozambique. "Pity I couldn't have been there," says one in a crisp British clip. He's young, maybe in his late twenties or early thirties, with a head of curly, dirty-blond hair. Though he's quite handsome, from the stoop of his shoulders he appears not to know it. He wears the instantly recognizable disheveled look of a newspaper reporter—hair needing a cut, shirt needing a button, a collar frayed and soft. His breast pocket holds a reporter's notebook, a ballpoint pen and a dime-sized ink stain.

"Yeah, well, next time," says the other, sipping his scotch. He's a middle-aged man, black, American, serious and dignified.

I walk over to their table. "Mind if I join you?" I ask.

"Not at all," smiles the young Brit, pronouncing the simple phrase with a mouthful of crisp *t*'s—*Naw-ta-tall*.

I lay down my paraphernalia and drag a metal chair over from my table, its legs scraping against the concrete patio. The younger one jumps up to take it from me, raising it aloft and placing it on the ground while motioning me to sit down with a polite "Please." The older one introduces himself. I miss his name because I'm staring at the younger one, but I do hear him say that he works for *The New York Times*. The younger one— his name is Julian, he says—reminds me of a shy British schoolboy. He can look me in the eye only for a second or two before staring back at his beer. He tells me he's based in Harare as a stringer for the BBC and for *The Financial Times,* and that he's been posted here for just under a year. "Did you just get here, then?" he asks me, rotating his glass in his hands to help the words come out.

"Yes," I answer. "I'm a photographer with Gamma, here to cover the rhino war."

The *Times* reporter laughs. "I wouldn't exactly call it a war," he says. "I mean, they have guns and all, but I don't really think they know what the hell they're doing up there. You covered any other wars?"

I brag a little, pretending to be a real veteran. "Oh sure. Israel, Afghanistan, I've been around . . ."

The men, in turn, pretend to be impressed. "Uh-huh," they say, "is that right?" but I can tell they'd rather get back to the much better discussion they were having before I interrupted.

I change the subject, getting right to the point. "Listen," I say, "Julian, uh . . ."

"Ken," says the man from the *Times.*

"Right. Ken. I have a bit of a problem." I tell them about my quandary with Nduku, trying to make light of the situation. The two of them laugh nervously, their expressions having turned from disinterested to sympathetic.

"Welcome to Africa," says Julian.

"Yeah, I don't know what to tell you," says Ken.

Julian takes another sip of his beer then pipes up with an idea. He says he knows a local journalist who covered Operation Stronghold and who might be able to offer some advice. He doesn't have the phone number on him, but he suggests I accompany him back to his house, where we could dig up the guy's business card and call him.

We say our good-byes to Ken and drive off together in Julian's white, slightly dented Ford hatchback toward the residential section of the city. To get there, we have to meander through busy downtown streets and outdoor markets alive with local Zimbabweans, some coming in and out of office buildings in Western clothing, others wearing richly colored batik cloths cinched around waists, wrapped around hair and draped over ebony shoulders. Most of the women have either a baby or small toddler strapped onto their backs with yet another one of these batik cloths, which they ex-

pertly tie and untie without breaking stride. A few of the babies are posi-
tioned in front, happily suckling at their mothers' breasts.

As we drive farther out, the terrain flattens, the jacaranda trees sprout
skyward in neat rows and the batik cloths disappear. Here, in the residential section of south Harare, blond, pigtailed children ride bikes on the
streets and frolic on well-manicured lawns with pink-flowered walkways
and delicate fountains carved from stone.

"Still pretty segregated, huh?" I say to Julian. It's 1989. The civil war
in Rhodesia, which began in the mid-1960s, had ended over seven years
earlier.

"Sort of," he says, turning onto a quiet side street. "This used to be an
all-white working-class neighborhood. Now some blacks have moved in.
Anyway, here we are."

Julian parks in his driveway, but before he can even step out of the car,
a small, rangy mutt runs out of the house and jumps into his arms, greeting him with an eager tongue and gales of puppy laughter. "This is Pablo,"
he says, holding out a paw for me to shake. "Pablo the puppy, named after
the Cuban embassy political attaché, if you can believe it. He keeps me
from getting too lonely." He stares at the puppy as he speaks, daring to let
his blue eyes make contact with mine for a brief second, until he reaches
the word "lonely." Though I resist the urge, something about the combination of that glance and the word and the accent and the blue and the air
and the sun makes me want to lick Julian's face, too.

We walk into the house, a modest yet airy structure whose bottom half
he rents. Julian tells me to make myself at home on the floor of the sitting
room—"I haven't really gotten around to furniture yet," he shouts—while
he rifles through the disorganized mess on his desk down the hallway. I
look around at the few decorative touches he's made: a black and blue
Lesotho blanket hanging from a stone wall, a colorful Swaziland flag on
the opposite wall, lots of haphazardly placed floor cushions, a rough-hewn
wooden chair. I grab an old *Economist* from a pile of many and settle down
to read on a large cushion in the corner of the room. A few minutes later I
can hear Julian speaking on the phone, but the friend must be doing most
of the talking because mostly I just hear a bunch of *Uh-huh*'s and *Right, I
see*'s. Then he says, "A small prop plane, is it? Okay, then. Appreciate it.
Right. Cheers," and hangs up the phone.

He comes back into the living room and plops down next to me on the floor. His legs are long, and he bends them into two khaki mountains, resting his elbows on his knees while holding his reporter's notebook between the two peaks. "Okay, I have the information," he says. "Here's what you need to do."

He tells me there's a local bus that can get me to Victoria Falls, a popular tourist sight on the Zambezi River where I won't have any problem finding lodging. He suggests that, because I'm a woman traveling alone, public transportation would be my safest and easiest option. Once I get to Vic Falls, any number of hotels should be able to help me arrange an inexpensive private flight to a small airstrip servicing the Mana Pools game reserve, a few miles from the base camp of the antipoaching squad.

"You see?" he says, ripping the piece of paper from its metal spiral and handing it to me. "Problem solved." I feel a pleasant jolt when Julian's hand accidentally brushes mine in the exchange, and I notice he smells nice, like soap. "Oh, and once you're there, ask for some chap named Mark. He's both the commander of Operation Stronghold and the chief warden of the park. The whole trip shouldn't take you more than three days or so, counting the bus travel and the day or two it'll take you to organize the charter flight. Do you like tuna fish?"

"Why? Do I need to bring some?"

"No, no." Julian laughs. "I was thinking of making some for dinner. Would you care to join me?"

"Sure. Yes. That would be nice," I answer. I fold the piece of paper with the notes on it and stick it in the back pocket of my jeans. "Uh, Julian," I say, "thanks. For being so nice, I mean. You know, restoring my faith in mankind."

"Ah, well," he laughs again, "when you taste my tuna salad, you might change your mind about that." He opens two beers for us to drink while he makes the sandwiches. As he's stirring in the mayonnaise, with his back turned to me he says, "So Afghanistan, that must have been some trip."

"Oh, yeah," I say, slipping once again into brag mode. "It was horrible. We were stuck in the mountains for weeks. I got a piece of shrapnel in my hand and . . ." But I slow and stop.

"Yes, shrapnel," says Julian, still stirring, "and so?"

"You know what, Julian? Forget the shrapnel. It was small, came right out. You want to know why Afghanistan was so horrible? There was this guy . . ." For the first time since getting back from Peshawar, I tell the full and complete story of Pascal. I tell Julian how I fell for him, how handsome and flirtatious and exciting he was, how badly I was beaten and duped by him, how he faked his photographs, how he left me alone to fend for myself.

"What an asshole," says Julian. "Here, grab the beers, let's eat dinner outside in the garden while it's still light."

We head to the backyard, where we sit down on some wooden lawn furniture, our paper plates on our laps, our beer bottles balanced on the slats between our knees. The early evening mosquitoes are out, everything looks orange and though the tuna sandwiches are bland, just as Julian had promised they'd be, the night has a magical, anticipatory feel to it, like an orchestra warming up. Julian is staring straight into the fading sun, taking a swig of his beer to wash down a bite of food. "So he beat you with a telephone receiver, and then he went inside Afghanistan without you?"

That Oxbridge accent slays me.

"Yeah," I say, slightly embarrassed at having poured my heart out to a stranger. "I don't know why I just told you that. I haven't really told anyone that."

"I'm a good listener," he says, smiling. "Besides, I don't charge by the hour."

I laugh, but then I open up even further, tell him about the rabbi who kissed me, about getting mugged, about lots of important things I usually keep private. As the sun finally sinks below the horizon, we sit in silence for a minute or so, side by side on our lawn chairs, listening to the crickets, eating tuna, both staring straight ahead at the darkening shadows on the jacaranda trees. Pablo the puppy runs around the grass, spending equal time furiously digging and running back to Julian for another pat on the head. When he goes back to his digging, I put down my plate and bottle on my chair and walk over to Julian. I sit down on the edge of his chair, my left thigh touching the side of his knee, and face him. I want to say something original, but as I lean over, just slightly, just to gauge his reaction, all I can manage is a banal "I like you."

Julian recoils. "I like you, too," he says, but it comes out more like a question than a statement of fact.

I immediately go back to sit on my chair. "I'm sorry," I say. "I misread the situation."

"Please, please," he replies, now sitting up to face me. "It's not that." There's a long, awkward pause and much nervous hand-wringing before he speaks again. Then he tells me about the girlfriend, the one who is coming to Harare to visit him. But the details seem sketchy, perhaps even made up for the benefit of my ego. Trying to ease the tension, I smile and tell him I've never known that to stop any man before. Julian laughs nervously and looks at the ground. Then he says that just means I've been hanging out with the wrong kind of men. "Look, Deborah, you're very young—"

I interrupt him. "You don't have to make any more excuses," I say. "I got it." I want to crawl into one of those holes puppy Pablo is digging.

"I'm not making excuses. And I'm not talking about age as a measure of years," he says, now staring at his fidgeting hands. "I mean young. Still trying to prove yourself. Trusting people you shouldn't trust." He finally looks me in the eye. "Think of it this way. When I'm covering a war, I can always tell who the first-time journalists are. They're the ones who run straight into the fray, not thinking. But when you're right in the middle of the action, you can't see anything at all. You have no perspective. Worst of all, you can get hurt. Badly. The more seasoned journalists know this. They hang back, they watch the situation develop, they run away if need be. Do you understand the analogy I'm trying to draw?"

"Uh-huh." I'm humiliated. Not only have I just been rejected, I've been psychoanalyzed, categorized and exposed for the green journalist I am. Julian stands up and walks over to my chair to put his arm around me. He tells me he didn't mean to hurt my feelings or sound pedantic. He pats my head as if I were Pablo and then plants a platonic kiss just above my right ear.

As we clean up dinner, we engage in a ten-minute conversation about the weather, and then Julian drives me back to my hotel. "Well, then, good luck with those rhinos," he says as I step out of the car.

I shut the door and lean into the open window. I thank him for calling his friend, for my tuna-fish dinner, for pointing out my flaws.

Julian runs his hand through his curly hair and sighs. "We're all flawed," he says. He apologizes for lecturing me and fumbles with the key in the ignition. The car makes a loud grinding sound as he accidentally tries to start the already idling engine. He apologizes for this, too, and drives off into the night.

Back in my room, I crawl into bed, and with Julian's words still ricocheting in my head, I recall the last time I accepted a dinner invitation from a stranger, barely a month or so earlier.

He's right. I am too trusting.

I MET SEAN AT AN AFTERNOON TEA at Shakespeare & Company, the small yet humbly famous English-language bookstore in Paris that lies just down the quay of the Seine from the Place St. Michel. By this time I was living in my small studio on the rue St. Denis, and because of my constant travel, I had few friends besides Marion. I spent almost every day in Paris alone with my cameras. The Sunday-afternoon teas on the second floor of the overstuffed bookstore became an eagerly anticipated fixture in my otherwise solitary life, and I was pleased that Sean—who was on a two-week vacation and who said he worked in advertising back in the States—wanted to continue our pseudointellectual conversation about Hemingway over dinner.

Sean was in his mid-thirties, with salt-and-pepper hair setting off his green eyes. He was well read, courteous and charming. We drank an entire bottle of wine, and we held hands during dinner, dreamily watching the pedestrians pass by our outdoor table on the serpentine and picturesque rue Mouffetard—which, because it featured prominently in *A Moveable Feast,* is where we decided to eat that night. When the sun dropped in the sky, Sean placed his sweater around my shoulders to keep out the evening chill.

At the time, I was seeing another photographer now and then—an older man, pushing forty, divorced with a five-year-old kid, hyperaware of his own charm—but our visits with each other were mostly afterhours, on a strictly need-to-see basis. Suffice it to say, ours was not a particularly chatty alliance. My friend Chantal, an editor at Sipa, called this a relationship *pour l'hygiene*—"for hygiene," which is what made me realize that French women are much more practical about sex than American women. They understand that the urge to copulate is just like the urge to eat or to urinate: strong, natural and necessary for proper personal maintenance.

Alas, the guy had been off shooting a story in Chile for almost an entire month by the time I met Sean. I was feeling, for lack of a better word, unhygienic.

After dinner, Sean and I walked to the Pont des Arts, a wooden pedestrian bridge straddling the Seine. We were leaning over the green, wrought-iron rail, watching the sky turn from pink to dark blue and admiring the Eiffel Tower in the distance, when he leaned over and kissed me. Suddenly, as if charged by our embrace—no joke—the lights on the tower illuminated. Nothing like a brightly lit, giant metal phallus to set the mood. Sean put his arm around me and suggested I accompany him back to his hotel. "Sure," I said, "let's go," and I took his hand in mine.

Now, I know there aren't a lot of women who would follow a total stranger back to his hotel room. I'm not one of them. Remember, unlike most women, I also chose to cover wars for a living. I was, in the parlance of a psychiatrist I once met at a cocktail party, a thrill seeker. He explained this had something to do with my neurons and their dopamine receptors, although I glazed over when he tried to elaborate. I say this not as an excuse, but as a means of explanation, and only a partial one at that. While I'm willing to entertain the notion that my dopamine receptors were more needy than other people's dopamine receptors, I also know that much of my behavior was very conscious and deliberate.

I was on a personal mission, a crusade against hypocrisy—with all of the self-righteous and blind religious fervor such a task entailed.

While my feminist forebears had paved the way for me to enter into any profession I chose, and maybe even to receive comparable pay, they had yet to make serious inroads into the sexual double standard between men and women in America. When a man pursues a number of different women, he's called normal—even a stud. When a woman pursues a number of different men, she's called a whore. We know this. Unfortunately, we have somehow allowed this dichotomy to become an accepted truth in our repressed society, and we bow to the psychobiologists foisting their Darwinian theories upon us about sperm and natural selection in hunter-gatherer societies to explain why this should and must be so. (If man's genetic inclination is to spread his sperm, it's okay for him to sleep around. But woman, O sanctified producer of eggs, dependent upon a single provider, must not.) Never mind that I never bought into any of that crap. (Two words: foraging grandmas.) For a girl just starting to understand her sexual persona, inflamed with seething teenage lust and desire, the idea that her behavior would be judged differently from a boy's behavior was nothing short of infuriating.

In my seventh-grade class, there was beautiful girl named Bebe. One afternoon after school—or so the titillating story goes—Bebe accompanied three of our male classmates to one of their basement rec rooms. There, one at a time, each had his turn with her. The rumors that swirled through the school hallways afterwards were outrageous and contradictory. They said she left her bra on. They said she was naked. They said she only went to second base. They said she had sex with all three. They said she gave head. They said she barfed when one of them tried to make her. The only thing upon which every single kid in that school seemed to agree was that Bebe was a whore. With a Magic Marker, someone wrote the word on her locker, and over the next week this was followed by graffiti ranging from "slut" to "cunt." In public, she was ostracized, humiliated, loudly insulted and quietly mocked.

As for the three boys, they became the most popular kids in the school.

I was outraged. What Bebe did, as far as I was concerned, was bold, brave and exciting. I was so tired of the game playing, the labels, the double standards and the Orwellian double-speak I saw my girlfriends having to resort to, saying no when they meant yes. But the morality tale of Bebe frightened us all. No one wanted to be the next girl to have "slut" written on her locker, even if many of us secretly envied her audacity.

By the time I hit high school, however, I was fed up. At age sixteen, raging with the hormones of puberty, starving for experience, I cast off my virginity like a pair of dirty socks I'd been wearing for far too long. (His name was Alex, he played defensive tackle, he said he loved me, I said it back, we did it, the earth moved—okay, maybe it just quivered—we cried, it was very nice, I felt relieved, we kept doing it, he left for college.) That taken care of, I jumped from bed to bed with the glee of a frog in a lily pond, gently deflowering boy after gangly teenage boy. Because of what had happened to Bebe, I was careful not to advertise this fact—if people were talking about me, I didn't want to know about it. And frankly, I was starting not to care. I liked sex, and I figured I should be able to act accordingly. In short, I was playing by the boys' rules.

But it's not easy being a one-girl revolution. Not that it got any easier once I became a woman.

When I moved to Paris and started speaking French, I was struck by the dual meanings of the word *aventure,* which can mean either "adventure" or "love affair." The correlation is obvious. Both describe situations requiring a willingness to leap from a safe precipice; both stimulate our adrenal glands, take us places we've never been, put us at risk. But what I failed to understand at the time—and what Julian would later have to point out—is that both adventures and love affairs require not just an eagerness and a willingness to experience them, but the instinct and the maturity to judge whether or not they are actually *worth* the risk. It's no coincidence that many of the war journalists who are killed in the line of duty are barely into their twenties when they die. They simply had no idea what kind of "adventure" they were getting themselves into.

And so it was for me with sex. Most of the time it was fun. But a few times it was awful.

Sean's room was located just above the lobby on the second floor of a small, slightly shabby hotel in the Marais. When we stepped inside, the room glowed with the amber rays from a streetlamp. We didn't even bother to turn on the light. We sat on the edge of the bed, kissing. We lay down. We undressed each other slowly, playfully tossing shirts, jeans and undergarments onto the floor. Then we slipped into bed. After half an hour of languorous caressing, Sean quietly suggested we make love. Smiling, I said I'd like that.

That's when everything changed. If what had come before was as dulcet as Chopin's nocturnes, what came after felt like the feedback from an electric guitar held too close to an amplifier. With our legs intertwined, he started to pound and thrust so hard, I thought my pelvic bone would crack. He began to shriek. "You fuck any stranger that asks you? Bad girl!" The bed's headboard was crashing repeatedly into the wall, Sean's screaming grew fouler and louder and as I tried to push him off of me, he grabbed me around the neck and yelled, "Behave, slut!" Then he sucked my breast so hard I screamed. His nails drew blood from my arms. Growing ever more excited, he began to slap me. He pulled my hair and licked my face, all the while pounding and pounding to the point where the rickety iron bed was literally bouncing off the floor. After a while, I stopped trying to fight him. I just prayed for the thrashing to stop.

When at last he finished, rolled off me and—thoroughly exhausted—started to snore, I stood up from the bed, my knees buckling under me.

Then I knelt on the hardwood floor in the dark to feel around for my discarded clothes. My underwear was missing. The thought of Mr. Madonna/ Whore finding them the next day so repulsed me, I took a minute more to try to locate them, but with no luck. I put my jeans on over my bare skin, my fingers shaking as they tried to maneuver the four metal buttons into the four empty buttonholes. I wandered out in a daze, tasting blood on my lip where Sean must have bit me. When I reached the lobby, the concierge stared at me with what I took to be a sympathetic look in his eyes. The floor of Sean's room was right above his desk. He had to have heard the banging and the screaming; he must have understood what I'd just endured. He looked me up and down, his lips pursed with concern.

Thank God, I thought. He's walking over to help me.

The concierge paused before speaking. And then in a stern, quiet, measured voice, he proclaimed, *"Nous n'avons pas besoin des putes ici."*

"Excusez-moi?" I said, assuming I'd misunderstood him.

"Nous n'avons pas besoin des putes ici," he repeated. *"Va-t-en!"*—"We have no need for prostitutes here. Be gone!"

I snapped. In a voice I'd never heard myself use—it could have shattered glass—tears flooding down, I screamed back in English, "How dare you! I am not a prostitute! Do you hear me? I am not a whore!" He pretended not to understand me, or maybe he actually didn't understand me, but I was so enraged I couldn't formulate a single thought in French. Our verbal communication thus limited, I lunged at him and began to pound his chest with my fists. I kicked him in the shins. I grabbed his tie, his shirt, anything I could hold on to, and screamed even louder. "Did you hear me, you asshole? I AM NOT A WHORE! You have a demented, violent guest up there," I pointed to the ceiling, "but you call ME a WHORE?! It's complete hypocrisy! Why's it the WOMAN who's always the whore, huh? Answer my question! Answer me! ANSWER ME!"

At this point some other guy dressed in a hotel uniform appeared, pulling me off of the concierge. Then the two of them hoisted me like a sack of potatoes and tossed me out the front door, where I landed with a thud on my back. The concierge couldn't resist yelling *"Pute!"* one more time before he dutifully locked the door. It was raining. Just like after Aidan, I thought. But that was a rape. This was . . . well . . . I had no idea what this was. Not rape, technically. But bad. Rage—rage directed at me, at my audacity, at any woman who might dare act like a man. I lay there on the sidewalk, stunned, my back feeling every wet cobblestone beneath me. I caught my breath, sat up and looked around to get my bearings. The street was completely deserted.

I opened my mouth to catch a few drops of rain on my tongue. Then, still sitting, silently sobbing, I let the water soak me through.

THE PHONE RINGS AT 3:30 A.M. "Good morning, Miss Co-paken, this is your wake-up call. Have a lovely day." Everyone who travels for a living knows that split-second feeling of panic that jolts through the body when you wake up in a strange hotel room: *Where am I? I DON'T LIVE HERE!* That's why, if the option's available, I always choose a sprightly wake-up-call operator over the electroshocking beeps of a hotel alarm clock; it's like a surrogate mom, a sunny, disembodied voice telling me, Calm down, silly girl, you're in a Hyatt Regency.

Years later, when Hal-like computer voices replaced most of the happy operators, I'd wake in hotel rooms feeling like an abandoned child.

I drag myself out of bed, shower and gather my stuff together. Back-pack? Check. Thermos? Check. Camera bag? Check. Box of food? Check. The food is in a large corrugated cardboard box that says "Clorox" on the outside, which the man at the grocery store gave me when I asked. It's got eggs (I'm an optimist) as well as less-fragile fare, such as canned soups and pastas and bread and vacuum-packed juice and dried fruit and nuts and granola and Snickers bars and those thin, little Kraft cheese and cracker packs, the ones with the small red plastic rectangles for knives—everything in the carton important—but the box is too heavy, and I wish I could leave it behind. I call a bellhop to help me get down to the lobby.

A taxi drives me to catch the 5 A.M. bus from Harare to Victoria Falls. It's still pitch black by the time I get there at 4:45, and the dusty open field/parking lot that serves as the bus station is teeming not only with lo-cals but with their huge jerry-rigged packages, wrapped in red-white-and-blue woven plastic with some twine, along with their cages upon cages of chickens. Of the five hundred or so faces in the crowd, mine is the only white one.

As the sky begins to lighten, turning first gray, then red, then orange and yellow, then blue, the bus has still not arrived. I'm sitting on the ground on my backpack, scanning the photo credits in *Time* magazine and looking at my watch every five minutes or so, but I'm the only one who seems to notice or care that the bus is now an hour late. The men are laughing, eating and smoking, helping each other move their bulky packages this way and that; the kids are all running around doing giggly, squiggly, hide-and-seeky kid stuff; the chickens and hens are clucking in their cages; and the women, wrapped in their brightly colored batiks, are talking to one another or breast-feeding or peeling oranges for their older children. One of the mothers walks over to me with a big smile and a peeled orange. "Here," she says, "you look hungry."

"Thanks," I smile back, "I am."

"And you better stop looking at your watch. The bus will be here when it gets here."

A helpful piece of information, I think, but just as the woman finishes her sentence, almost on cue, three buses pull up into the dusty parking lot. Suddenly, all of these seemingly laid-back locals start scrambling. It's pure bedlam, with dust rising everywhere and bodies jumping over one another. Most of the men hoist each other and their packages onto the top of the bus, shouting, laughing and cursing all the while. The women, carrying children, suitcases and chicken cages, maneuver their way past one another to reach the stairs and secure a seat. I look around, calculating the number of people left to board versus the number of seats I believe to still be vacant, and I quickly join in the fray. But when I finally get on the bus, it's standing room only.

The bus looks like it's been around since before the start of the Rhodesian civil war. The plastic upholstery on the seats is either falling apart or nonexistent, many of the windows are either broken or just missing. A fine film of dust and grime covers the floor. Before I even realize what's happening, the bus driver grabs my box of food and passes it from passenger to passenger until one of them spots an empty space on the shelf above the seats in the back. I hope I'll see it again. I'm standing in the middle of the aisle, squished between two other unlucky souls. I carry the overburdened backpack on my back, and my camera bag is on my shoulder, but it keeps slipping off because of the backpack. "How long is the trip to Victoria Falls?" I ask the woman standing sardinelike next to me.

"Sometimes six hours. Sometimes twelve," she says with a smile.

"Excellent," I say, wondering how the hell I'm going to last, but then a seated woman takes my camera bag and puts it under her feet and a man grabs my backpack and puts it under his seat, and then the woman who offered me the peeled orange picks up her toddler and her caged chicken off the seat next to her, yanks me down and places the child and cage on my lap. Okay, that's better.

The little girl on my lap is squirmy but friendly. We spend about an hour laughing and making silly faces at each other until she falls asleep hugging me, the weight of her warm, fragrant head pressed snugly against my shoulder. I take the chicken cage and put it on the floor, resting my feet on top of it, and bury my nose in the sleeping girl's neck. I inhale deeply so as to better take in her perfect smell. That's when her mother turns to me, an infant suckling at her exposed breast. "Where are your children?" she asks.

"My children?" I smile. "Oh, I don't have any."

"You have husband?"

"No, no husband either," I answer.

"That's a pity. An old woman like you with no family."

"Oh," I laugh nervously, "I'm only twenty-three. Plenty of time for all that later."

"I'm twenty-two," she says, placing the baby's mouth on her other nipple.

I watch the infant's cheeks suck in and out, his eyes rolled back into their sockets in ecstasy. Soon, all five of us—the woman, her two kids, the chicken and me—are all snuggled up together, sleeping. Four hours later, halfway to Victoria Falls, I help them off the bus and place the toddler in the arms of her father, who has come to the bus stop to wait for his family. He thanks me and gives his young daughter a playful kiss, eliciting peals of laughter when he tosses her up into the air. As I'm mounting the steps to get back on the bus, the woman grabs my arm and whispers in my ear. "Find yourself a husband, make some children," she says. "You have too much love to be all alone."

I smile and tell her it's not that simple. She smiles back and says it is that simple. I return to my seat, which now feels spacious but empty, and pull out the book I've brought along for the trip: Gabriel García Marquez's *One Hundred Years of Solitude*.

THE PILOT LETS GO OF HIS CONTROLS. "You're the copilot, so you fly it," he shouts over the noise of the engines, chuckling to himself.

"Nothing to it. Pull out to go up, push in to go down. Simple. Go on, grab the controls." He puts his hands behind his head, pretending to stretch out and relax.

Instinctively, I clutch on to what looks like a half-circle steering wheel and pull it out. The nose of the plane tips up. I push it in. The nose of the plane tips down. I turn right. I turn left. "I'm flying!" I yell, like Wendy in *Peter Pan*. The plane is a small prop plane—just two seats with two sets of controls in front and four empty seats behind us—and I've paid the pilot 150 U.S. dollars in cash to fly me east along the Zambezi River from Victoria Falls to the airstrip at Mana Pools. Just as Julian's friend had promised, chartering the flight had been fairly easy. Below us, a sea of tiny green trees flows by.

"So, who's meeting you when we get there?" the pilot asks me, quickly grabbing his set of controls when the plane starts to tilt sideways.

"No one. Hey, give me another chance. I promise I won't make it tip again." The pilot relents, and once more, I'm flying the plane.

"What do you mean 'no one'?"

I explain my predicament—the faxes promising transport and an escort, the Operation Stronghold troops and their lack of telephones, Nduku, the money I've already spent to get here.

The pilot just shakes his head and laughs. "So no one knows you're coming, then, right?"

"Well, they don't know I'm coming today," I answer, "but they must have received a telex from the consulate saying I'd be coming at some point."

"Oh, boy," he says, taking the controls. "Here, you relax. I'll fly."

Later, when we begin our descent, the pilot points out a grassy clearing in the middle of the trees. "You see that?" he says, grinning slyly. "That's the airport."

"I don't see any airport."

"You're not using your imagination. Look over there," he points to the trees on the right, "that's the arrival hall. Over there," he points to the trees on the left, "that's departures. And over there," he laughs, pointing off into the distance, "those are the taxis!" I follow the path of his finger and spot, trotting along the outskirts of the clearing, a herd of a dozen elephants.

"Very funny," I say, but I'm not laughing. When Julian said "airstrip,"

I didn't exactly picture a real airport, but I did picture, well, something. Like a tarmac. Like a tiny building. Maybe a road.

When we land—on a packed-dirt strip in the middle of the grass—the pilot helps me out of the plane and unloads my backpack, camera bag and cardboard box of food, which he places in a neat pile on the ground. The clearing is no larger than a high school football field, surrounded by trees on all sides. It's midday, the hot sun burns directly overhead and the birds and the insects sing a cacophonous opera of chirps, squeaks and trills. Then, over the pleasant din, I hear a distinct roar. "What was that?" I ask the pilot. As if to answer my question, another roar emanates from somewhere inside the trees behind me.

"Probably a lion. Try to avoid them if you can," he says, with about the same amount of gravity as a morning-commute radio host warning his audience about a traffic jam on the interstate. Then, jumping back into his plane, he shouts over his shoulder, "Well, I've got to get back to Vic Falls. Got another flight at two. You take care of yourself."

"Thanks. Oh, hey, which way do I go?" I shout, but by now the pilot has shut his door, the propellers are spinning, and the plane is turning around to begin its runway sprint. I stand there, watching it take off and then disappear into the ether. Then I look around, surveying the situation. There's me. There's my backpack, my box of food, my camera bag. There's an open field, grass, trees, sky and sun. There's a roar.

I am completely alone. No, that's an understatement. I'm by myself, somewhere in a jungle in Zimbabwe, surrounded by wild animals, loaded down with stuff, lacking both a compass and a map, devoid of a single frame of reference.

And no one is expecting me.

How do I get myself into these situations? It's easy to blame Nduku, but that's like blaming Pascal for my solo trip inside Afghanistan. No, I get myself into these situations because I'm stubborn, because I'm impetuous, because I allow my judgment to be muddled by pride. Just like Julian said, I throw myself into the fray without thinking. And now, here I am once again, flying solo and scared.

Okay, I think, time to use my head. For a fucking change. Julian's friend had said that the airstrip is a few miles south of the Operation Stronghold base camp. That means I must walk north. From my photographer's vest, I dig out the crumpled piece of paper he scribbled on—just moments before I leaned over to try to kiss him, oh, God, how embarrassing—and try to decipher the hieroglyphics. It says: *Mana Pools. Airstrip. Road takes you to base camp/Zambezi River.* Road? *Road?* I don't see any road. But there has to be a road. Why would anyone build an airstrip without a road?

I leave my bags and boxes in the middle of the field and walk along the tree-lined perimeter, searching for any sign of a thoroughfare. What I find doesn't so much look like a road as a narrow dirt path through the trees parallel to the airstrip, but it leads toward somewhere and away from here, so I decide to take it. Only problem is which way do I go? With the sun directly overhead, I can't figure out where north is. Besides, if I'm south of the equator, how does that work? Is the sun in the northern part of the sky? Must be, right? The bathtubs drain in the opposite direction. Winter is summer. So north must be south. Thing is, the road looks like it's heading east to west. Or west to east. Or neither. If only my Girl Scout troop had spent a little less time sewing and selling cookies and a little more time navigating the woods like the boys, I'd probably know this stuff.

I head back to my bags, once again slinging my backpack on my back and my camera bag on my shoulder. I pick up the heavy cardboard box of food and try to walk. This is ridiculous, I think. I'll never make it twenty yards, let alone a mile. And Xavier wanted me to bring a light kit. What an asshole. The image of me trying to drag three cases of lights along with everything else I'm carrying makes me crack up. Here I am, loaded down like a bag lady in the middle of the jungle, laughing hysterically. This must be what insanity feels like.

I carry everything to the small clearing that leads to the road. Okay, right or left? Which way is it going to be? *"Two roads diverged in a yellow wood . . ."* And what, Mr. Frost? What's the next line? I know it ends with *"And I, I took the one less traveled by. And that has made all the difference,"* but what comes in between? I used to know that poem by heart back in seventh grade. We had to recite it in front of the class. I loved that poem. A twelve-year-old girl can decide to model her life on a poem like that.

I choose right, but not because it looks any less traveled than left. At this point, I just have to make a choice. Any choice.

I briefly toy with the idea of leaving the food box here and coming back for it, but I'm sure there are animals who are far bigger and far hungrier than I am who'd just love to devour a few of my oatmeal-raisin-granola bars. There's little to no chance the box will be here when I get back, and I'm in no mood to add starvation to my list of woes. So I put it on the ground and try kicking it. But every time I kick the box, my camera bag is jolted off my shoulder. So then I get the bright idea of putting the camera bag on top of the box, and now I'm in business. For the next hour, I push and pull that box and my cameras along the dirt path, traveling probably no more than a mile and with no idea if I'm even heading in the right direction. Though it's still hot, the path is shaded by tall trees. Once I've committed myself to the rhythm of this futile exercise—push, scrape, stop, pull, scrape, stop, push, scrape, stop, sigh, rest—sweating and exhausted, I start to relax, to listen to the life whistling all around me.

Noise vaults through these lush, quiet trees like a Mozart symphony. The monkeys are the string section, their high-pitched squeals forming the underlying melody. The birds are the flutes, the insects the rhythm section, the distant trumpeting of elephants the brass. Then there's that strange, low-pitched snorting, which reminds me of a bass (and which, I would later find out, was actually the sound of a hippo; this should have tipped me off, had I been more jungle savvy, to my proximity to water).

But beneath the clamor of the animal orchestra is a silence so profound it's immobilizing. I'm too tired to go any farther anyway, so I drag my stuff to the side of the path, sit down on a rock, close my eyes and listen to it. It's one of those cinematic, self-conscious Zen moments, the kind where you're aware of the absurdity of the act—*I'm sitting here all alone on a rock in the middle of the jungle with my eyes closed, listening to silence and thinking Big Thoughts*—but you're doing it anyway and actually enjoying it.

Unfortunately, the biggest thoughts that pop into my mind involve my flesh being ripped by a lion. Do lions hunt humans in a game reserve park? Or are they so used to seeing tourists staring out at them from Land Rovers, they could care less? Am I in danger? I'm not sure what is worse—knowing what hazards lurk just beyond the trees or being completely oblivious.

I stand up from the rock and start all over again. Push, scrape, stop. Pull, scrape, stop. Sigh, rest. And then, just as I've started to give up any hope, I hear the rumble of an engine. And then laughter. And then a jeep appears from the direction I've just come, carrying three shirtless men. How auspicious—three muscular *deus* in a rugged *machina*.

"Hey, there, mate!" the driver calls out. "You look like you could use a lift." Must be an Aussie: the *h* is "hey" is silent, and "mate" comes out sounding like "mite."

"Oh, yeah?" I say. "How could you tell?" I brush the strand of hair that's come loose from my braid behind my ear and wipe the sweat off my forehead as an afterthought.

"The name's Darien. These are my mates Will and Connor. We're on holiday." In the back of the jeep is a case of blue and gold Foster's Ale. Why is it that wherever you go on this immense planet, you can always find Australians on holiday? It must have something to do with growing up in a former penal colony. They're probably culturally programmed to seek freedom, roam.

I introduce myself. A round of hi's and handshakes ensues.

"Where are you heading, then?" asks Connor. Or is that Will? All three of them look alike—blond, brawny and bare-chested. I feel like an unwitting, overdressed extra in a beer commercial.

"Where am I heading?" I look at the Aussies, at the dappled light hitting the dirt path, at the seemingly endless forest of densely packed trees. "You know," I say with a smile, "I have no idea."

The men help me load my stuff into their jeep. I sit on top of the Foster's, and Darien drives off in the direction I'd been walking. They're on safari, they tell me, driving around in search of wild animals by day, eating, drinking and being merry around a campfire on the banks of the Zambezi by night. I should join them, they say. I tell them it sounds fun, but that I'm here to cover a rhino war. I explain about the poachers, the shoot-to-kill policy, Operation Stronghold. "A rhino war?" says Darien, shifting into third gear. "So that's what those guys are doing with those guns." His blond ringlets fly back off his forehead in the wind.

"You've seen them?" I ask.

"Yeah. They've got a bunch of machine guns and an old helicopter. Every day it takes off with a couple of them, and every night it comes back. I figured it was some sort of military training."

"You're a photojournalist, then?" says Will, consciously trying to make conversation. I'm practically sitting on his lap, squeezed between the Foster's and his naked chest. "Must be fascinating." He raises his eyebrows when he says this. Darien, watching us in the rearview mirror, tells Will to cut out the flirting. He found me first, he says.

"You know what?" I reply with a yawn. "Sometimes it really sucks."

We drive a bit farther, then the trees give way to an open field on the banks of the Zambezi. There must be at least forty hippos happily bobbing and snorting away in the calm pool of water. An elephant family drinks. Hundreds of birds flitter about. A couple of monkeys frolic in the trees. I can't help thinking it looks fake, like a movie set.

We drive still farther, until we come upon a couple of ramshackle wooden cabins, the kind that are painted olive green with mesh screens instead of windows, like the ones in my summer camp.

"Here we are, then," says Darien, stopping the jeep to let me off. "This is where the men with the guns live." He unloads my gear and, making the dramatic gesture of kissing my hand, urges me to hike the half mile down the river to help him and his "mites" polish off the Foster's later that evening. "You could pitch your tent with ours. We'll protect you from the lions," he says with a wink.

"I'm sure you will," I wink back, "but I don't even have a tent to pitch. Thanks for the lift and everything, but I think I'll just sleep alone tonight, if that's okay with you boys."

I say this with enough sarcasm that Darien looks offended. Then I feel bad. He's just saved me from at least another hour or two of dragging my stuff through the jungle on foot, and I repay him by insinuating that he and his drunk friends would try to have their way with me (like Bebe! I think), when they're probably just harmless jack-a-roos, trying to be nice to a stranger.

But I'm tired of paying the consequences when my instincts are wrong. I've now been around long enough to know that such a scenario isn't out of the realm of possibility. It's just like earlier, back at the airstrip. Maybe the lions roaring beyond the trees were harmless, already sated by an enormous antelope carcass or two. Maybe they were not. But why on earth would I ever stick around and give them the benefit of the doubt?

IT WAS FIVE O'CLOCK in the afternoon at the end of my sophomore year of college when Jack, Greg and I finished editing our section of the

Boston Ballet documentary we'd been working on for film class, and the warm spring air beckoned. The three of us had become close friends while collaborating on it, and for the past thirty-six hours, we'd been holed up together in a small editing room in the basement of Harvard's Sever Hall, meticulously snipping and taping small pieces of film and plastic brown sound stock together and trying to keep synch on a Steenbeck. Jack suggested we buy a six-pack of beer and drink them on the roof of my dormitory, Adams House, to celebrate. Giddy from both the lack of sleep and a sense of accomplishment, we bought the beer and climbed the staircase to the roof.

With the sun falling lower in the sky, we sat and laughed and smoked and drank toast after toast to our success at finishing on time. Our team had worked well together, rarely bickering like some of the other groups still trying to complete their sections. We had made all decisions through mutual consensus, respected one another's opinions.

Which is why I was confused when Jack whispered something into Greg's ear. "Hey, no secrets!" I laughed, taking another drag from my cigarette. Then Greg, looking at me, whispered something back to Jack. And then, before I could even grasp what was happening, the two of them were pushing me down on my back. I could see the purple sky, a sliver of a moon, the first few stars waking up. I could smell the tar on the roof. Jack's hands were on my breasts, his tongue trying to find entry into my mouth. Greg was at my waist, unzipping my jeans.

I was dumbfounded. In the entire time we worked on our film together, I could not recall ever flirting with them. I never made any sexual references, innuendos or ambiguous comments. I felt no attraction toward either of them. We were partners, I thought, working together, a creative team. How long had they been planning this little scenario? Was I so oblivious as to not have seen it coming? Or is it impossible to predict what men will do?

Screaming obscenities at the two men, I pushed them off of me and stood up, zipping my jeans with my mouth clenched in hatred. They didn't try to hold me back, but I ran away anyway. I ran down the stairs of the dormitory, fumbled with my keys, opened the door to my room and, once safely inside, slammed it shut and bolted the lock. I undressed as if my clothes were on fire, wrapped myself in a towel and started the shower. Within minutes I heard a loud knocking at my door.

"Deb, Deb, we're sorry. We didn't mean to freak you out. Please, just let us in." It was Jack's voice.

"Fuck you!" I shouted. Then I slipped into the shower to drown out all the noise.

Unfortunately, this small violation was only the dawn of the grim and bizarre pattern to come. The next year, my junior year, the muggings began. In the late fall, a drunk homeless man with bloodshot eyes broke into my dorm room, where I was alone working on a Shakespeare term paper. He shut my bedroom door behind him with a thud and threatened to rape me if I didn't give him money. I had no money on me, so I lied and told him I'd seen him in my window and had already called the police; being drunk or high or stupid or whatever, he believed me and bolted. The police found him the next day, shoplifting a sweater at an Urban Outfitters, but when I went to court to testify against him, he'd been let out on personal recognizance and never showed up. I switched bedrooms after that. That same winter, I was taking an early evening walk through a crowded Harvard Square when I felt a combat boot kick me in the face. I remember feeling the impact and seeing a man run off, but since I passed out, the rest is hazy. A fellow student I barely knew—I think his name was Bob— saw me lying there on the sidewalk surrounded by gawking bystanders and picked me up like a baby. He then carried me to the *Lampoon* castle, where he called the police and made me a cup of hot chocolate, the kind with the tiny floating marshmallows.

That June, a man mugged me and my roommate at gunpoint when we were heading home from dinner at a Chinese restaurant in Cambridge. Two weeks later in New York City, where I was working for Magnum, a man posing as a taxi driver stopped his cab for me in front of Penn Station. When I got inside, his accomplice, who'd been crouched down in the backseat, pointed his gun at me and stole the new wallet I'd just bought to replace the one pilfered by the first mugger. That same summer of my discontent, a luggage salesman who was trying to sell me a Samsonite on wheels led me to the back of the store, where he said the suitcase would be and where he promptly mauled me. A few months later, already well into working on my "Shooting Back" thesis photographs my senior year, three drunk guys wearing Boston College hats confronted me on a darkened street and tried to push me to the ground. "Wanna fuck?" one of them said. I was so infuriated by my lack of control over the world at this point that I actually beat him over the head with the only weapon I had at my disposal, the plastic case covering the video I'd just rented for my tutorial on men and violence, *A Clockwork Orange*. When I was finished with him, blood was squirting from the corner of his eye and running out of his left nostril.

The next day, during my one-on-one tutorial at his quaint little house on Athens Street, my professor William Alfred fixed me a martini. Then, in place of a lesson, he allowed me to just sit in his well-worn armchair and cry for the entire hour.

Then came the flasher, then Aidan, then the ultra-Orthodox rabbi, then Pascal, then the stabbing in Zurich, then Sean, then Nduku, and, in between, lots of boyfriends and lovers ranging from extremely kind and generous to just this side of evil.

There was a pattern. There was no pattern. It didn't matter if I invited them into my life or if they barged in uninvited. Men were predictable. They were completely unpredictable. They gave me intense pleasure. They caused me profound pain.

It was complicated.

It would be easy to say I invited these attacks, and believe me, I've often berated myself for doing so. I have no doubt that my eighteen-year sojourn inside the padded walls of suburbia stunted my instincts, turned me into a poodle with a "kick me" sign amidst wolves. Plus I'm short, female, slight of build and friendly. The perfect lethal combination, if you want to blame the victim. But for every time I may have, for lack of a better term, "invited" an assault—Jack and Greg, Aidan, the flasher, Pascal, Sean and, okay, maybe even the stabbing in Zurich, if you want to take it that far—there were just too many other random events and violations. To wit: two attempted rapes (in my dorm room, outside the video store), two sexual assaults (the luggage store, the rabbi), two armed robberies (on the street after dinner, in the back of the taxi), one regular assault (combat boot in the face), and one demand for sexual favors in exchange for safe passage into the jungle (Nduku), which is pretty funny, because when you actually think about it, there's no such thing as safe passage into a jungle.

MARK, THE WARDEN OF MANA POOLS and thus the pro forma commander of Operation Stronghold, looks at me as if I'm an alien. "A pho-

tographer? From Paris, you say? That's funny. No one told me you were coming." He says this with the quiet civility of a man who has never been in a
rush. We're standing in one of the cabins, and Mark walks over to the wall
calendar above his clutterless desk to look for some scribble that might prove
him wrong, but not even a birthday mars its crisp white boxes of empty days.
He's white, dressed in a short-sleeve olive uniform shirt, olive shorts and hiking boots. On his right sunburned knee is some mud; in his beard, some
crumbs. He politely explains how he can't let me accompany his soldiers on
patrol unless I have written permission from Nduku. "But you're more than
welcome to camp out by the river. It's beautiful this time of year."

"But I have written permission from Nduku," I say. I show him my
fax, never mentioning the whole sexual-favor-as-bribery mess. I figure
now that I'm here, what's the point?

"That's odd," he says. He flips over the fax in his hand as if searching
the blank backside for enlightenment. "Usually the press office informs us
when someone's coming. Did you meet with Nduku in Harare?"

"No," I lie.

"Oh, well, that's probably it. You should have, you know. He could
have arranged your transport. How'd you get here anyway?"

I tell him I chartered a plane from Victoria Falls.

"Well, then, never mind," Mark says, reaching out to shake my hand.
"Welcome to our little war."

"Thanks." We chat for a bit about schedules. He tells me the soldiers go
out on patrol at 8 A.M. every morning, searching for any signs of poachers—
vultures circling above, debris from a campfire, dead rhinos with bloody
stumps where their horns should be. "And if you find a poacher?" I ask.

"We shoot him," he says, distracted by my pile of stuff. "Did you bring
a tent?"

"No."

"That's okay, I think I probably have an old one around here somewhere." He scratches his beard to help him think.

Though the soldiers sleep in dormitory-like cabins, Mark advises
against my joining them. "It's not a good idea," he says in a tone that
makes it clear that his statement requires no further explanation. Which it
doesn't.

I don't know why I simply assumed I'd have a place to sleep. Oh, well,
I think. Camping will be fun.

Mark searches around the crevices of his cabin, but he can't find the extra tent. I briefly contemplate joining the Australians in their tent, but since no rain is forecast for this evening, I figure I'll wing it in the open air with my sleeping bag. I borrow a pot from Mark, carry my stuff no more than a quarter of a mile down to the campgrounds by the river, find a rock to sit on, gather some wood, make a fire and boil three eggs for dinner. It's dusk, and the Zambezi stretches before me, wide, calm and alive. The hippos are still there, bobbing around, snorting, doing their hippo thing, fat and innocent-looking. But I've been told about hippos. They're vegetarians, Mark said, but if you get in their way, they'll rip your head off.

A lone elephant ambles by less than ten yards in front of me. He stops to take a drink, sees me and moves on. In the fading light, he looks two-dimensional and dark, like a big, black, cutout elephant paper doll. Two crocodile eyes and only the hint of a snout swim like a whisper on the surface of the river, a ghostly V-shaped wake trailing behind them. Even the monkeys know to be quiet now, allowing the crickets to have the final word of the day.

I peel one of my now hard-boiled eggs, letting the pieces of shell fall to the ground. I'm so hungry, I eat it in two bites, savoring the heaviness of the yolk as it squeezes through my esophagus and plummets like a rock into my stomach. I gobble down the other two equally fast, chasing them with some apple juice. Then I peel an orange, the rind getting underneath my fingernails, the sweet fruit bursting between my teeth. When the last section is gone, I light a cigarette and blow the smoke across the river.

Who knew covering a war could be so peaceful?

I stare up at the thickening soup of stars and think about the mother who shared her seat with me on the bus to Victoria Falls. How nice it must be to have such firm convictions about one's role in life, to be able to say, "It is so simple." I am envious. For me, nothing is ever that simple. Not men, not work, not morality, not love, not trust, not people, not politics, not sex, not God, and especially not motherhood. Especially not that.

I fall asleep. In my dream, I'm on the crowded bus to Victoria Falls, only this time I am cradling a little girl who looks like me in every way except for her black, straight hair. I feel her breath in small, sleepy spurts of air on my neck. I rub my hand across her tiny back, her vertebrae stretched like a single strand of pearls beneath her taut skin. I tell her it's okay, everything will be okay. When we finally reach our stop, I try to rouse her. But she's dead. I shake her. I cry out for help. It's no use. With all the breast-feeding and chicken clucking and package shuffling and orange peeling and children laughing, no one on the bus can hear my screams.

THE NIGHT BEFORE our abortion, Gabe asked me, "Are you sure you want to do this?"

We were seventeen, sitting on my childhood bed with the rainbow sheets and stuffed animals. I had just received my acceptance letter to Harvard. Gabe would be going to a college far away in Louisiana.

"Of course I'm sure," I said.

"Just think about it for a second. We love each other. We'd make great parents. I just don't want you to think you have to rush into this." In retrospect, these were heady, mature statements for a seventeen-year-old boy to make. But that was Gabe. While his other friends were busy playing pinball and smoking bongs in one another's basements, Gabe preferred to spend all of his free time with me: driving around Potomac with the top down, blasting "Little Red Corvette" or Howard Jones singing "What Is Love?," holding hands, laughing, debating the existence of God with the wind whipping through our hair. While the other boys relied on whatever myth and hearsay they could gather from their bragging buddies—"*Oh, yeah, dude, a girl can't come unless you're doin' her*"—Gabe understood and was an avid student of the female anatomy. And while most of the boys in my high school used the phrase "I love you" as nothing more than a conduit for getting laid, Gabe felt these words in the depths of his melancholy teenage soul.

"I don't need to think about it. I'm doing it," I said, full of adolescent bluster and self-confidence. I had plans. Big plans. College, some sort of career, then maybe—just maybe, and much later—a family. But after a silent minute, I felt tears, love, trying to erode my resolve.

"Yeah, you're right. What was I thinking?" Gabe said. He stroked the threadbare fur on my yellow stuffed bunny. Then, with a sigh and a quivering lip, he slumped over, his head in his hands. I felt his chest heaving up and down against mine as I held him close and tried to kiss away the briny mess from his cheek. But soon I was sobbing too hard to comfort him anymore.

"Everything will be okay," I whispered, more to myself than to him. "We're doing the right thing." I let my fingers run through Gabe's straight black hair, my mind already composing the elegy for the hair, the face, the fingers I would never see.

"I know," he said. But I could tell he didn't believe it.

Early the next morning, as I was getting ready to leave, Gabe called me on the phone from his mom's house. "I can't go with you to the clinic," he said. "I just want to make sure your parents are going with you." He paused, leaving me ample room for a reply.

"Yes, they're going," I said. "We're all going. But I'd like you to be there, too."

"I'm sorry," he said. "I can't be there." He didn't elaborate. His voice cracking on the other end of the line, he ended the short conversation: "Just know I love you. I really do."

I loved him, too. So much that I ached. So much that I would never really get over it. So much that I would spend the next half decade or so actively avoiding love, keeping my heart buried under layer upon internal layer of cement and barbed wire.

But not enough to give up my life.

SOMETHING WET AND SLIMY falls on my forehead, waking me. "Oh, gross!" I say out loud, startled more by the sight of the sunrise and the Zambezi (*Where am I? I DON'T LIVE HERE!*) than by the mucuslike substance now dripping down my face. I slept in my clothes, so I unzip my sleeping bag, stand up and try to shake the heaviness of morning from my body, wiping the stuff off my face with the bottom of my T-shirt. It's clear and fairly odorless, so it can't be bird droppings. Maybe it's some weird tree sap I've never heard about. I glance up into the tall trees above me to investigate and suddenly understand everything. There, on a branch, are two very pleased monkeys, crushing egg after egg in their hands and sucking out the potent liquid within, screeching and hollering with joyous monkey glee. A third one is trying to rip into a box of cheese and crackers with his mouth. I quickly look down at the spot where my carton of food used to be, knowing it will be gone before even confirming its absence.

I'm such an idiot. I should have left the carton in Mark's cabin. But this doesn't actually disturb me as much as the fact that I've just dreamt about the child Gabe and I never had, only to be woken up by a glob of falling albumen. What's that all about? A sign? I don't believe in signs.

I formally declared my doubts about the existence of a higher power to my parents when I was nine, on the day my Hebrew school teacher taught us about Auschwitz. The teacher told us, his sleepy, Sunday morning classroom full of Jewish boys and girls, that because the Jews actually survived such a hell, God must therefore exist. I didn't buy it. I mean, slavery in Egypt, the Crusades, the Inquisition: all comprehensible to me in the context of history and ignorance. But Auschwitz? In the middle of the twentieth century? In Europe? No fucking way.

"I don't believe in God," I told my father between bites of a pumpernickel bagel after class. As far as I was concerned, no real god would ever let Hitler strip, shoot, starve, asphyxiate, torture and shove six million Jews into the ovens. It didn't make sense.

"Then you're an atheist," he said, without passing judgment. "Atheists are people who don't believe in God." Dad was always looking for excuses to slide another vocabulary word into the file cabinet he was building in my brain (*"My, what a truculent doggie!"*; *"You're eating the penultimate cookie."*). "I'm an agnostic," he said, "which means I'm not willing to place my bet on either side of the debate."

This sounded more reasonable to me than dismissing God altogether. "Nagnostic?" I asked.

"No, *ag*-nostic."

"Oh. That's what I wanna be, too." And a lifetime of skepticism was born.

I stare back up at the monkeys, my stomach rumbling from hunger. I smoke a cigarette to calm the rumbling. Then, just as I'm wondering how I'm going to eat over the next week or two, Mark's army buddy Ray arrives at the campgrounds in his blue pickup truck. The flatbed is filled with a padlocked trunk full of food, three cases of beer, a rifle, a kerosene lamp, bottled water, a tent and even a couple of folding lawn chairs. Ray and Mark fought side by side in the Rhodesian civil war, he tells me, so whenever Ray has any vacation time socked away, he drives up to Mana Pools to camp out, to help his friend shoot poachers and to reminisce about those halcyon days—"You know, when Rhodesia was Rhodesia and everyone knew their place," he says wistfully. Ray is in his mid-forties, white, unmarried, thin and balding, and he wears kneesocks with his army boots and khaki shorts. He also has the fattest Swiss army knife I've ever seen. I get the distinct impression that for Ray, Operation Stronghold—with its predominantly white commanders shooting poor black poachers—is a glorious excuse for revenge.

But Ray also makes a mean spaghetti carbonara, and I have no food. Hang out with a racist and eat or shun him and starve? The answer seems pretty clear. And while I would never defend bigotry, Ray did see a lot of his friends die in that war. That could make anyone bitter and angry, right?

What's worse—because I really want to hate him—is that underneath Ray's unreconstructed colonialism, his heart is kind. One morning, instead of waking up with the sky as my ceiling, I wake up inside Ray's tent, utterly confused. I walk outside to find him sleeping on the flatbed of his truck, covered with a plastic tarp as a blanket but for the most part soaking wet. "It started to rain last night," he says, shivering. "I didn't want you to get wet."

Over the next few days, I go out on a couple of patrols with the troops. Sometimes we drive a Land Rover. Sometimes they take me in the helicopter. But while we see a lot of elephants—and I mean *tons* of elephants—we never spot a poacher or a dead rhino or, for that matter, even a live rhino. We just spend hours and hours driving around the Mana Pools game reserve, tourists on safari who just happen to have a couple of Dutch FN automatic assault rifles at the ready.

Because I know Xavier wants only well-lit photographs, I shoot most of my pictures in the early morning or the late afternoon to avoid the harsh midday shadows. I prefer magic hour—that moment of burnished-gold brilliance just before sunset. If you've ever seen Terrence Malick's *Days of Heaven*, which was shot almost exclusively during magic hour, you'll know what I mean.

This leaves the hours of ten to four wide open. I spend most of them sitting in one of Ray's plastic lawn chairs, either gazing out at the Zambezi or reading my García Márquez book or worrying about money. This is an expensive trip, and the only pictures I have are of a bunch of smiling soldiers driving around in a Land Rover, which hardly looks like anything approximating a war. This is a problem. As usual, I can't afford not to sell this story.

So late one afternoon, right before magic hour, I ask three of the soldiers to come with me down to the Zambezi with their guns. I arrange them in a triangular formation in the tall reeds and tell them to squat in the grass and hold their guns as if they'd just heard a rustling in the trees that might have sounded like a poacher. "Look angry," I tell them. It's hard to keep them from laughing, but when they stop, the image in my viewfinder looks great—well composed, beautiful color saturation, great depth of field, shiny guns, scary soldiers. It's just photo montée, I try to convince myself, every photojournalist out there does it. But I feel like a criminal.

I spot an elephant walking through the reeds on the banks of the river, his skin practically red from the fading sunlight. I dismiss the soldiers with a "Thanks, guys, appreciate it" and shoot off an entire roll of that elephant to make myself feel better.

MANA POOLS NATIONAL PARK, ZIMBABWE, 1989

The next day, in the cool crispness of the early morning light, I ask Mark to accompany me to the pile of rhinoceros skulls he keeps in his front yard. "Were all of these killed by poachers?" I ask him.

"Probably not," he says. "I'm sure some of them died from natural causes. I just collect 'em. I find them lying around in the grass or people bring me some—"

"Never mind. Just sit in the middle of the pile and look at me as if these skulls make you really sad." I shoot off a roll. "Great, Mark, thanks a lot."

MANA POOLS NATIONAL PARK, ZIMBABWE, 1989

It's just photo montée, it's just photo montée, it's just photo montée . . . Fuck. I might as well go into advertising photography at this rate. It certainly pays better, and you get a stylist and a makeup artist to boot. Let's see, I've befriended a bigot because I was hungry, and I'm shooting staged photographs so that I won't starve when I get back to Paris. At this rate, I'll sell off my last remaining principle in less than a day or two.

"So is that it? Do you have everything that you need now?" Mark asks me, carefully stepping over the skulls so as not to crush them. "Or are you like all the other journalists who tell me they need to see a dead poacher before they'll get out of my hair?"

"Well, now that you've mentioned it . . ." Sure, go ahead. Kill a man because I need the picture.

Mark tells me they haven't found a poacher in over three months. Some war. He says I'm welcome to stay, but Ray will be leaving to go back to Harare in a week, taking his food and his lawn chairs with him.

"Don't worry," I say, "I won't stay indefinitely. I'll leave when Ray leaves." At least it'll be a free ride back.

Two days before we're scheduled to return to Harare, I'm on late afternoon ground patrol with Mark and a few of the soldiers when we spot a flock of vultures circling slowly in the distant sky. Mark throws the Land Rover into fourth gear and we zoom over the dirt road, the wind tousling my hair into a tangled frenzy. The last time this happened, we found a dead elephant, so I'm not overly excited. But when we reach the vortex of vultures, there he is. A dead rhino. And in the spot where his horn should be is dried blood and ripped flesh.

We all step out of the vehicle and walk over to the slain beast. The stench of decay soaks the air, and the hundred or so vultures on the ground barely give way when we approach. Mark walks over to examine the carcass. "This guy's been here at least a day or two, if not more," he says, holding his nose and gagging. The gray skin of the rhino's body, covered in white vulture shit, looks like something Jackson Pollock might have done. Mark steps away from the rhino, pulls out his map, and marks the spot where we're standing with a red x. Then he calls over his soldiers. "Okay, men, this is the area to search." He makes an invisible circle around the x with his hand. "Tomorrow morning, you'll go out and look for their smoke. Let's head back. I've got to radio this one in."

"Smoke?" I ask.

Mark looks at me and smiles. "Even poachers like a hot breakfast," he says.

The next morning, when I wake up, Ray is gone. He isn't in his tent, he isn't in his truck, he isn't taking a piss in the woods. Dammit. I hope he didn't leave on patrol without me. I find a dirty bowl, clean it out with the water in my canteen, add in some powdered milk and granola, and sit down in the lawn chair to eat. I watch yet another crocodile trying to look nonchalant while slithering thieflike through the water. Suddenly, I see Mark running down to our campsite, sweating and out of breath. "Deborah, you better come quick. Ray went out with my men in the middle of the night. They left on foot. Snuck up on the bastards. We'll take the chopper. Come on!"

I grab my camera bag, overturning the cereal bowl in my haste. The adrenaline is gushing through my veins, half of me hoping that Ray will wait to shoot the poacher until I get there, the other half chastising myself for being such a sicko.

MANA POOLS NATIONAL PARK, ZIMBABWE, 1989

Once airborne, I feel the whip of the rotating helicopter blades vibrating in my rib cage. Mark's staring out the bulbous window and searching through the trees below, yelling orders at the pilot. "There, there! Right over there!" he shouts. We land in a clearing and duck under the still rotating blades as we exit the chopper. Just inside the treeline, I spot Ray and five soldiers. They're standing around, casually chatting, waiting for us. Behind them are the remains of a campfire, still emitting tiny tufts of smoke and encircled by the kind of things men don't usually leave behind as trash—a sweatshirt, a knapsack, a couple of blankets, a pair of boots, a battered canteen. Oh, and two rhino horns.

"Hey there, Deborah," says Ray, looking ragged and tired. He's got a rifle slung over his shoulder, and he's smiling. "We got a little present for you.

Wanna see him?" He steps aside and points down to the ground at his feet, where a young black man (maybe eighteen, twenty at most) lies on his stomach with the side of his face in the underbrush. He looks like he's sleeping, his eyes closed, his expression peaceful. There are only two signs of anything amiss: the pool of blood that has started to spread out from under his body, and the bullet holes in his back. There are at least eight holes pierced through his brown, wide-gauge sweater, as if it had been consumed by a closet full of hungry moths. I have never seen human death this close. "The other two got away," says Ray. "But we'll get 'em. We'll get 'em."

Instinctively, I grab my camera and start shooting, crouching and circling in a small orbit around the dead man, trying to get the best angle so that the bullet holes feature prominently in the frame. I circle the body again, my movements like a feverish waltz—circumnavigating, twirling, whirling, spinning around and around and around.

I am a vulture. I don't even try to pretend otherwise.

BACK IN HARARE, Julian picks me up at my hotel to drive me to an afternoon croquet party hosted by one of his diplomat friends. "You're looking rather thin," he says, as he opens the car door.

"Some monkeys stole my food," I say, offering up my newest adventure story with a perfect dead-pan delivery.

Julian laughs and musses my hair with a friendly pat on the head. "How perfectly rude of them," he says.

The truth is that I haven't been able to eat anything since that bowl of cereal I spilled while rushing off to board the helicopter. Later that night, Mark had organized a celebratory barbecue up at his cabin, but when I sat down with my plate of chicken and corn, I couldn't make the food go down my throat. Instead, in search of numbness, I drank a beer and four shots of really bad whiskey. But the alcohol backfired. I kept thinking about the poacher's family. Who would be missing him across the river in Zambia when he neglected to return home within a few days' time? His parents? A wife? Maybe a child? I asked Ray what would become of the corpse, and he just grinned. "What corpse?" he said. "This is a jungle." Then he started to laugh. I spent the rest of the evening staring out over the Zambezi, drunk and crying.

The croquet party, hosted on the lush grounds of an enormous home in north Harare, is in full swing by the time we arrive. It's an older crowd, many of the guests chasing after their small, flaxen-haired children through the grass. Some teenage kids are flirting with one another while playing a game of badminton. Black servants wander through the yard carrying silver trays full of tiny cucumber sandwiches with the crusts cut off, while the few black guests try valiantly to look comfortable in such a setting.

Julian brings me a gin and tonic from the bar. Everyone at the party seems to know him, and before long he's swept away into one conversation or another. I'm not feeling very sociable, so I take the remainder of my gin and tonic and sit down at one of the empty, ornate metal tables on the patio. I watch as a mother and father swing their giggling daughter like a jump rope between them, the dad holding her ankles, the mom tightly grasping her forearms.

It is so simple, the woman on the bus had said. *So simple.*

Julian finds me out on the patio, toting a handsome couple behind him. They're writers, he tells me, freelancers for *Sierra* magazine. They were just up in Mana Pools a couple of weeks before me, reporting the Operation Stronghold story. They need photographs. Perhaps I can help them. He leaves the three of us sitting there together.

"Julian tells me you got a picture of a dead poacher," says the man.

"Word travels fast," I say.

I'm distracted by the two boys who are chasing their little sister through the grass, their fingers pointed into tiny finger guns. "Bang, bang!" they're yelling. "You're dead!" She's petrified and crying, calling for her mommy.

"So it's true then?" the writer asks, shooting his wife a knowing glance.

"Oh, yeah," I say. "He's dead. Dead, dead, dead. Excuse me for a second."

I run over to the crying girl in the grass and pick her up. Then I chastise her brothers, who quickly turn their finger weapons back into hands. On my way back to the journalists on the patio, I carry the little girl, in her pink smocked pinafore, to the refuge of her mother's arms. The woman thanks me and turns to her daughter. "Oh, honey, were they shooting you again?" I hear her ask as I walk away. From the corner of my eye, I can see the little girl nodding, her lower lip trembling, the words staying safely inside.

"We'll need your photos for our article," says the man when I return. He hands me his business card. I take it, promising to send a complete slide set to *Sierra* when I get back to Paris. The sale will just about cover my expenses. But the steady money will come from the elephant pictures. Every magazine seems to need a good elephant picture now and then.

"I'm so glad we met you," says his wife, all smiles. "I mean, hate to say it, but without a dead poacher, there isn't really a story, now, is there?"

"No," I say. "There isn't."

VULTURESTI, ROMANIA, 1990

IT'S 3 A.M. IN BUCHAREST, and there's not a coal miner in sight.
I'm shivering, bouncing the balls of my feet against the car floor
and rocking back and forth to stay warm. Gad's wrapped in a blanket, and his head rests on a pillow that he's placed between himself
and the steering wheel. He's snoring. It's my turn to be on miner-
lookout patrol, but I don't think I'm going to make it. I keep clearing small, streaky circles on the fogged windshield with the side of
my fist, but all I see are a couple of other photographers pacing,
smoking cigarettes, jumping up and down and rubbing their hands
together to stay warm. The protesters in the streets are either huddled together sleeping or gathered around makeshift campfires, listening to their radios and chatting about the revolution. All of us
are waiting for something, anything to happen.

"Gad? Hey, Gad?" I say, gently shaking his back.

Gad sputters awake, mumbling something in German. Then,
jolting upright, he throws off his blanket and grabs for his camera
bag, which lies open and ready between the two of us, wedged in
against the stick shift. "What? Are they here? What's happening?"
His brown, wavy hair is matted to his head, and it blends manelike
into the matted but more reddish hair growing on his chin and
upper lip. His front tooth is missing. He lost it in a motorcycle accident, and I know he has a replacement, but I haven't seen him wear
it for a couple of days now. Gad has little patience for grooming.

"Relax," I say. My own teeth are chattering. "Nothing's happening out there. I'm just cold. It's late. Can you drive me back?" We're parked in front of the Inter-Continental Hotel, which is at most a fifteen-minute walk from the apartment building where I'm staying, but there's no way I'm trekking alone with a bag full of expensive camera equipment at three o'clock in the morning. Ceaușescu and his communist dictatorship have only been dead for a little more than two months; if sold on the still-thriving black market, my cameras could feed, clothe and house a medium-sized Romanian family for the next year or so.

"Sure," Gad says, starting the engine, "let's go. I'll crank up the heater."

Gad and I have been friends since our junior year at college. Only back then I knew him as Johannes. Gad was his middle name, and he used to introduce himself by saying, "Hi. My name is Johannes. But you can call me Gad," which, because of his heavy German accent, came out sounding like "Hi, my name is Your Highness, but you can call me God." Somebody finally pointed this out to him, which cracked Gad up because he could never understand why people were always giving him such bizarre looks upon meeting him. So he simplified his life and became just plain Gad.

Gad and I used to spend hours giggling and printing photos in the Adams House darkroom together, where we'd inevitably end up in some convoluted philosophical conversation about the nature of good versus evil. "Lighten up!" I'd tell him. "You take things way too seriously." He'd reply, with a smile on his face and a Kafka book in his hand, that he couldn't because there was just too much social injustice and malevolence in the world.

We danced in the darkroom to Paul Simon's "You Can Call Me Al," which Gad could play forty times over without getting bored. We gave each other love advice, criticized each other's work. But our favorite thing to do was to gossip about Gilles Peress, who we worshipped for different reasons. Gad was intrigued by Gilles's obsession with mortality; I just dug the man's pictures.

Though I am well versed in Gad's philosophy, however, his history remains much more vague. Gad rarely talks about his past. In fact, when I ran into him here in Bucharest a couple of days ago in the lobby of the Inter-Continental Hotel, I was surprised not so much to see him again—because of our similar career paths, we were bound to run into each other at some point—but to hear him speaking fluent Romanian. After a quick embrace, I asked him how he managed to learn the language so fast.

"I was born in Romania. We moved to Germany only when I was ten," he said, and left it at that.

We've been sitting here in Gad's car, which some of the time doubles as his residence and smells like it, for a little over four hours. Someone told someone who told Gad that a bunch of coal miners might be coming into Bucharest tonight, armed with sticks and bludgeons, to join in the mass protests that have been taking place here every day in University Plaza. The protests have been for the most part peaceful, and sometimes musical, with hundreds of people singing in unison *"Olay, olay-olay-olay . . ."* while waving their blue-yellow-and-red-striped flags, the ones with the holes cut out of the middle where the communist seal used to be. Though inspiring to watch, peaceful demonstrations are boring affairs, photographically speaking. There are only so many pictures you can take of yet another earnest Romanian kid sticking his head out of yet another flag hole. It's a rich metaphor, but it's been done to death.

But miners are often angry—being miners—and they tend to enjoy good, bloody skirmishes with the police. Which would mean good pictures. Because as every photojournalist knows, violence sells.

Gad backs out of our parking space. "I don't know about you," he says, "but I've had it."

"Me, too," I say, "I'm exhausted."

"No, not just tonight," he says, laughing. "I mean I've had it with this job. With photography. With sitting around in a car waiting for some miners to show up and beat up a policeman so I can sell a picture. It's bullshit."

"I know, but—"

"No. No but's. It's just bullshit," he says, now turning the corner. "Your place is just down here, right?"

"Yeah, second entrance from the left. So, what exactly are you saying?" I ask.

Gad pulls the car in front of my building and wiggles the stick shift into neutral. The motor idles. "I've been thinking about it a lot. I want to go to law school, study international law. Help people for a change."

I stifle a laugh. "Law school? Help people? Oh, please, Gad. How will a law degree allow you to help these miserable people?" I point up at the darkened buildings around us. These people are so screwed, I think, they don't even realize it yet. They've been shafted by everyone. Ceauşescu, his government, the secret police, even their neighbors, who could turn them in for no apparent reason if they felt like it. Nobody trusts anyone around here. They all run around paranoid and scared because—poof!—people disappear and never come back.

"It will," he says. He looks slightly hurt.

With the car still idling, Gad and I spend the next ten minutes talking and debating in the dark, just like back in college. He tells me the whole reason he got into photography in the first place was to help people—the refugees, the oppressed, the victims of war—but that he now realizes he was just being naïve to think his camera could fix the world.

"Gad, it's naïve to think you can fix the world period," I say.

He winks at me, smiling that gap-toothed grin. "Yeah, but I can always try."

Before I leave, I tell him about the vulture dreams I've been having ever since my trip to Zimbabwe. Gad says he doesn't need to have vulture dreams. He feels like one every day.

"Yeah, but law school, Gad," I say, smiling. "That's like trading one species of vulture for another. Besides, if you become a lawyer, you'll have to shave your beard. Shower. Maybe even wear your tooth."

"But law's a powerful tool for change," he says. "Always has been. Photography is losing that power. Anyway, I'll get a razor. Buy some soap. Find my tooth. What's the big deal?"

"So you're serious then?"

"Absolutely."

I thank Gad for the ride and the discussion, tell him it feels like old times. He watches to make sure I get into the building, and I hear the escalating whir of his car backing up as I step inside. The elevator smells like urine, but I'm used to it by now. I open the door of the apartment, take off my coat, attach my flash unit to the charger plugged into the wall, disrobe, brush my teeth and slip quietly into bed next to Doru. His back feels warm and smooth as I press my stomach against it, and I kiss him between his lank shoulder blades.

"Merci, ma biche"—"Thank you, sweetie"—he says, groggily turning to kiss my lips. Doru doesn't speak English. I don't speak Romanian. So we've had to settle for French, which feels odd, like a cat quacking with a dog. Since both of us, though fairly fluent, are somewhat deficient in French nouns, we're always using the word truc, which means "thing," and having conversations like "Where's the thing? You know, the thing. The thing that stops up the thing in the bathtub."

"Oh, you mean the thing!"

"Yeah, the thing."

Doru's long fingers cup my face, and he buries his nose in my neck. *"Et alors?"* he says. "Your face is so cold. Any miners?" I'd invited Doru to come sit in Gad's car to wait for the rumored rampage, but he thought we were nuts.

"No. You were right," I say. "No miners."

"Ha. Told you so. When are you going to learn to trust me?" he says, now kissing my nose, now my cheeks with those enormous lips of his. "Did you have fun with your little friend?" The last two words puzzle me. *Petit copain*—"little friend"—can also mean "boyfriend" in French. Communication between two people is difficult enough when both speak the same language, let alone two different languages. Add in a third, and simple words and phrases become tiny grenades, waiting to explode. But while I'm trying to figure out whether Doru meant "little friend" or "boyfriend," his lips begin a far more feverish dance across my face. Conveniently, my brain shuts down.

"You mean Gad? ... Yeah ... We talked ... Reminisced about college ... Things like that ..." I say, punctuating each phrase with a kiss along the length of his wide forehead.

"Uh-huh, things like that," he says. I'm just about to reach down between Doru's legs when he says, "So, tell me, did you fuck Nicolas or not?"

I WAS IN JAMAICA, on a Christmas vacation with my family at the end of 1989, when the Romanian communist dictatorship collapsed in a violent heap. I had just spent three weeks covering the eighteen-city round-the-world scavenger hunt I'd been assigned for *Géo* magazine, before that I'd flown to San Francisco to cover the earthquake, I was about to head to Los Angeles to do a story on girl gangs and I was exhausted. Sunbathing in my flowered bikini, looking out over the calm blue waters of Montego Bay and sipping pineappley drinks, I followed the events of Ceauşescu's undoing through day-old newspapers. I skimmed articles about the bloody street fighting in Bucharest and Timişoara, about the French cameraman who was crushed and killed under a tank, about the firing squad who had assassinated Mr. and Mrs. Ceauşescu in the middle of a picturesque outdoor courtyard.

I wondered whether I should cut my vacation short and head to Bucharest immediately. I went for long swims and tried not to think about it.

My twin sisters, Julie and Laura, were in their senior year of high school. My sister Jennifer was finishing her last year of college. I had not seen any of them for over a year. My mother and father had made one trip to Paris to visit me, but it had been almost a year since I'd seen them as well. We were having a wonderful time on the beach together, laughing, talking, reading books, eating coconuts, slathering suntan lotion on one another's backs, being a family. I was happy to be on furlough.

Reluctantly, guiltily, I decided not to go to Romania.

A few days later, I flew to L.A. and hung out with a girl gang for two weeks. With a cold call to *The New York Times*'s L.A. bureau—"Hi. I'm about to shoot a girl gang initiation ceremony. I'm at a pay phone on Grape Street. They're scheduled to beat each other up in half an hour. Wanna meet me here?"—I convinced Seth Mydans, the reporter who answered the phone, to jump in his car and come join me. Which meant I'd have a shot at selling the photos to the *Times*. I was learning not to count too much on Gamma, even if they were entitled to fifty percent of my meager earnings, regardless of the assignment's origin.

LOS ANGELES, 1990

In fact, I was starting to figure out that if I wanted to get paid assignments, I had to do most of the footwork by myself. I took photo editors out to lunch, schmoozed them at cocktail parties and exhibit openings, called them incessantly with story ideas or to simply remind them I existed.

So, just before heading back to Paris from L.A., I called a bunch of French editors to let them know I would be in the States in case any of them needed an American story to be shot. "As a matter of fact, I do," said Jacques. Jacques Haillot, the teddy-bear-like photo editor for *L'Express* magazine, had a soft spot for me. And I for him. Because in a microcosm like photojournalism, a place inhabited predominantly by sexist pigs, Jacques was a rare gentleman. He assigned me two stories: crack and violence in D.C. and one of those vague, slightly lefty French examinations of race relations in the U.S., entitled "Being Black." Few things fascinate the French as much as stories about other countries' racism. I suppose it makes them feel better about their own.

Jacques asked if I wouldn't mind spending a month and a half in and around Washington, D.C., working with my favorite French journalist, Michèle. Michèle was fortyish, single and brilliant. She smoked at least a pack of Gitanes a day, drank wine like it was water, was forever misplacing her pens, incessantly twirled the short front lock of her black hair and liked to walk around her hotel rooms buck naked while dictating her illegibly written articles to her editors back in Paris. She was a wickedly funny impersonator, who could lampoon fat movie-going Americans eating their enormous buckets of popcorn with the same venom she reserved for French Catholic priests. But one of the best things about working with Michèle was that I never had to worry about her making a pass at me.

I told Jacques I'd be delighted to hang out in crack dens with Michèle. And except for the addict who bullied us into paying him $15 after I shot a photo of him getting high, we had a rip-roaring time. Michèle especially loved the part where we got to drive around and watch the police arrest people. "I just adore American cops," she said, fascinated by the policeman who helped tackle, cuff and book a perp without ever letting go of his Dove bar.

While working on the various stories with Michèle in D.C., feeling particularly self-confident, I agreed to let Matthew join us for dinner. Matthew was the old boyfriend from college, a blue-eyed preppy with ringlet curls and the requisite Dead tapes and tapestry-covered bedroom walls. He had the distinction of being the only other person after Gabe I'd finally allowed to slip through the barbed wire protecting my heart after a string of meaningless, if fun, college affairs. He'd seduced me at the end of my junior year with his guitar, playing a soulful rendition of "Tangled Up in Blue" for a large, drunken crowd of people at a party while staring me straight in the eye. Afterwards, we decided to go skinny-dipping. Two weeks later, I was visiting him on Nantucket, where he was painting houses for the summer.

By fall, we were inseparable. We sat in on each other's classes, we went out for weekly dim sum brunches, we cooked enormous Thai feasts for *Lampoon* dinners, we read books to each other, we slept together almost every night. Mostly in his bed, because my roommate was involved in some illicit substance trafficking, which meant way too many doorbells ringing after midnight, as well as loud 4 A.M. screenings of *Pee-wee's Play-house* for all the acid heads tripping in our living room. Matthew's small, single room became our own little Eden: a place to sleep, to work, to talk, to think, to dance around in the buff, to play music, to write, to make love, to escape from the madness and clamor of everyday life. Isn't that what love is, after all? That mythic place where two can dwell—alone together—connected, naked and joyful?

But as winter set in, the relationship started to falter. Or rather, while I was falling deeper and deeper in love—allowing myself to imagine our future together, the shape of our children's faces even, the ones we'd have after roaming the world for a couple of years together as journalists, his text accompanying my photographs, why not?—Matthew began to look for the exit. The transition was subtle at first. A night here and there spent apart. Less ardor in bed. Entries in his sacred leather-bound journal I was no longer allowed to read. But then the pace picked up. The withholding of sex. Small barbs about my physique: my nose was too big, my legs too short, my hair not blond enough, not straight enough, not good enough. Hey, I knew I was not beautiful. Then again, I'd never really considered myself so monstrously ugly until Matthew began slipping away.

"You mean I look too Jewish," I'd said.

Matthew was half Jewish. He liked his WASP half much better. "No," he laughed, turning crimson, "it's not that." But I could tell I'd hit a nerve.

The final coup de grâce—the apple, if you will—was when a girl he'd met in Nantucket (very blond, long legs, small nose, no noticeable imperfections, annoyingly nice) came for a visit on a weekend a big, formal party was planned. "She's just a friend of mine," he said. He explained that we—meaning Matthew, his friend Richard, the girl and I—would all go to the party together, double date. Unfortunately, he neglected to mention that I would not be *his* date that evening but rather Richard's. And he kissed the pretty girl from Nantucket right in front of my eyes.

I hated him after that. And I vowed, for the second time, to never, ever let myself fall in love again.

Two years later, when he joined Michèle and I for dinner that night in a seafood restaurant in Georgetown, Matthew seemed changed: contrite, humbled, even slightly needy. He told us he'd been hired as an associate producer on a documentary being produced in D.C., but that the job was a place holder, something to do until he figured out what it was he actually wanted to do, to be. He was living with his parents, trying to save money. He did not appear to be happy about the whole situation.

Later in the evening, when we were alone, he confessed that graduation and the realities of the workaday world had opened his eyes, made him understand things he hadn't understood before. He apologized for insulting me, for his idiocy, his immaturity. He asked for my forgiveness. Because I was going to be stuck in D.C. for two months shooting, because I was bored, because he used to think I was ugly and now apparently didn't, because I'd never recovered from seeing him kiss that perfection of a girl in front of me—because, like all spurned lovers, I wanted him to fall in love with me again so I could gain back my dignity—I agreed to forgive him. But in my heart, of course, I never did.

Hell hath no fury like a woman made to feel like a hideous, big-nosed midget.

One night, after a romp in my quaint Georgetown hotel room, I was caught off guard when Matthew actually did declare his love for me. He should have never let me go, he said. I had no idea how to respond. I tried to reciprocate the sentiment, thinking maybe I should try to love him back, reattach the apple to the tree with some Super Glue and twine. Thinking that I should force myself to love him back because maybe my life would be more meaningful with a tiny bit of love thrown in it. But even as the words were coming out, they felt false. In fact, after his kindhearted and rather endearing admission, I felt little more than a sense of bittersweet vindication.

Michèle, the consummate *française,* said she was glad at least one of us was getting laid. But though she put up with Matthew during our many dinners as a threesome, she warned me against taking in stray mutts. "Mark my word," she said, as we drove to Dulles airport, "he'll come to visit you in Paris, and then you won't be able to get rid of him."

When I got back to Paris, there was a message from Matthew on my answering machine. He'd booked himself on a flight. He was scheduled to arrive in Paris mid-May, after the documentary he was working on was completed. His ticket was nonrefundable. And it was one-way.

It was March, a few days before my twenty-fourth birthday, and as I wandered aimlessly around Les Halles that first day back I felt restless and unsettled. I chalked it up to jet lag and to having been away for so long, but I also knew it was more than that. The reunion with Matthew had unhinged me. I'd enjoyed hearing him tell me how stupid he'd been; I'd relished the caresses to both body and ego. But now I was angry at myself for allowing it to happen, apprehensive about his arrival. Also, the stories I'd been working on had unhinged me. I was having dreams about pregnant women smoking crack pipes. A couple of the girl gang members had left angry messages on my answering machine when a group picture they posed for—and specifically asked me to put in a newspaper to make them famous—appeared on the front page of *The New York Times.*

I called Tiny, the bleached-blonde gang leader, at her parents' home in Watts. "You got us in trouble," she said. "My mom grounded me for a whole month." This from a girl who was trying to raise enough money to buy her own gun.

"Tiny, I told you I was taking pictures for the *Times.*" I looked out into the bright, ivy-covered courtyard of my Parisian home. My neighbor, the portly nudist, was cooking himself some eggs. I pictured Tiny sitting all alone in her dark, airless house, with the Jesus commemorative plates and posters plastered all over the living room walls.

"Yeah, but I didn't know people actually read the fucking thing," she said.

On some level, I sympathized. The more I hung out with those girls, the more I realized how much of their tough-chick act was just that. An act. Sure, they beat each other up during initiation ceremonies, collected money to one day buy an arsenal of weapons, engraved tattoos into one another's arms and shoulders and threatened classmates who dissed them.

But they also giggled and talked about boys and ate Oreos and snuggled teddy bears and had crushes and wrote bad poetry and read *Tiger Beat* together. When one of their homegirls gave birth to a baby, the whole gang showed up at her house with an enormous bag of chips, a jar of salsa and a pink onesie they'd all chipped in to buy, and they each took turns feeding and burping the child. With the girls' fathers in jail or dead or nonexistent and their mothers working double shifts to pay the rent, the gang was one of the only real families they had ever known.

Sitting there listening to Tiny yell at me over international phone lines, I realized I should have taken this lack of parental influence into consideration. I should have removed my journalist cap, with all of its high and mighty principles of impartiality and neutrality, for just a brief moment, just long enough to warn the gang what the notoriety might do to them. I should have explained that the world might not be ready for underprivileged girls—or any girls, for that matter—who aggressively stick up for themselves. Perhaps I should have made it clear that millions of people read *The New York Times* every day. I apologized to Tiny for getting her into trouble. She told me if she ever saw me again, she would kill me.

A WEEK LATER, on a cool day in mid-March, I stopped for a morning coffee at the Père Tranquille and stared out the window at the well-tailored people sinking down the escalator into the Les Halles Métro station. They had briefcases and newspapers stuffed under their arms, important-looking coats, shiny shoes, purposeful strides. They knew where they'd be for the next eight to ten hours, and they knew the following day would bring more of the same. I glanced down at my heavy camera bag and at my rugged, scuffed Paraboots with their thick rubber soles and wondered what it would be like to trade places with one of them, to have the type of job where work meant commuting to an office in delicate leather pumps.

I called Marion from a smoke-filled phone booth in the café to tell her I was on my way to the agency. She said she had a meeting outside the office, but she suggested we grab a bite at the Pizzapino in our neighborhood for dinner, reminding me that the last two times we'd made plans, I'd had to call her from the airport to cancel. I apologized and told her I'd meet her there at eight, come hell or high water.

"What does that mean, 'hell or high water'?"

"It means I'll be there," I said. "Don't worry."

A half hour later, I strode into the Gamma office just as the noisy AFP machine was spitting out a wire report on new violence that had just erupted in Tîrgu-Mureş, a small Romanian city 150 miles north of Bucharest. There had been more gunfire, the report said. Many tanks. Angry mobs with truncheons. Something about ethnic Hungarians fighting Romanians or vice versa, which in retrospect was just a tiny, canapé-type appetizer of the simmering ethnic hatred that would soon be unleashed in that corner of the world.

I tried to sneak out of the agency quietly, but Henri grabbed me by the collar. "Copaken!" he hollered, pronouncing my last name incorrectly as usual (accent on the first syllable instead of the second, short *a* instead of long. It came out sounding like a Native American war cry: "Koh-pă-KEN!").

Henri handed me four 500-franc notes, less than $400, along with the wire story ripped from the machine and told me that while I'd missed the last flight to Bucharest, a plane was taking off from Charles de Gaulle airport and flying to Budapest, Hungary, in exactly one hour, and if I didn't have my ass firmly planted on one of the seats of that plane . . .

"I know," I said, "you'll break my face."

Henri allowed himself a proud, fatherly smile.

"But how do I get from Budapest to Tîrgu—Tîrgu what is it called?" I asked, now running with Henri down the hallway to Gamma's photo-filled reception area.

Practically pushing me out the front door, he said simply, "Tîrgu-Mureş. Figure it out."

The next flights out to either Bucharest or Budapest weren't until the following afternoon, which would mean arriving in Tîrgu-Mureş, wherever the hell that was, a full twenty-four hours later; by then, the story could be over. My apartment was a fifteen-minute Métro ride from the agency. The airport was a forty-minute taxi ride from my apartment in light traffic. Doing the math in my head, I figured if everything was running smoothly, I'd have exactly five minutes to pack. That left zero minutes to argue. Or even think.

I'd had short notice for stories before—two hours, sometimes three—but one hour would really be pushing it. On autopilot, I sprinted out of the agency, down the stairs of the Denfert-Rochereau Métro station and into a car of the express RER, whose doors were closing as I jumped in. During the whole short ride, I stared at my watch, whispering, "Come on, come on, come on . . ." whenever the train stopped. At Châtelet-les-Halles, I ran up the escalator, bumping into annoyed passengers in their delicate leather pumps who cursed at me in French, and then I wove my way through the mazelike underground shopping mall. I rode up another three escalators, out the entrance, past the Père Tranquille, through the tiny crowded streets of Les Halles and finally up the stairs to my third-floor apartment, two steps at a time. I yanked my suitcase out of the closet and threw everything that looked moderately clean into it.

From the refrigerator, I took out an enormous rectangular Tupperware container filled with eighty rolls of Fuji 100 ASA color slide film and a dozen or so rolls of Tri-X black-and-white film, which, to save space, had already been shucked out of both their cardboard boxes and their little black plastic cylinders. Then I grabbed forty more rolls of Tri-X that I hadn't had time to dislodge and compact, but you can't go anywhere without an ample supply of black-and-white film because who knows when you might need it? Tîrgu-Mureş? Where the hell was Tîrgu-Mureş?

Just as I was about to leave, I realized the phone situation in Romania would probably range from difficult to impossible. Phones in communist countries had no international direct dial and were notoriously unreliable. Control the flow of information, and you control the population. So I pressed the outgoing message button on my answering machine and recorded the following fast and frantic message: *"Bonjour. C'est Deborah. S'il vous plaît, laissez-moi une message après le beep sonore*—Hi. It's Deborah. Please leave a message after the beep. Mom, Dad, I'm in Romania. I'll try to call."

The answering machine was still making its strange clicking noises as I locked my front door and ran down the stairs. Then it was back through the streets of Les Halles again and out to the Boulevard Sébastopol. It only took three minutes to find a taxi—a record in Paris—but it felt like twenty. I had a brief panic attack on the way to the airport until I located my passport in the zippered pocket of my jacket. Normally I kept it in the camera bag, but since I'd just recently returned to Paris from D.C., it was still in the jacket along with my cardboard stub from the transatlantic flight.

At the airport, I cut the line at the ticket counter, yelling, *"Journaliste! Journaliste!"* and waving my Gamma press pass. Another guy carrying a giant Nagra tape deck and microphone was trying to do the same.

"Excusez-moi, mademoiselle," he said. "I was here first." He was over six feet tall. He had enormous black leather boot–clad feet, thick black hair, a thick black leather jacket, black jeans and a black T-shirt stretched taut against his chest. It wasn't bright inside the airport, but he wore a pair of black Ray-Bans anyway.

"Oh, yeah?" I said, puffing out my puny chest, ready for a fight. "Well, I have to get on this flight, too, okay? So just calm down, uh"—I picked up the name tag off his suitcase and turned it over with a quick flick of my wrist—"Nicolas." Then I turned to the beleaguered man behind the ticket counter. "One ticket to Budapest, please."

"No, you calm down," Nicolas said gruffly, turning over the name tag on my suitcase with even more gauntlet-throwing fanfare, "DÉ-bo-rah."

"It's DE-bra, okay, DE-bra. Not DÉ-bo-rah. You people never get it right."

The ticket vendor, a Romanian, looked at both of us with exasperation. "Both of you calm down," he said, handing us our tickets simultaneously. "If you run, you might make it."

Just then, a TV camera crew of four panting men came sprinting up to the ticket counter. *"Journalistes! Journalistes!"* they shouted, waving their TF1 press passes in the air. Nicolas and I made a mad dash to the gate just as the stewardesses were closing the doors. The TV guys missed the flight.

I sat down in my seat. Nicolas, laughing, threw his bag into the overhead compartment above me. "That's just great. Adjoining seats," he said, trying to squeeze his enormous body into the narrow cushioned slot assigned to him.

After ignoring each other for the first half hour, we gingerly started to speak. Nicolas was a reporter for Radio France International. He'd been in Timişoara. He'd covered Bucharest. His mom had escaped from Romania, and he had grown up speaking Romanian at home. Best of all, he knew where Tîrgu-Mureş was, and he knew how to get from Budapest to Tîrgu-Mureş. He thought it would be a good idea if we drove together. Knowing not one thing about the country I was about to enter, least of all how to get from Budapest to some place called Tîrgu-Mureş, who was I to argue?

We checked into a hotel in Budapest, where, after a tortured exchange with the international operator, I called Marion from my room to apologize into her answering machine for missing dinner once again.

The next day, at the crack of dawn, Nicolas and I rented a car and drove to the Romanian border. I slept most of the way from Budapest until Cluj, where we were waylaid by a group of angry Romanian demonstrators. Nicolas recorded some sound, I took a few shots and then we jumped back in the car to drive the seventy-five miles or so still remaining until we reached Tîrgu-Mureş. The roads between Cluj and Tîrgu-Mureş were barely paved, cutting through hilly green farmland and bordered every now and then by a tunnel of trees planted at precise, identical intervals. We were in the heart of Transylvania, legendary stomping grounds of Count Dracula. "You have a boyfriend? Live with someone?" Nicolas asked.

I stared out the window. We were stuck behind a barely alive horse pulling a rickety old cart and an equally rickety old man slowly down the road. There was no room on either side to pass them. "You're not my type, if that's what you're asking. Try driving on the grass."

"I can't. Too many rocks." Nicolas looked insulted. "And that's not what I was asking. I was just making conversation. Boy, are you defensive." He was wearing the exact same all-black outfit he had worn the day before. When we were picking up the rental car, he had to fish something out of his suitcase, so I took the opportunity to peek inside. Every piece of his neatly folded clothing, with the exception of a few white T-shirts, was black. Even his briefs were black. "Must make it easy to get dressed in the morning," I'd said to him, but he didn't laugh.

It was still light when we neared the main square of Tîrgu-Mureş. The crowds were thick, impenetrable by car, so Nicolas just left the car where it stood in the middle of the street and yelled at me to follow him. We ran, pushing our way through the sea of people, until at last we reached ground zero. There, in the center of town, a column of tanks and a line of heavily armed soldiers encircled the open plaza, totally in control. Despite our psychotic sprint, we were too late. There would be no more fighting. For Nicolas, it was a total bust. Without the sound of gunfire and shrieking mobs, radio reports about purported violent clashes between ethnic Hungarians and Romanians tend to lose a certain amount of gravity. As for me, I wasn't thrilled to have missed the fighting, but columns of tanks and soldiers standing guard are not bad, as photo opportunities go. I started shooting, circling the scene looking for good angles.

TÎRGU-MUREȘ, ROMANIA, 1990

About an hour later, as darkness fell, Nicolas found me. "I got a good interview with one of the soldiers. It'll have to do. You on an expense account?" he asked.

I told him I wasn't.

He told me he was. "You're welcome to share my room," he said.

I thought about it for a moment. If we'd arrived in the middle of an angry ethnic battle, my pictures would sell, I'd get an assignment or two, some magazine would pay for my room. But as it was, we'd arrived too late. I'd thrown the tickets to Budapest on my nearly maxed-out credit card. Once again, I seemed to be hemorrhaging money to pay for my job. "If we can get a room with two beds, sure," I said.

At this point, Nicolas looked exasperated. "Of course we can get a room with two beds. My God, what do you take me for?"

"A man," I said, under my breath and not really to him.

That night, in his black underwear and black T-shirt, Nicolas fell asleep in his bed. I fell asleep in mine.

The next morning, when I returned to the town square, the tanks and soldiers were still there. I was in the middle of framing a close-up of the barrel of a gun, with blurred tanks and a line of soldiers in the background, when I spotted the word "Gamma" in my viewfinder. Surprised and curious, I pulled my camera away from my eye, and there, right in front of me, was a tall, lanky man with enormous lips and two large Gamma mailing labels stuck to both the front and the back of his acid-washed jeans jacket.

"Excuse me," I said, approaching him. "Where did you get those stickers?" The man had a smooth, feminine chisel to his face, but also the jutting chin, prominent Adam's apple and aquiline nose of a nobleman. He wore sneakers with his jeans, and his straight, dirty-blond hair appeared to be soft and feathery, like a baby's. Around his neck hung a single Nikon with a 20-millimeter lens.

"Sorry, no English," he said.

"*Français, tu parles français?*" I asked. The man nodded. I asked him, in French, where he got the stickers.

"*Bonjour,*" he said, ignoring my question, "I don't believe we've met. My name is Doru. What's yours?" He kissed my hand. Then he blushed.

"Deborah. Nice to meet you. Now tell me where you got those stickers."

Doru said my boss Henri had sent the stickers to him and to his best friend, Ovidiu, last month during the revolution, when they'd become permanent stringers for the agency. Gamma kept a stable of hundreds of stringers all over the world to cover the random spot-news events that their France-based staff photographers might not be able to reach in time.

Ovidiu waved at us from behind the column of tanks. He was much shorter and darker than Doru, but he was dressed almost identically. And right there, in the middle of Ovidiu's own acid-washed jeans jacket, was another package-sized Gamma mailing label. Ovidiu shouted something to Doru in Romanian, which I could tell from his body language must have been "Do you need me?", but Doru waved his head no and motioned his friend to keep shooting.

"You do know you and your little doppelgänger over there are wearing mailing labels," I said, an arrogant mock to my tone.

Doru played along, pretending to be shocked. "No! Really? I had no idea!" He had an angelic smile. He told me that he and Ovidiu, being Romanian, were nervous about getting beaten up by a mob of angry Hungarians. Since they didn't have press passes to prove they were working for Gamma, they figured the stickers were the only solution.

I was angry at Henri. It was hard enough making a living as a photographer. Not only had I arrived in Tîrgu-Mureş too late to shoot any battles,

I was stuck spinning my wheels with two oddball, wild-'n'-crazy guys from the same agency. If any of our pictures should happen to sell, we'd automatically have to share the profit, which, on a $250, quarter-page photo would produce exactly $41.66 per person after Gamma took it's 50 percent cut.

After shooting a tense late-afternoon demonstration by a mob of agitated Hungarians carrying signs and candles in their clenched fists, Doru, Ovidiu and I found a French television crew who would be returning to Paris the following day and who promised to carry our three envelopes of film back with them. When we got back to the hotel, Nicolas was in the lobby, trying to politely seduce the hotel operator into getting him an outside line to France so he could file his story. I introduced him to my new sticker-covered friends and told him to join us for dinner after he'd filed. He promised he would and dashed off to the phone.

"I'm sorry," Doru said when Nicolas was out of earshot, "but who's Johnny Bravo Ray-Ban Man?"

"I met him on the plane," I said. "He's harmless. And pretty smart. And he's letting me stay in his room for free, so be nice to him."

"Oh, I get it," said Doru, with a tone that implied he was no fool.

"No, you don't. Really. We're just sharing a room," I said.

After a dinner of greasy chicken Kiev, where the conversation was held half in Romanian (for Ovidiu's sake, who spoke little French) and half in French (for my sake, who spoke not a word of Romanian), the four of us went back to Nicolas's hotel room for a drink. Doru produced one of those ghastly communist cigarettes, the kind where you have to squash the paper end between your fingers. "Don't smoke that stinky thing in here," I said, taking out my pack of Marlboros. "Here, have one of these."

Doru took a cigarette from my pack and rolled it through his fingers like a fine Cuban cigar. He lifted it up to his nose to breathe in its aroma. "Ah, Marlboro. The symbol of free markets, capitalism, liberty." He was smiling, trying to pretend his whole poor-little-commie act was a joke, but the overall effect was far more wistful than ironic. He lit the cigarette, took a tentative first drag. Then, slowly, he exhaled. "My first one," he said, his eyes moistening, if barely, despite himself.

As we smoked, Doru explained that because his father was a career diplomat, he and his brother were able to spend many of their early childhood years living in Switzerland, years that he recalled as an endless fantasy world of rich cheeses, sweet chocolates and fresh, unpolluted air. Then, the posting was over, and Doru's family was forced to move back to Bucharest. They lived better than most, but that wasn't saying much. Doru's father had to resort to things like smuggling in a tape of *Animal Farm* so that his sons might begin to understand their contradiction-filled lives.

"I used to cry myself to sleep, dreaming about chocolates," Doru said. He smoked the remainder of his cigarette slowly and carefully, savoring both it and the moment with equal affection. Then he stubbed it out. "You want to work together again tomorrow?" He pulled a drunk Ovidiu to his feet.

No, I thought. Tomorrow, I want to save you. I want to stuff you with chocolate and take you home with me. I want to bring you to a library and let you pick out any book you want. You thought Orwell was good? Wait until you read Bulgakov, Kundera. There's so much I can show you.

"Sure," I said. Then I showed him to the door, where he kissed me playfully on both cheeks and where, once again, he lifted my hand to his mouth. Doru had explained earlier that this hand-kissing business was not an affectation but rather a Romanian tradition. Hey, I'd said with a smile, I'm all for tradition.

The next day, Nicolas and I both received calls from our bosses telling us in so many words to get our butts down to Bucharest. Rumor had it that the demonstrations would be getting bigger and angrier. Something was bound to happen. We were to leave Tîrgu-Mureş immediately. At about the same time as the phone calls, Doru and Ovidiu showed up, wearing the exact same clothes as they had worn the day before.

"We're leaving for Bucharest. You two want a ride?" Nicolas asked, nonchalantly packing his piles of precisely folded black clothes into his black suitcase. He repeated himself in Romanian for Ovidiu's sake.

Doru looked at me and blushed. "That would be great." Ovidiu just nodded, his eyes betraying the frustration of his limited tongue.

I told Doru to go get his bags, but he sheepishly explained that neither he nor Ovidiu had any bags. "It's just us and our cameras," he said. "We're ready to go right now."

We checked out of the hotel, jumped in the car and drove south into the foothills of the Carpathian Mountains, where the road began to twist and turn as the hills grew ever steeper. About an hour outside of Bucharest, Doru suggested we stop for dinner at a charming hotel in the picturesque mountain village of Piteşti. "They have dancing there," he said, "live music. It'll be fun." Nicolas was all for fun, Ovidiu was hungry and I live for dancing to live music, so we all agreed to stop.

When we walked into the cavernous restaurant, the tables were covered with heaping plates of food, clear green bottles of water, darker bottles of wine and full ashtrays. But all the patrons, save for a few too drunk to stand, were crowded onto the dance floor, swaying maniacally to the loud beat of the wedding-band version of "The Lambada." The female singer, wearing a gaudy red sequined dress, belted out the tune as if inspired by God. A few of the revelers were actually weeping with joy.

"Why are they crying?" I yelled into Doru's ear so he could hear me.

He grabbed my hand and yanked me onto the dance floor. "It's the Lambada!" he yelled back, as if the tears required no further explanation. When I looked confused, Doru repeated himself. "The Lambada! You understand?"

"No," I yelled back.

The noise was overwhelming, and Doru looked like he was searching for a way to explain something very complicated with as few words as possible. "They are free," he shouted, suddenly picking me up and cradling me in his arms like a child. He began to spin me around. "They are crying because we are free."

After a while, the band stopped trying to play anything else. Every time they'd start up with a Romanian song, the patrons would sit back down at their tables and begin to eat, or smoke their cigarettes, or drink their wine. "Lambada!" one would yell from one corner of the room. "Lambada! Lambada!" shouted another, and then soon the whole place was begging to hear that silly melody just one more time, simply because it was foreign, Ceauşescu was dead and they could. The lady in the red dress capitulated and sang the song eight more times while we were there, and as we left to continue our voyage, we could still hear her voice echoing through the mountains behind us.

That night, when we arrived in Bucharest and I saw a crowd of demonstrators gathered in front of the Inter-Continental Hotel, I decided to check into my own room. This had all the trappings of a potentially big story—masses of people, a recently collapsed government, poverty, breadlines, anger, upcoming elections, colorful flags with holes in them. I figured

Gamma would definitely find me an assignment. Besides, Nicolas was starting to get on my nerves.

"Why the separate rooms? You and Nicolas have a lovers' spat?" Doru asked me, as he helped me carry my bags up to my room.

"Doru, I told you. We're not sleeping together. I was just trying to save money."

"Uh-huh," he said. Then he thanked me for dancing the Lambada with him, kissed my hand, and walked out the door of my room, which, at $120 a night, was more money than a typical Romanian could ever have hoped to have earned in an entire month.

Procuring a steady assignment to cover my costs, however, proved more difficult than I had assumed. Within the next few days, every news organization, every journalist, every photographer I'd ever met on the roving international war circuit had all convened on Bucharest. The lobby of the Inter-Continental was filled with enormous metal cases of television equipment, burly men wearing photographer's vests and carrying cameras, frantic daily writers wearing their deadlines in the creases of their brows and a murky, almost impenetrable cloud of cigarette smoke. The whole situation was, in the delicate vernacular of my fellow news gatherers, a pig fuck. A gang bang.

Doru and I were out in the streets every day shooting demos. He only owned one wide-angle lens, so I shared mine. Every time he asked to borrow one, he would look down at his feet and hunch his shoulders as if apologizing, his face stricken with a mixture of embarrassment and rage. Doru, like every Romanian barking in the streets, was angry.

Ceauşescu had been buried for nearly three months, but life in Romania had not improved. Bread was still hard to come by, and when a loaf did become available, it was usually stale. The Securitate—the infamous Romanian secret police force—still seemed to hold sway. Gas was scarce, toilets and elevators didn't work, you couldn't find a pair of shoes even if you had the money to pay for them. People needed a scapegoat, and for the moment, it was the provisional new guy in charge, Iliescu. Conspiracy theories abounded. Iliescu had stolen the gold faucets from Ceauşescu's palace. Iliescu was a pawn of the Securitate. Iliescu was the anti-Christ. The Romanians had been lied to for so long that basic concepts such as fact and logic seemed to be utterly immaterial.

When Doru and I would finish shooting the desecrated flags and the raised fists and the open mouths filled with petulant songs, we'd write our captions in the backseat of a taxi heading out to Otopeni airport. There, we'd scour the departure hall for a kindhearted and open-minded passenger to carry our freshly exposed film back to Paris. "Don't worry. We do this all the time. Just try not to put the film through the X-ray machine. Make them hand-check it. A messenger will be waiting for you when you exit customs," we'd promise.

Then, to make good on our promise, we'd have to immediately leave the airport and zoom back to the phone queue in the basement of the Inter-Continental, where at least thirty journalists at any given time were all waiting—while cursing and pacing and smoking and scribbling—to place an international call. The hotel had dedicated ten clunky red plastic rotary-dial telephones for this purpose. They were all lined up next to one another on the far wall, which made it an ideal place to spy on your colleagues if, like me, you were so inclined.

When we finally made it to the front of the line, we'd call Henri and give him a physical description of the incoming passenger—"tall, brown hair, beard, carrying a guitar case" or "short, fat, pimples, Madonna T-shirt"—as well as any news, hearsay or gossip we might have overheard on the current situation in Bucharest. Being Bucharest, it was mostly just gossip: "We hear the police might arrest people tonight," "Someone told us the Securitate has hundreds of spies pretending to be demonstrators," or even, "We spoke to a guy who said Ceauşescu is alive and living in Bulgaria."

Henri in turn told us he was able to sell our demo pictures here and there, but he had yet to procure any steady assignments. Meanwhile, my hotel bill was growing ever larger.

Over yet another inedible dinner of fried potato cubes and burned meat ("What kind of meat?" I once dared ask, to which a surly waiter replied, "Why do you care?"), I was trying to decide whether or not to cut my losses and head back to Paris when Doru, blushing, suggested I move in with him. I could sleep on his couch. He would be a gentleman. We were working together and sharing our meager profits anyway, he said, so we might as well share cheap accommodations.

I politely thanked him and said I would gladly accept his offer.

That evening, after helping me unpack my clothes, Doru covered his living room couch with fresh sheets and a blanket while I changed into an oversized T-shirt and brushed my teeth in the bathroom. When I came out, he was sitting on the floor, watching the news on television. "This is your space," he said, pointing to the couch. "I will sit here on the ground."

"That's ridiculous. You can sit on your own couch to watch the news," I said, slapping the cushion next to me, but Doru remained on the floor.

"No," he said, his voice firm. "I am a gentleman. I will stay here."

When the news was over, he stood up from the floor and once again kissed my hand before heading off to his own bed. "Good night, my little Deborah," he said, pausing for just a moment to stare into my eyes. "Sweet dreams." There on his couch, alone in the dark, I tried to sleep with my fingers still tingling from Doru's lips. And my dreams, when they finally came, were far from sweet. (They were lewd. With a Lambada soundtrack.)

The following night, we were in the same odd formation—me on the couch, Doru in front of me on the floor, lights off, television blaring—when Doru, staring straight ahead, complained of a bad back. This was a normal complaint, coming from a photographer, but in his voice I heard a small trill of innuendo. He asked if I wouldn't mind rubbing his left shoulder. I told him I'd be glad to rub both.

Still sitting on the floor, he removed his T-shirt and pretended to pay attention to the images of Romanian demonstrators on the news, the light on his chest varying in intensity with the relative brightness or darkness of the TV screen. "That doesn't look like Bucharest. Where is that?" I asked him, now straddling him from behind and kneading my fingers through the knots in his shoulders.

"Timişoara. We should go there tomorrow. Too many photographers in Bucharest right now."

"Yeah, okay," I said. "Let's do that. I'd like to see Timişoara." Then, suddenly, overwhelmed with a tenderness that I can only describe—if oddly so—as half maternal, half carnal, I bent over from my perch on the couch and kissed the back of his neck.

Doru quickly turned around and offered me his mouth. We stayed like that, locked in an awkward embrace, for a few minutes longer until he placed his head in my lap and hugged my legs tightly to his cheek, like a child. Then he stood up, sat down next to me on the couch, and began to gently undress me, pausing to kiss and caress any newly exposed skin. We made love on that couch in an almost trancelike slow motion, both of us trying to get the dance right.

Afterwards, weighed down by fatigue, I felt Doru pick me up and carry me from the living room into his bed. There, he covered me with his quilt and lay down beside me. When I opened my eyes, I caught him staring at me.

A few minutes later, Doru began to sob. I could tell he was trying to do it quietly, but the muffled sounds and the small vibrations woke me up.

"What's the matter?" I asked. I turned to face him.

"Nothing, nothing," he said. "I thought you were sleeping. Good night, my little Deborah. You gave me a beautiful gift tonight. I'm just happy, that's all." Then he turned away from me.

I hugged his back tightly to my stomach, wanting to understand.

After awhile, his crying jag now finished, he turned back around and said, "I don't think it's a good idea for me to fall in love with you." I detected a slight tinge of anger in his voice, a sudden sense of detachment in his demeanor. "You're going to finish up here, go back to Paris, walk on the Champs-Elysées and sit in a quaint little café with a glass of Beaujolais watching the sun set behind the Arc de Triomphe." His features then softened, and he cupped my face in his hands. "And I'm going to be stuck here forever, pining."

"JESUS, DORU, do we have to go through this bullshit again? No, for the eighty-fifth time, I did not fuck Nicolas." The first time Doru asked me this question, I was confused, because I thought *baiser* meant "to kiss" or just "a kiss"—the way I'd learned it in French class back in junior high school—and not "to fuck," its more common and colloquial definition. Doru mistook my confusion for waffling and has been angry about it ever since. "And I did not fuck Gad either, if that's what you were actually asking."

I push him away from me and scoot to the edge of the bed, where I bury my head in a pillow. If I were to move another inch, I'd fall off.

"That's not what I was asking," he says.

"Yes it was," I say. I pause, trying to decide if it's even worth arguing anymore. "Besides, why does it even matter? Even if I did have sex with Nicolas, it would have happened *before* I met you. I've had sex with lots of men in the past. Why do you even care?"

"Because I do," he says.

"Well, you shouldn't," I say.

I take small solace in the fact that he and Ovidiu, friends since child-hood, have lately been arguing as well. I'm not exactly sure what is going on because they yell at each other in Romanian, but Doru tells me it has something to do with money.

"Gad's quitting photojournalism," I say, trying to ease the conversa-tion away from yet another minor explosion of misunderstanding.

"Is that so?" Doru answers, not really interested. He inches over to me and cradles me from behind. His limbs are so long, my whole tiny body fits snugly between his neck and his knees. "I'm sorry. I shouldn't be jeal-ous. I know you and Gad are old friends."

"We are." I'm still not looking at him.

"I love you." He kisses my ear.

"I love you, too," I say, which is neither entirely false nor exactly true. In fact, I'm having a hard time understanding precisely what I feel for Doru.

"Sure you do." He sighs.

"Stop it," I say, wondering if Doru will ever feel comfortable sitting at a café sipping Beaujolais in the shadow of the Arc de Triomphe.

DORU, OVIDIU AND I are in the parking lot of the Inter-Continental, scanning the license plates of the cars and searching for the little white Oltcit we've just rented. When we finally locate the car, a Romanian knock-off of the Citroën Visa, Ovidiu takes two Gamma mailing labels out of his camera bag and affixes one on either door. I point to a label and mime the word "why" with my palms facing up.

He just shrugs as if it should be obvious and says, "Securitate."

Because Ovidiu and I cannot communicate verbally, except through Doru (which is tiresome), we've become adept at using our body and ex-aggerated facial expressions to converse. Ovidiu has a kind, plain face that lends itself to this task. He wrinkles his nose to show disgust. He rolls his eyes whenever Doru gets into one of his paranoid huffs. If he wants to thank me, even though he now knows how to say "thank you" in English and in French, he prefers to just squeeze my two hands tightly in his while looking into my eyes. If he catches Doru kissing me, he holds his hands to his heart, raises his shoulders and smiles. If the kissing between Doru and me goes on for too long, as it often does, he throws his head down in third-wheel angst and pretends to sulk. Either that or he taps on his watch.

But pantomime has its limits. Without words, it is not obvious to me why Ovidiu is worried about the Securitate. I ask Doru to translate.

Doru explains that because the license plates on our rental car are the type normally assigned to foreigners, we'll be more prone to getting stopped by the Securitate, who, once they stop us, will want to extort our money. The press stickers will make them think twice before doing so.

We've rented the car to take us away from Bucharest. Doru thinks we shouldn't waste any more time shooting political demonstrations in University Plaza when there's an entire undocumented country full of post-communist ruins. A friend of his has just come back from Copsca Mica, for example. It's a mining town that is so polluted with black ash that color pictures of soot-covered faces come out looking as if they'd been shot on black-and-white film.

We drive out of the city on a mission to find orphans. Doru has heard rumors of Dickensian-type conditions in some of the Romanian orphanages, which for some reason he keeps calling *Les hopitaux des irrecuperables.*

"Hospitals for unrecoverables? What do you mean by that?" I ask.

Doru stares at me with a look I'm starting to recognize. It's the one where he's standing on the far bank of the river, I'm standing on the near, the river is very wide, and we have no bridge. "You know, unrecoverable. Children who can't be saved," he says.

"Oh, I see. Children who can't be saved . . ." I repeat absentmindedly. Doru checks his rearview mirror and looks pleased, like maybe the river is not as wide as he thought. Like maybe he could try swimming. Except now I'm actually digesting the words, translating them into English in my head. "Doru, excuse me, but what kind of a kid can't be saved?"

Doru furrows his brow in confusion. "What do you mean?" Now he turns his gaze away from the road to look at me. "Lots of kids can't be saved. Lame ones, retarded ones, the bastards, the blind . . ."

And I think to myself, the chasm is too wide. If either of us tries to swim to the other side, we will drown.

Since there are no Yellow Pages in Romania, the only way to search for orphanages is to drive around the country and look for them. On Doru's hunch, we drive to a small town called Becini and start questioning the locals. I sit in the car while Doru and Ovidiu question shopkeepers, street sweepers and random pedestrians, but they all shrug their shoulders and shake their heads. No. Sorry. Can't help you. Never heard of such hospitals. Try the next town. Maybe they have one.

Doru spots the former communist party headquarters of Becini and figures it's as good a place as any to continue our inquiries. The local bureaucrat, a pudgy, chain-smoking man with pockmarked skin, assures us that no such orphanages exist anywhere in Romania. Pointing at me, he asks Doru where we plan to spend the night, since the one hotel in Becini has rules against lodging foreigners. When Doru can't come up with a proper alternative, the man insists that we sleep in his office, which comes out sounding much more like an order than an invitation.

I spend a restless night. I'm snuggled between Doru and Ovidiu, wishing I'd brushed my teeth before bed and staring up at an enormous marble bust of Lenin. In the darkness, I can't help thinking he looks like a cross between Mr. Clean and the red cartoon devil from the Underwood ham commercials. I'm about to tell Doru this, but then I remember he'll have no idea what I'm talking about.

Sometime before morning, I need to go to the bathroom, but I don't know where the bathrooms are. I rouse Doru, but he says that all the bathrooms are locked until morning, as are the doors leading to the outside. "What if there's a fire?" I ask.

Doru looks slightly annoyed. "We'll burn. Now go back to sleep." He covers me with his jacket and his arm.

But I cannot fall back asleep. I stare up at Lenin, with his triangle eyebrows, his triangle nose and his self-satisfied smirk, and I am unable to shake the feeling that the man is mocking me.

The next morning, freed by the janitor, we pee and drive out of Becini. Ovidiu, who normally prefers to sit quietly in the backseat, starts to hum the notes from "The Lambada." Doru joins in and soon all three of us are absentmindedly crooning together. We're searching for a town called Vulturesti—where Doru thinks we might finally find an orphanage—but since there's no Vulturesti indicated on the official map of Romania we bought back at the hotel, we resort once again to asking around. One man tells us it's twenty miles north. Another says it's forty-five miles to the east. A few people have never heard of the city. Ovidiu suggests we stop for lunch and continue our search on full stomachs.

Since restaurants in Romania are scarce, we've brought along some sausage, stale bread and water. We stop to picnic atop a hill in the middle of an open field, overlooking a town that could very well be Vulturesti. Or not.

When the food is gone, Ovidiu goes for a walk. Tells us he has to go relieve himself, but both Doru and I know he's just being nice, trying to give the two of us a moment alone. Doru takes out a pack of Marlboros from the carton I bought for him and offers me one. With his Zippo lighter, also a present from me, he lights first my cigarette, then his own. Then he kisses me gently on the forehead. "What am I going to do when you're gone?" he asks, smiling and blowing smoke rings into the spring air.

Gone? Don't be silly, I think. I won't go without you. We can make this thing work. We'll get you a visa. You'll come live with me in Paris. I'll tell Matthew to cancel his ticket. You'll move into my tiny apartment, and we'll make love every night. Okay, every morning, too. You'll work for Gamma, start earning some money. Okay, maybe not right away, but soon, like in five years or so when your archives start generating some cash—you know, the stuff you don't necessarily want to shoot, but the stuff that'll sell, like that picture I took of the Eiffel Tower during the Bicentennial with the fireworks behind it. That one stupid picture sells all the time. Of course, while you're busy building up your archives, your debt to the agency will pile up. You won't be able to help me with the rent, and you'll probably get angry when you can't even find fifteen lousy francs in your pocket to buy a ham and cheese sandwich for lunch. You won't have time to read *Master and Margarita,* or any of the other books I've carefully picked out for you, because you'll be too busy just trying to survive. You'll think every male friend of mine wants to sleep with me, and you'll ask me suspicious questions about where I've been. You'll meet my parents, who will fly to Paris for a visit and take you out to a dinner of oysters and champagne at La Coupole, and you will resent this as well, because you grew up listening to smuggled *Animal Farm* tapes and pining for just the tiniest taste of Swiss chocolate. In time, you might even grow to hate me.

"Let's not talk about that right now," I say.

Vulturesti, when we finally find it, is a small, pastoral hamlet with gingerbread houses nestled into cozy hillsides. The smell of horse dung seeps into the car as Doru rolls down his window to ask a buggy driver for directions to the Hospital for Unrecoverables. To our surprise, the man knows exactly what we're talking about. His wife happens to work there as a nurse. Horrible place, he says. Then he tells us to follow him.

When we pull into its gravel driveway, the orphanage looks like any other of the quaint gingerbread houses scattered through the hills of Vulturesti: it has a whitewashed exterior, an orange-tiled roof, a couple of windows with green shutters and a wooden door. This surprises me somehow. I guess I had imagined it would look more Gothic, more like a set design from *Oliver Twist*. Ovidiu and I stay in the car, while Doru goes in with the French lipsticks we've brought along as bribes.

A half hour later, Doru comes back to the car. The lipsticks are gone, and his face is ashen. "What's the matter?" I ask him. "Where are the lipsticks? Can we go in and shoot now?"

Doru says something to Ovidiu in Romanian. Ovidiu just shakes his head and looks down at the ground.

"What? What?" I ask. "Speak in French, please. Doru, what's going on?"

"They took the lipsticks. We can go in and shoot. But Deborah, it's pretty bad in there." Again, I picture a scene out of *Oliver Twist*: children in worn clothing, overcrowded rooms, broken toys, watery gruel, some dirty-faced kid holding out his bowl saying, "Please, sir, I want more."

"Doru, I've seen bad before. I think I can handle it."

But nothing—no thing, no place, no photograph, no film, no experience, no nightmare—could have ever prepared me for the Hospital for Unrecoverables.

Before we even get inside, we are surrounded by a chaotic swirl of children. They've seen us from a small, barred window, and they've come running out of the orphanage, squinting. Some of them are naked or nearly so, their bodies covered with bruises and layers of dirt. The ones who are clothed are dressed in ripped night garments in hues ranging from soot gray to muddy brown. Many of the boys have large holes torn in the crotch of their tattered leggings, and they stare at us while tightly grasping their penises in the way a normal child might clutch a favorite stuffed animal. One of the girls has fastened herself to my leg, wailing, "Mama! Mama!", but most of the others just grunt. A dark-haired boy, maybe five years old, opens his mouth to scream. Nothing comes out. Another boy, nearing puberty, just rocks back and forth on the tips of his toes, slapping his own face at regular intervals. His penis—a man's penis—hangs out of his underwear, flopping to and fro. I try to avert my eyes by turning back to the mute screamer, but he looks so much like that Edvard Munch painting, I can't rest my gaze there either.

"Welcome to my country," says Doru. His eyes are slits, and he bites into his upper lip with his bottom teeth. Then he spits on the ground. "Welcome to my fucked-up country." He looks more embarrassed than horrified. The mute boy now reaches up to Doru, his hands stretching and trembling. Pick me! Pick me! Doru scoops him up, slings him over his shoulder, and begins to shoot. The boy holds on to his neck and refuses to let go.

A few minutes later, two custodians, dressed in crisply starched nurses' uniforms, accompany us inside to the main room of the orphanage, a filthy, dank and airless box, its six bare planes created with equal parts poured-concrete and indifference. The place reeks of urine. I look over just in time to catch one of the boys taking a piss in the far corner of the room, his wet stream hitting and temporarily staining the surface of the wall slate gray. In the center of the room is a narrow aisle, bordered on either side by a single row of metal bed frames, all of them flecked with white paint chips. There are no mattresses.

Doru asks one of the women why there are no mattresses, and she explains that they were all destroyed by incessant bed-wetting.

One of the boys, emaciated and naked from the waist down, squats on one of the bed frames, his toes curled around the cylindrical slats, his right ankle tied with a piece of ripped cloth to its headboard. He screams and bangs his head against the cold metal, grasping the bars like an angry caged monkey. "Untie me! Let me down!" he says. The two nurses—can they even be called that?—ignore him.

Neither Doru, Ovidiu or I say another word, because language has suddenly become inappropriate. So we pull out our cameras, hide our faces behind them and start to shoot, each for our own particular reasons—Ovidiu because he's human, Doru because he's furious and me because, for the first time in my career as a photojournalist, it seems like the most morally appropriate action to take.

We know we have to record them all, each and every filthy orphan face, so we fan out across the room and begin to work. I start with the tied-up boy. When I approach him, he barks at me and tries to bite my hand. The nurses are off in the corner, playing cards, so the girl in the torn blue nightgown, the one who called me Mama, intervenes on my behalf. She whispers something to him, calming him down. Snap. I shoot the two of them together. Snap. I shoot another boy screaming hungrily into his rusty lunch bowl. Snap. And another one jumping up and down. Snap. And another one just sitting there, alone in his thoughts on a bed with no mattress.

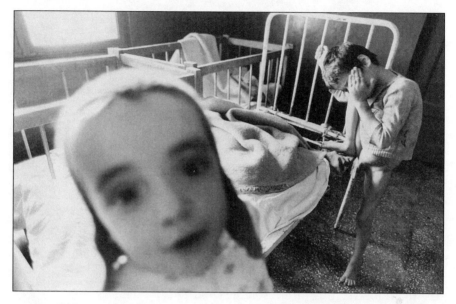

VULTURESTI, ROMANIA, 1990

VULTURESTI, ROMANIA, 1990

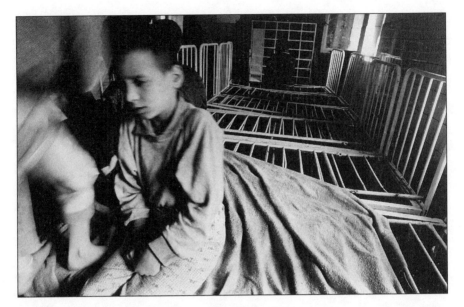

VULTURESTI, ROMANIA, 1990

"Is there another room?" we ask. The women in the white uniforms tell us there is, upstairs, but there's no need to go up there because that's the room for the truly unrecoverable children.

Before they can say no, Doru and I run out to the hallway and bound up the stairs three at a time. We hear the soft, plaintive moans before we even enter the room. There, crammed together into a single crib, on a blanket sodden with their own urine and feces, lie five listless toddlers. They range in age from perhaps one to four years old. Two have no legs. Another looks like he (or is it a she?) has cerebral palsy. One has drool running down his chin, and the fifth one seems mentally retarded. When the children notice us standing over their crib, they flap their hands expectantly, five little baby birds, patiently waiting in their soiled nest for the return of a phantom mother.

I start to shoot, and Doru follows, our faces hidden behind lenses, our minds trying to concentrate on camera mechanics: f/2, 125th, shit, not even a 6oth, but that hand fluttering is going to be too blurry. The smell! Don't throw up. Flash? No flash. The picture will lose all emotion. Okay, just focus on the one kid lying still. The others can be blurry. Yeah, that'll look good. Wish I had a step stool. I'm too low. Doru's taller, he's got a better angle. Let him shoot the wide shot. Baby birds. They look like baby

VULTURESTI, ROMANIA, 1990

birds, flapping. So much flapping. *Oh my God.* What is *wrong* with this country? I've got to get out of here.

"I'll be right back, Doru," I say, which makes him jump, because up until now we haven't spoken a word to each other. I run down the stairs clutching my mouth and pinching my nose, the sight and the stench finally overpowering me. There's got to be a bathroom around here somewhere. I'm poking around closets and administrative offices along the corridor when I stumble across a door that leads to a moldy shower room. A trickle of tea-colored water leaks from one of the shower heads, splattering onto the mossy concrete floor. I step inside, hoping to find a toilet, and that's when I see him.

There, in the middle of the room, lying on a wooden plank suspended midair between two chairs, is a tiny, naked, blue corpse.

I start to scream.

Doru is the first to arrive, shouting in French, "What is it?", then Ovidiu, then the two nurses, lumbering lazily behind.

What is it? *What is it?* I think. I'm pointing to the body, my finger shaking. Oh, it's nothing, nothing at all. Just a *dead kid,* that's all. Here in the middle of a shower room. What kind of a fucked-up place is this anyway? I catch myself hyperventilating. Breathe normally, I think to myself. Breathe normally.

"Shit," says Doru.

Ovidiu shakes his head.

The nurses take one look at each other and try to stifle a laugh. It's nervous laughter, to be sure, but it's laughter nevertheless. Laughter in a shower room at the foot of a child's corpse. I stare at them, my mouth agape. "My God, Doru, tell them shut up." But no translation is needed. My voice is stern enough that the women fall silent.

Romanian words pass back and forth between Doru, Ovidiu and the nurses until finally Doru translates: "They are sorry for laughing. Children die here all the time, so they were only laughing because you screamed. He committed suicide yesterday. He hit himself against a wall. Just kept hitting himself against the wall until he—"

I interrupt him. "Suicide?!" I scream. The boy was six years old. Eight at the most. Children die here all the time? What, one a day? A couple a month?

Doru snaps at me, more out of defeat than anger. "I'm just translating, okay?"

My voice rising in pitch, I tell Doru to ask the nurses how many children die here a month. He refuses. He looks at me with pleading eyes. "Deborah, please calm down. You're trying to understand something that is incomprehensible."

But I can't calm down. "So why is this dead body here?" I ask. "Do they plan on burying him, or are they just going to leave him here to decompose?" Breathe normally.

Doru sighs. More Romanian words fly over the corpse. He tells me that they're waiting for the doctor to perform an autopsy. "It's Romanian law," he says. "Anyone who dies in an institution has to have an autopsy."

Of course, I think. It's the law. I'm trying to remain calm. "Can you ask them if they follow any laws about feeding orphans? You know, making sure they don't die of starvation?" I feel like hitting someone. "What about mattresses? Any laws about mattresses?" I glare at the nurses, and even if they don't understand my French, they catch the drift.

"Calm down, Deborah." Doru scowls at me. "It's not their fault. They're just following orders."

Right. They're just following orders. And there's a dead body in a shower room. And there are children tied to beds. And flapping hands. And expressionless stares. And tattered clothes and emaciated bodies. You can't fool me. I have seen footage like this before. It was black and white and grainy, the camera slowly panning across men, women and children standing gaunt behind barbed wire, branded with numbers and yellow stars, staring out with the wide-eyed dissolution that comes from knowing—really knowing—that there is no God.

Okay, so there's no Zyklon-B coming out of the shower nozzles. Just water and rust. And no ovens. And obviously the scale and the scope and the impetus and the infrastructure are all completely different. A child in the camps would have felt his innocent laughter turn to screams then to suffocated silence within the short span of fifteen minutes. Here, at the Vulturesti Hospital for Unrecoverables, life is snuffed out the Romanian way—slowly. Asphyxiation by neglect.

After my Sunday school teacher taught us about Auschwitz, my dad took me to the bookstore to buy *The Diary of Anne Frank*. I read it so many times, the pages fell out. I started having recurring gas chamber dreams, and these dreams followed me into adulthood. In the dream, I'm naked and shorn and all alone amongst naked, shorn strangers when the gas is turned on. Like all the other women shrieking and thrashing and clawing and trying to breath, I throw myself against the door, hoping to pry it open or at least to find a crack for oxygen. Just when I realize that the door is locked and the seal is airtight, just as I feel myself being smothered and squashed by the other bodies trying to push their way up against the door, a hole appears in the wall. It's small, just big enough for one mouth. My mouth. I breath through the hole, filling my lungs with fresh oxygen. When I turn around, everyone else is dead.

"Yisgadal, v'yisgadash, shmay rabah . . ." I stare at the stiff, cold cadaver lying naked before me and recite what I can remember of the mourner's Kaddish. I'm not religious, but the words bubble up anyway, as if they'd somehow been encoded into my DNA. "Oseh shalom bimromav . . ."

Doru lets me finish my ancient mumblings, grabs my arm and leads me out to the dusty courtyard behind the orphanage. He offers me a cigarette. While we smoke he rubs my neck between his thumb and forefinger. "Stop trying to understand it," he says, breaking the silence. He stubs out his butt on the ground. "It will only make you crazy. Like me."

When the doctor finally shows up, smelling of whiskey and stale Romanian tobacco, he greets the nurses with familiarity, and they accompany him into their administrative office for a cigarette break. This leaves no one but Ovidiu, Doru and me to watch over the orphans.

The little girl in the blue nightgown will not leave my side now. "Mama, mama!" she yells, trying desperately to make her point. Her face is heart-shaped, with a huge forehead and flirtatious blue eyes partially hidden behind blond wisps of hair. She looks to be about five years old, maybe six. I put down my cameras, sit on a bed frame, lift her up and hold her in my lap. At first she hugs me, nuzzling her head deep into my shoulder. Yes, okay, I'll take this one home. Just wrap her up, and I'll take her straight home. I hug her back. Suddenly, the girl recoils. She sits up, arches her back. Before I realize what's happening, she has grabbed my right breast in her hand and is clamping down hard on my nipple with her teeth. I scream and push her off me.

Just then, the two nurses emerge from the gray cloud of smoke in their office. They are carrying a small, corroded saw and walking toward the shower room.

"Ask them what they are doing," I say to Doru.

Doru stops them in the hallway, then runs back to the administrative office. I hear him yelling at the doctor. The two emerge, a wall of ice between them, and head to the shower room. "Follow me," Doru says.

"What's going on?" I ask, practically running down the hallway to keep up. Ovidiu is right behind me.

"The autopsy. Let's go."

As we approach the entrance to the shower room, we spot the two women. They have already started to saw into the dead boy's skull, two lumberjacks cleaving a log between them, bisecting the forehead just above and parallel to his eyebrows. They chat amiably together as they go about their macabre task, their faces glistening and their armpits stained with sweat from the effort of trying to cut bone with a dull blade. The doctor walks into the room with us and leans against the far wall. Then he pulls out a toothpick and begins fishing around in his teeth with it, bored and otherwise idle.

What the hell is going on? I poke Doru and ask him why the nurses are performing the autopsy rather than the doctor, never mind that they're using a rusty old saw to do it. He just shakes his head and shrugs, defeated. "Because they are," he says. "Because the doctor is a fucking lazy bastard. I told you. This is Romania. Don't try to understand it."

I am simultaneously repulsed and fascinated by the gruesome sight before me. I grab my Leica and hold it up to my eyes. Doru reaches for his Nikon. Ovidiu takes a last look at the sliced forehead and walks out. A few minutes later, I hear him retching in the courtyard.

I know, above all else, that I must keep myself from thinking. I shoot a medium shot of the saw cutting into the skin, trying to concentrate on lens and shutter and light, but I am caught off guard by the lack of blood. Theoretically, I understand dead hearts. But somehow it's still surprising to see an incision that doesn't bleed. I become hyperconscious of my own breathing, picturing platelets and plasma streaming through my arteries, branching off into the capillaries, then racing back up through my veins, darker, weaker and screaming for oxygen.

At what point after the boy bashed his head against the wall did his blood cells finally realize it was no use going back to the heart for more oxygen? And at what point *before* the boy bashed his head against the wall did he reach a similar conclusion? That it just wasn't worth it, that there was no oxygen to be had.

One of the nurses holds the bottom of the boy's face, her palms clamping down on his cheeks, her elbows braced on the table, while the other one tries to stick her fingers underneath the top of the incision just along the hairline.

The rapid-fire clicking sound of Doru's motor drive echoes in the cement room. The nurses are now peeling the boy's face off, pulling at it as if stripping the skin from a mango. Hair disappears under the retracted scalp. Eyes, then nose vanish under the folded-down forehead flap, leaving nothing more than exposed sinew—shiny, red, anonymous.

When the women finally extricate the brain, they motion for the doctor to come take a look, but he stands defiantly with his arms crossed, his back still leaning up against the far wall. He and Doru exchange angry Romanian words, but the women just shrug, poke the wrinkled organ a couple of times with their fingers and start in on the chest cavity.

They cut a vertical slice in the center of the boy's rib cage, again with the rusty saw, and pull out, one by one, his vital organs: a liver, two kidneys, the stomach, the coiled-up intestines and, finally, the heart, silent and still. This time, one of the nurses actually walks over to the doctor with the heart in her hands and asks him to examine it. Once again, he refuses. Doru glares at the doctor but does not speak. The nurse looks back and forth from Doru to the doctor, sighs and returns to the body still carrying the flaccid heart cupped in the palm of her hands. She lays it down on the plank right next to the boy's elbow, and starts to throw everything else back inside, in no particular order, the way you'd pack a bag if you were in a hurry.

I've got to get out of here.

I stop to change my film. Without the camera to shield my eyes, I start to feel weak. Queasy. The room tilts. I see the heart lying there, inert and cold. I see the women shoving it back inside the chest cavity. I see them sewing up the opening with a needle and black thread. I see the doctor, lighting a cigarette and blowing smoke over the corpse. I see him holding up some official-looking papers, leaning them against the wall and signing them, his cigarette dangling from his mouth. But I see all these things in slow pixilation, a slide show punctuated by the sound of Doru's shutter release, my eyes darting around from image to image in what feels more and more like a two-dimensional space. I picture the cavity behind my eyes, and instead of a brain I imagine an enormous roll of film, winding maniacally inside a bloodless metallic skull. A simple recording device, nothing more.

The women throw the body into a burlap bag, carry the bag to the broom closet, open the door to the closet and push the bag inside, wedged between a mop and an old cardboard box.

I ask Doru if the nurses plan to just leave the body in the closet like that.

He says it wouldn't surprise him if they did, but after consulting with the women, he explains to me that someone from the morgue should be by soon, in a week or two tops.

I wander by myself out into the courtyard, and with one whiff of the puddle of vomit Ovidiu left behind, I throw up. Once I start, it's hard to stop, and by the end I'm dry heaving, trying to regain control over my body. I am in bad shape. My hands won't stop shaking. My left knee is in spasm. I can't catch my breath. The sounds vibrating in my ear are garbled, as if muffled by a towel. My nose is running, my heart feels arrhythmic, my eyes are watering.

The brain, unlike a roll of film, seems to have an infinite capacity to record and, even worse, recall. Especially the more shocking images. It would be so much easier if, after every thirty-six gruesome frames, I could toss it out and replace it with a fresh brain. That way I wouldn't have to re-member or interpret, for the rest of my life, the faceless, disemboweled dead boy with the heart ripped out of his chest.

When the heaving finally stops, I wipe my mouth and eyes with the back of my sleeve and look up. I concentrate on breathing. After a while, my knee stops trembling. My hands fall limply to my sides. I look up into the sky, and it's as if I've opened the pages of a pop-up book or put on a pair of cardboard 3-D glasses. First the clouds pop out, then a bird. I see the sun and the way its rays hit the newly formed buds in the trees. I see the separate planes of the orphanage building, I see the horizon receding in proper perspective. Everything that had previously turned flat now has heft, shadow, dimension, depth. I see a broken tricycle. It's the first toy I've seen all day.

"DEBORAH, THESE ARE TOO GRISLY! I can't distribute them! No one will publish them!" I waited an hour and forty minutes down here in the basement of the Inter-Continental for this phone call to Paris, and now Henri is barking in my ear, telling me my orphanage pictures are too hideous to publish. It's been two days since I sent him the film. I was sure some magazine or another would have bought the story by now. But of course a magazine can't buy a picture that its photo editor never gets a chance to see.

I tell Henri to just leave out the autopsy photos and send the others around to the magazines. I suggest that he might want to consider just sending the black and white I shot instead of the color, which would be less "grisly." I ask him if he received my fax with the handwritten text I wrote to go along with the photos.

He tells me I should know by now that magazines don't normally ac-cept text written by photographers for publication. Or black-and-white film, for that matter, which is why he hasn't even developed the Tri-X yet. Then he chastises me for disappearing for three days without any contact. "I found you an assignment to cover pre-election demos in Bucharest for

Libération, and you were off on a honeymoon with Doru in the country-side!"

I tell him it wasn't exactly a honeymoon. I remind him that I found the *Libération* assignment myself, and that it would not be starting for another couple of weeks. I ask him to please, when he gets a chance, send the black-and-white film to the lab to be developed.

He tells me to get off the phone, to get my ass outside and to start shooting.

I feel numb. I hang up the phone and go for a walk outside, leaving my cameras inside my bag. I walk through the demonstrators milling about in University Plaza, past the empty shops with their long lines of Romanians spilling out of them, waiting to buy bread. Or shoes. Or scraps of tough, inedible meat. I meander my way back to Doru's apartment. "What did Henri say?" he asks when I walk in the door.

"Not much," I say.

"Did he sell the orphan pictures?" There's an edge of frustration to his voice.

"No. Not yet." But I do not elaborate. Since returning back to Bucharest from Vulturesti, we've been bickering a lot over small, stupid things, resorting to a mostly monosyllabic discourse. I can't tell if it's our emotional reaction to what we saw at the orphanage or if it's Doru's way of protecting himself, distancing himself from me. For my part, because Doru is counting on those orphan pictures to sell, and because I just don't have the heart to tell him that Gamma is sitting on them, I feel a little devious. Which makes me snappish.

Doru gathers his equipment together and shoves it inside the new Domke bag I had my mom ship over for him from the States. He said he'd pay me back for it one day, but I told him, "Don't be crazy. It's a gift." Doru now has two cameras in his bag, his Nikon F3 and the Nikkormat I gave him. The Nikkormat is the camera I shot my thesis with, and before that the Pussycat Lounge. It's the camera that made me fall in love with photography in the first place. I told him it was too heavy and clunky for me when I presented it to him as a gift. He was polite enough to pretend he believed me.

A few days after I gave him the camera, he asked if he could borrow a thousand dollars to buy a used car his brother had located in Geneva. I had only $1,300 to my name. What's more, if I agreed, it would mean that at some point I'd have to fly back to Paris to take out the cash, meet Doru and the car in Geneva, then drive back to Bucharest in time to cover the elections. But I said yes and booked my flight back to Paris. That's when the bickering started in earnest. Doru hates himself for asking me for the money. He hates himself for his future debt to me. I hate myself for not realizing that he would.

So, naturally, we take it out on each other.

Doru tells me he has to run over to the AFP bureau. They have an assignment for him, and he needs the cash. Normally, a photographer working for Gamma is not allowed to simultaneously shoot for a wire agency, but Doru could care less. The way he figures, the more money he can earn, the quicker he can get out of Romania.

When Doru leaves, I sit on his bed and stare out the window. My view is partially blocked by the two bricks of black-and-white film—a brick being a package of twenty rolls—which are sitting on top of Doru's dresser. They are the rolls of Tri-X I grabbed on my way out of my apartment in my mad rush to Charles de Gaulle airport, when was that? Two weeks ago? Three? It feels like a year. The boxes are still tightly wrapped in their shrink-wrap, just sitting there between me and the window, gathering dust.

Yesterday, I bumped into a colleague in the lobby of the Inter-Continental Hotel, a photographer named Jim from New York whom I'd run into a few times in the past. He asked if he could buy some black-and-white film from me. He'd arrived in Bucharest from some other godforsaken place, I could never keep track of where, and he was low on supplies. I told him I'd think about it, see how much film I had left, even though I knew I had the two bricks sitting unopened on the dresser in Doru's apartment.

One of the most talented, well-respected and scrupulously honest photojournalists around, Jim was a member of Magnum, had a contract with *Time* magazine and had won many prestigious awards for his toils. Some people called him "The Monk." He drank only Perrier, never smoked, never cursed, had never divorced (or ever married, for that matter), kept his lean body in perfect physical shape and every night, at least as far as any of us could gather, he went to bed both early and unaccompanied. There were rumors of hearts Jim had broken during the small pockets of downtime he had between stories, but no hard evidence.

Jim's reputation among us mortals was practically mythic, as if he were not human but rather a deified Hollywood version of himself. They said that his khaki wardrobe was always pressed and unsullied, no matter the war or how long he'd been covering it. That his straight brown hair remained combed and perfectly coiffed even in the midst of shooting a battle. That his handsome face was always scrubbed and clean-shaven regardless of the scarcity of razors, soap or running water.

In reality, he was simply a focused, well-groomed ascetic whose talent, clout and strong jaw fueled the petty jealousies and snarky comments of his less competent, less comely, more grass-stained colleagues.

I liked Jim, appreciated his idiosyncrasies. I understood that, unlike the majority of us photographers who were shooting for the thrill of it, Jim was a man on a mission. He truly believed he'd been put on this planet to record its every misery and to try to save it, and he could not see the point of being distracted, clouded or exhausted by earthly temptations. Which pretty much ruled out all but one of the *w* words (war) most photojournalists love (wine, women, whiskey, Winstons, weed, whoring, whatever.)

"What have you been up to that you've run out of film?" I asked Jim when I saw him in the lobby.

In typical Jim fashion, he answered, "Oh, a bit of this, a bit of that," which probably meant he'd just completed a lengthy assignment in some far-flung destination like Namibia or Burma for *National Geographic.* He wasn't being rude; Jim just never liked to brag.

When he inquired about my recent exploits, I was equally vague. But not, like Jim, out of modesty. I didn't tell Jim about Vulturesti because I was afraid of getting scooped. I knew that if I told him about the orphanage, Jim would want to shoot it, to add it to his archive of human suffering. Then, because of his skill and his stature in the world of photojournalism, the magazines would buy his pictures, not mine.

Now, staring at the film on Doru's desk, still numb from my conversation with Henri, I suddenly realize what I must do.

I shove the two bricks of black-and-white film inside a plastic FNAC bag. Then I take out my reporter's notebook and a pen and hastily scribble down directions from Bucharest to the orphanage in Vulturesti. I tear the sheet of paper from the spiral, fold it in half, and throw it in with the film. I grab the bag, run out of the apartment and dash back through the streets of Bucharest until I reach the Inter-Continental, sweating and out of breath. As usual, the lobby is swarming with journalists, so it doesn't take long for me to locate Jim. "I just saw him, eating lunch," Gad tells me, pointing in the direction of the restaurant.

"He just went back up to his room," his fixer tells me, when I find him sitting all alone at a table.

Jim's room is on the same floor as the AFP bureau, and as I pass by the office, Doru is heading out the door. "Where are you going?" he asks, surprised to run into me.

"To see a friend," I say, caught off guard. I don't want to have to explain to Doru what I'm up to, because that would involve telling him about my telephone conversation with Henri. Which I know will not only crush him, because he's counting on paying me back the thousand dollars he owes me with his earnings from the Vulturesti story, it will dredge up his ingrained Romanian paranoia. He'll think Henri, instead of just being stupid, is trying to fuck him over. And I don't need that right now. Recently, after Ovidiu planted the notion in his head, Doru has become convinced that Henri has been tampering with his sales reports and withholding his money.

I try changing the subject. "So, what did they assign you?" I ask.

"Miners. Again. Can you believe it? I'll bet you not a single miner shows up tonight. They'll come when no one's waiting for them. But as long as AFP is paying me, I don't really care." Doru pauses, raising one eyebrow. "What friend?"

I'm stuck. "Jim. That guy from Magnum. You know him?"

Doru looks at me suspiciously. "Of course. The god of photojournalism. No, I don't know him personally," he says.

"Yeah, well, I don't know him that well either. I just have a package for him, that's all."

He eyes the FNAC bag, its lower-case, late-seventies-style white letters against a gold backdrop. Any French photographer would immediately know it contains film, the Fédération Nationale des Achats des Cadres—the National Federation of Executive Purchases, how French is that?—being the one chain store in France where all photographers buy their film. But to Doru it's just a plastic bag. "I see. A package," he says, his voice tinged with a mixture of doubt and sarcasm. "So, will I see you later?"

"Sure. I'll find you in the streets," I say, running off down the hallway to Jim's room.

"You do that," he calls after me, in a tone meant to convey that this conversation is far from over.

Jim answers the door to his room dressed, as usual, in various shades of tan and olive. The room itself is spotless. I let my eyes wander around, looking for clues, but nothing speaks to me. There's not even an iron in sight, no object to tell me anything more about Jim than he allows to be known.

I walk over to the bed and turn my plastic bag upside down, letting the film and the note fall on the blanket. I tell him about what I saw, about the beds with no mattresses, about the dead boy, about the ripped clothes and the starvation. I tell him about Gamma sitting on the pictures. As I speak, Jim listens politely, his face betraying little emotion. Any other photographer would be salivating by now. I show him the note, make sure he can read my manic scribbles. "Vul-tur-es-ti," I say. "That's *V-u-l-t-u-r-e-s-t-i*. It's hard to find." I tell him at this point I don't care whose pictures get published first or where; my only concern is that they do get published.

What I really want to tell him about but don't is those dreams, those horrible gas chamber dreams in which everyone dies except me because I hog the air hole. That the dreams are now sprouting new characters, birdlike kids with flapping wings, a boy with his face peeled off walking around, zombielike, with his dead, bloodless heart in his hands. That somehow I imagine that if I can save a couple of orphans by handing the story over to Jim—who, because of his clout, will most likely get his pictures published—the dreams might stop. Which I know is just selfishness and survivor guilt masquerading as philanthropy, but I don't care.

Instead, when Jim looks me in the eye and with a vaguely nonplussed tone asks me if I'm sure I want to hand the Vulturesti story over to him, I say only, "Yes. I'm sure."

"I understand," he says, sounding more like a clergyman than a journalist. He takes my hands in his and thanks me. Says he can probably get *The New York Times Magazine* interested in the story. Asks me how much he owes me for the film.

"Nothing," I say. "Just promise me you'll go."

"I promise," he says. He shows me out the door. "And thanks. Really."

"No problem."

I walk out of the hotel and find Doru sitting on some steps overlooking University Plaza, smoking one of his acrid-smelling Romanian cigarettes and waiting for miners. The plaza is wide, teeming with people and their banners, surrounded by buildings that fall into two distinct schools of architecture. The older buildings, oversized and overly ornate, look like they might have been designed by Haussmann if he'd been sneaking steroids from under his drafting table. Though they are now crumbling and decrepit, some with big chunks of pediment simply missing, they hint at a glorious if pompous past. Then there are the hideous modernist buildings like the Inter-Continental, a giant, stretched-out shoe box of an eyesore, obviously constructed under the whip of communism. It is anonymous, drab and ugly, nothing more than gray slabs of concrete slapped carelessly together.

Every visible surface in University Plaza—not only the facades of the buildings, but the sidewalks, the roads, even the street signs—is covered with soot. Even the protesters themselves seem to be covered with a layer of grime.

"How can you smoke those things?" I say, sitting down next to Doru. "Don't you have any Marlboros left?" I bought Doru another whole carton on our last trip to the airport.

Doru scoots his body away from me, leaving a gap between us. He mutters something in Romanian, and then, switching to French, says, "I have many Marlboros left." He stares straight ahead at the growing crowd. "I just wanted to smoke one of my own, if you don't mind." He pretends to adjust the ASA dial on the Nikkormat, my beloved old camera. Then, as if thinking better of it, he removes the camera from around his neck and shoves it into the Domke bag at his feet.

I tell him of course I don't mind, but he stubs the half-smoked cigarette out anyway. I'm not sure what to do, so I take out my own pack of Marlboros and offer him one. He waves it off. Then I remember the Toblerone bar in my camera bag, the one I bought with my American dollars in the hotel gift shop when I couldn't face another breakfast of stale bread and rancid butter. "Hey," I say, opening the foil and breaking off a triangle, "how about a piece of this?"

He finally turns to look at me, his eyes filled with animosity. "I don't need your charity," he says. Then he stands up to leave.

I go after him, finally grabbing his arm to keep him from escaping. "Please, Doru, don't do this," I plead.

He yanks his arm free. "Leave me alone," he says. "Just go away. I love you. But I don't want any more of your fucking charity." His voice is louder now, but because of the noise of the crowds, no one else seems to notice. He tells me to stop treating him as if he were one of the orphans. He's not unrecoverable. He doesn't need my help or anybody else's. He doesn't need to be fixed. He doesn't need to be saved. He doesn't need my presents. Okay, well, he needs the car I'm about to buy him, but he says that he's thought that one through, and that I'll end up saving money by not having to rent one during the elections when we get back. He says that while I was off with Jim, maybe even having sex for all he knows, he was out here in the street, earning a living, trying to make enough money to get himself out of this hellhole. That he doesn't really need chocolate anyway. In fact, if he never eats another bite of chocolate in his entire life, he'll be just fine.

I don't even know where to begin to respond. I can barely speak, and when I do I can only address the one statement I know, without any doubt, to be false. "I did not have sex with Jim," I say.

"Yeah," says Doru, "just like you didn't have sex with Nicolas. Give me a break, okay? I'm not stupid."

I finally snap. "Jesus, Doru, for the ninety-eighth time, I didn't sleep with Nicolas! Or Gad or Jim or anyone else since you and I have been together! Why are you doing this?" I'm yelling now, my body coiled, my fists in tight little balls. Then, unable to stop myself, I unfurl my right hand and slap Doru's face. The impact leaves a red welt on his cheek. He instinctively clutches at it and stares at me through stunned eyes. Furious and tripping over my own words, mixing English with French, I tell him the jealousy has got to stop. That I went to Jim's room to give him some film. That I don't want to ever hear Nicolas's name mentioned again. That I'm sick and tired of him not trusting me. That the presents I give him, I give him out of love, not charity.

Doru still stares at me, looking befuddled and holding his slapped cheek in his hand. He says nothing. I can feel the mucus running down my throat, my nose running, my eyes stinging with tears.

"Love?" he says. "Love?" He shakes his head, lets out a small, angry burst of laughter. "Please, Deborah, don't confuse pity for love." He rubs his eye and pretends that it's nothing more than a piece of dust that's caused it to water. Then he picks up his camera bag, walks down the steps and heads off into the crowd of demonstrators. It engulfs him and he disappears.

MARION AND I TAKE the elevator to the top floor of the Inter-Continental, laughing together as usual. Marion has arrived from Paris to spend her twenty-fifth birthday with me in Romania. I called her to cry about my newly miserable situation with Doru, but by the end of the conversation I was comforting her because she'd just found out that her boyfriend, Philippe, who would not commit to celebrating her birthday with her, had recently impregnated another woman. I said this was probably not a good sign, and then I jokingly suggested she come join me here. "Romania is a shit hole," I said, "but it can't be any worse than the place you're at." The next day (and this is why I love Marion), she bought a plane ticket to Bucharest.

She's squatting with me at Doru's apartment. Since Doru and I are not sleeping together anymore, or even talking much anymore, Marion and I have been relegated to the living room floor. After my fight with Doru, at the end of April, I went back to Paris for ten days to deal with his car and to buy more film to cover the elections. During that short stay in Paris, as strange as it may sound, I happened to meet and fall in love with the man I would eventually marry. The timing could not have been worse.

If Doru was merely jealous beforehand, he is furious now. In fact, he hates me. And rightfully so. I just don't know what to do about it. I tried to get *Libération* to pay for a hotel room upon my return, but I was told their budget wouldn't allow for it. They said they hired me to cover the elections because I had assured them (back when Doru and I were getting along, back before I accidentally met my future husband during the furlough in Paris) that I would be covering my own lodging expenses, which I found not only annoying but mildly insulting, as I'd been imagining they hired me for my proficiency as a photographer. Since I have no savings left after lending Doru the money for his car, and since *Libération* is counting on my coverage, Doru has very graciously suggested a cohabitation based on the late-eighties French political model: peaceful but icy, like Mitterrand sharing his government with Chirac.

Sure, I wanted to say, except Chirac never felt a strangely maternal love—the kind of love he never knew he was capable of feeling—for Mitterrand. Chirac never saw Mitterrand get misty over his first Marlboro. He never danced the Lambada with Mitterrand, six times, in a Transylvanian mountain hideaway. And he never once felt an electrical surge pulsating from his heart to his extremities after a single kiss from Mitterrand's lips.

After that short trip to Paris, the situation for both Doru and me became almost untenable. Which is why I called Marion crying in the first place. And why things are better now that she's here, to act as a buffer between us.

Marion and I are the first of our group to arrive for dinner in the formal dining room at the hotel, and we take our seats. The formal dining room serves the same lousy fried meat and soggy fried potato cubes as the less formal cafeteria on the ground floor, but it has what in Romania passes for atmosphere—gaudy, too-bright chandeliers, garish synthetic linens, waiters in polyester suits with bow ties, enormous open space and triple-height ceilings. While it is hardly an intimate setting, it does have big round tables that can accommodate up to twenty people, which is helpful because we've made a reservation for seventeen.

Because of new rumors about marauding miners, I probably should have come dressed to work—the pockets of my vest filled with film, my cameras loaded, my flash battery charged. But I'm so sick of all the lies and false intelligence, I can't be bothered. As the other photographers arrive one by one, however, I notice they're all wearing their Banana Republic vests, all carrying heavy bags of equipment. The rumor, as usual, has traveled fast.

Our group is mostly Paris-based photojournalists. As each photographer arrives, he completes the exact same ritualistic motions as his predecessor, as if everyone had read the same instruction manual. Step one: shove camera bag under table. Step two: extract Leica and place on top of table next to bread plate. Step three: fish package of cigarettes and Zippo lighter out of breast pocket, put lighter on top of pack, place between wineglass and ashtray. Step four: smile conspiratorially and say, *"Salut, les potes!"*—"Hello there, mates!"—but don't mention the word "miners" or let on that you've heard that they're armed and heading into Bucharest tonight. Step five: reach for wine bottle, pour and drink. Step six: deride the Romanian vintage as undrinkable, then, while continuing to drink it, allude to the cultural superiority of the French. Step seven: ask, "So, what have you all been up to?" then laugh at your funny joke, because no one in this group would actually be stupid enough to answer.

I've tried to save the seat next to me for Doru, but he arrives late and is forced to take his place a couple of chairs down from mine. After a few minutes, I lean over to sneak a glimpse of him. He's talking to another photographer seated next to him, his back toward me. When someone across the table from him starts insulting Romanians, calling them stupid and clueless, Doru sits there listening to him stoically, bristling but saying nothing. Because of his fluency in French and his almost perfect Swiss accent, Doru passes easily as a Westerner. So when the waiter comes over to take our orders, and Doru says no thanks, he doesn't want any dinner, most of the photographers just assume that the Swiss photographer in the funny-looking acid-washed jean jacket is simply not hungry. It would never occur to them that Doru can't even afford to order a Coke, let alone a small appetizer or soup, and that he would rather starve than lose face.

Doru was right. I did pity him. I do pity him. He grew up in a shitty country with an evil dictator, informants for neighbors, deadly levels of pollution, lousy employment prospects, urine-stained elevators and inedible chocolate. What he doesn't understand, and maybe never will, is that the pity was commingled with love. I loved him for his black humor and for his Lenin jokes. I loved him because he was not afraid to cry. I loved him because, instead of fleeing Vulturesti at dusk, when the fading light made shooting pictures next to impossible, he insisted we stay through dinner, at which point he rolled up his sleeves, grabbed a ladle and served the orphans their soup himself. I loved him because he knew he was damaged goods, he knew he'd been deprived, and he knew that there was absolutely nothing he could do about it except maybe to make sure a couple of neglected and abused orphans had some soup to eat on the one night he happened to pay a visit. I loved him because I knew that, underneath all that jealous paranoia and scar tissue, he loved me, too.

But had I been *in* love with him? Did we fall *in* love with each other? No. I had not. We did not. It was a hard truth to face.

Love, I realized, has many forms.

In Hebrew, the word for love is *ahavah,* which is related to the word for giving, *hav.* This is not a coincidence of etymology. (I was a Sunday school teacher for five years. I used to spend a lot of time thinking about this stuff.) In fact, it reflects an ancient and entrenched Judaic value system: to love means to give, to give means to love. But Judaism does not value all types of giving equally. In fact, Moses Maimonides, twelfth-century Jewish philosopher, codifier of the Talmud, went so far as to define eight different types of charity—*tzedakah,* in Hebrew—and to assign each type of *tzedakah* a descending level of value.

At the ethical pinnacle of Maimonides' scale is the teach-a-man-to-fish school of thought: help a person help himself. Second, third and fourth are unsolicited gifts ranked by levels of anonymity, the more anonymous the better. At the bottom are levels five through eight, ranked last because both donor and recipient are known to each other. These are further broken down by the degree of solicitation, the generosity of the gift and the willingness of the donor to actually give.

Seen in this light, my charity to Doru could either be interpreted as the highest form of charity or the lowest, depending upon the viewer. The way I saw it, I was giving him tools to help him succeed in his chosen profession—a camera, a camera bag, then later the car. But Doru saw things differently. In his version, also a valid version, he had to ask for help, and then he had to face me, his "donor," every morning. I was the capitalist master, throwing him, the "less equal," communist dog, a few scraps from my dinner table. Until finally, his pride could no longer take it.

"Nothing? Nothing at all? Not even a small salad?" the waiter asks Doru.

"That's right," says Doru. "I don't want anything."

Just then, Peter and David make their grand entrance, filling in the last two empty seats at the table. They walk slowly, deliberately, nodding graciously to the barnyard riffraff.

Peter and David have become the darlings of the photojournalism world. Identical twins with identical manes of shoulder-length curly blond hair and identical brown leather blazers, they pride themselves on doing the international war/demo/strife/revolution circuit with style and panache. Both twins work on contract, which means that unlike the rest of us agency shlubs, they never have to worry about footing half their bills or procuring day rates for their extensive travels. Hence, the expensive blazers. And nice apartments in Paris. And many, many camera lenses, of all shapes and focal lengths.

David takes his seat. Peter, still standing, addresses the assembled group. "Does anyone want to see the galleys of our latest book?" he asks, and before anyone can demur, he produces a copy he just happens to have brought along to dinner and starts to pass its pages around the table. Then he holds up his wineglass to make a toast. These photos, he explains, represent a year of hard work and commitment. He feels privileged and lucky to have been able, with his brother, to bear witness to the crumbling of the Iron Curtain during this historic moment of social upheaval. And he feels confident that the photographs enshrined in this, their latest book, will live forever as the document that will best tell the story of the last days of communism.

Marion looks at me, and with her back toward Peter, pretends to stick her finger down her throat. "At least he didn't take credit for knocking Lenin off his pedestal," she whispers. Doru leans over the table to catch my eye. He smiles, shaking his head in disbelief. I smile back, happy enough to be sharing a simple comic moment with him. I catch some of the other photographers trading snide glances with their colleagues—men who covered the same events, the same Prague spring, the same Solidarity, the same Berlin Wall, the same *perestroika* as the twins, with what I'm sure they considered the same if not greater skill.

And then, suddenly, from outside, a shot rings out. It's a single shot, and it vibrates off the brick wall of the hotel, the wall that faces University Plaza. The shot is immediately followed by a distinct scream. We all drop our cigarettes and our wineglasses, our forks and our mock-up pages of Peter and David's book. Shit, I think. The one night I didn't bring my cameras. Like synchronized swimmers, the others simultaneously reach under the table for their camera bags, grab their Leicas from on top and run toward the window. We hear a second shot, then a third, but we are too far up, too far from the crowd. Someone in our group, I don't know who, shouts, "Miners!" Then another one, in English with a French accent, yells, "Rock and roll!", which is the international journalist cry for "Let's go shoot pictures and dodge bullets!" In an instant, a dozen or so adrenaline-pumped journalists are running for the exit.

Marion, sprinting next to me, is giddy. "Rock and roll? This is much more fun than waiting for Philippe to call!" she says.

"In a manner of speaking, yes," I say.

Only Doru stays behind. "Come on, Doru!" I yell. "Let's go. I've got to go back to your place and grab my cameras."

"But who's going to pay the bill?" he says. He looks confused.

"Fuck the bill," someone yells from the top of the stairs, when the elevator takes too long arriving, "we'll pay it when we get back."

"But we can't just leave without paying the bill . . ."

When I look back, I see Doru standing there, all alone at our abandoned table, desperately fishing around his nearly empty pockets for money he knows he will never find.

"DÉJÀ VU, HUH?" I say to Gad, staring out his car window at the peaceful demonstrators. I found Gad parked as usual in the Inter-Continental parking lot, about an hour after our group from dinner fanned out into the quiet, minerless plaza. I never even had to go back to Doru's to fetch my cameras. "I wonder what those shots were?"

"Probably some joker," he says. "Probably some idiot who just wanted to watch a bunch of frantic journalists run around chasing their tails."

I roll down the car window and breathe in the night air. It's spring now, the beginning of May, not quite warm but mild enough to leave the window open. Gad looks at me. "Did you hear about Jim's orphan photos? Six double pages in *The New York Times Magazine*," he says.

"Yeah, I heard," I say. I also heard that, two days after Jim's pictures were published, some anonymous donor sent a whole truckload of new mattresses to Vulturesti. A mere three on Maimonides' scale, but pretty damned great as far as I'm concerned.

Jim's published pictures also had the effect of forcing Gamma to distribute my own photographs of Vulturesti. (Although not the black-and-white ones. Those I would have to develop, edit and print myself upon my arrival in Paris.) Henri even called me a few days ago to tell me that one of my orphan shots had just won the Déclic du Mois, a picture-of-the-month photo contest cosponsored by Kodak and *Photomagazine*. The prize? Free publicity and a quarter-page photo in *Photomagazine*, as well as eighty rolls—four bricks—of film. Exactly twice the amount of film I donated to Jim.

Karma? Divine intervention? Coincidence? You decide.

"Now, see," Gad says, getting excited now, "if I were a lawyer, I could actually do something for those kids. I could figure out how to get around the red tape of international adoption laws, get each one of those kids placed in a happy, stable home." He pauses, smiles, his head seemingly filled with the endless possibilities. "Do you understand now why I want to go to law school? Do you?"

Yes. Of course. Adoption trumps mattresses.

"I do. I understand," I say. I pat Gad on his knee. And I think to myself, Maimonides would have really liked my friend Gad.

Ovidiu peeks his head in the car. He has learned a lot of English in the past two months, what with all of the Western journalists who've descended upon Bucharest. "Hi, Deborah," he says in English, "you know Doru where is?"

"Yeah," I say. "He walked Marion back to the apartment." That is, he walked Marion back to the apartment after emptying his pockets of every last bill and coin he had to his name to try to make a dent in our seventeen-person dinner bill. When the rest of us came back to finish our meal, we saw it sitting there in a neat little pile. Seven American dollars, two dimes, forty Romanian lei, eight Romanian coins, a deutsche mark and a British pound.

"Okay. Thanks. Need find him. He owe me. Fifty dollars. Orphan pictures," he says. Then he walks away.

"What's that all about?" Gad asks.

"I'm not sure," I say, opening the car door and stepping outside.

DORU AND OVIDIU eventually stopped speaking to each other over that alleged fifty-dollar debt. Similar petty squabbles over money later alienated some of Ovidiu's other friends as well. When he visited me in Paris at the beginning of 1991, Ovidiu absconded with one of my wool sweaters, worth approximately fifty dollars, which I chalked up to retribution for the money he felt Doru owed him. As the years progressed, he fathered a son who, as a toddler, watched Ovidiu mysteriously keel over dead in the middle of his living room. Some friends, including Doru, suspected he had somehow killed himself, with pills or whatever. His corpse underwent the requisite autopsy required by Romanian law, but the coroner was never able to prove definitively whether Ovidiu did, in fact, commit suicide.

Doru, with help from his parents' diplomatic connections, moved to Geneva, Switzerland, the day after angry Romanian miners invaded University Plaza, wielding truncheons and baseball bats. There, he earned a scholarship to complete his graduate art degree. After finishing his studies, he then moved to Paris, where he was finally able to sit on the Champs-

Elysées drinking Beaujolais and watching the sun set behind the Arc de Triomphe. He married a French woman, ran out of money and found himself having to manage an American-style fast food restaurant in order to survive. After his divorce, he headed back to Eastern Europe, settling down in Prague as a staff photographer for a Czech business journal. When he found out about his boyhood friend Ovidiu's apparent suicide, he sat in his car and wept.

As for Gad, the summer before his matriculation at law school, he traveled inside northern Iraq behind enemy lines on an assignment to cover Kurdish refugees for *Newsweek*. There, he was captured, shot and killed by Iraqi soldiers while trying to protect his Kurdish guide from harm. At first, *Newsweek* claimed that since Gad was only shooting for the magazine on a freelance basis, they should not be held responsible for recovering the body. When people in the photo community cried foul, the magazine finally reversed its stance. But by then it was too late. The only thing Gad's mother was able to retrieve from the battlefields of northern Iraq was her son's bloody passport.

GAD WATCHES OVIDIU disappear into the darkness. "People are so strange, aren't they?" he says.

"They sure are." I slam the passenger door shut. "Anyway, no use waiting around here for miners anymore. I'm going back to Doru's to get some sleep." I lean my head in the window, tell him I'll be leaving for Paris the following morning. "Got a boy back there who says he loves me," I say, beaming. "Pretty cool, huh?"

Gad flashes me that cockeyed toothless grin. "Yeah, pretty cool."

"If I don't see you again before the fall, good luck with law school." I kiss the tips of my fingers and reach them through the open passenger window to touch his nose.

"Thanks," Gad says, grabbing hold of my hand, squeezing it tightly, then letting it go. "And you have a safe trip home." He yawns. "I think I'll get some sleep, too." And with that, he climbs in the backseat of his car, covers himself with a blanket and closes his eyes.

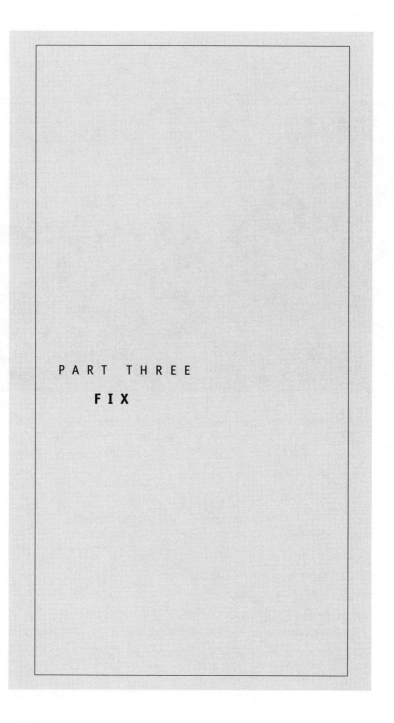

PART THREE

FIX

MOSCOW, USSR, 1991

"N O. *D O B R O Y E H   D Y E N* I S ' G O O D   D A Y.' *Zdrastvootyeh* means 'hello.' Three syllables, *zdra-stvoo-tyeh*. You see, it's right here." Paul points to the Cyrillic letters in my textbook. His voice is loud to compensate for the rhythmic clatter of wheels and tracks beneath us.

"*Zdra . . . stvoo . . . tyeh?*" I repeat slowly. While Paul nods, I return his smile with a scowl. "You've got to be joking." I snap the book shut. "That's not a hello. It's a compound sentence."

Paul laughs, his deep-set blue eyes flickering as they catch the sun strobing into our train compartment. Because the windowpane is filthy, the light is refracted, creating a nimbus of feathery follicles on top of his head. "Don't worry, before we get to Moscow, you'll be speaking fluent Russian. I promise," he says. He plants a kiss on my forehead. Outside, Polish farmhouses rush by. I stare out the window and feel a shiver run down my spine.

"It's sort of creepy, isn't it?" I say.

"What? Being a Jew on a train in Poland?" he asks. I nod. "Yes. It's creepy."

Paul can read my mind. At first I was convinced that there were tiny elves in my skull who were sending telepathic messages to his, but then, as Paul and I got to know each other, I realized his brain just makes the same erratic connections as mine. Whatever else we might choose to discuss, eventually it all comes back to either sex or the Holocaust.

"*Zdrastvootyeh, tovareeshch!*" Andy sticks his head in the doorway to the compartment, smoking a Camel. His bicep is massive, and it bulges as he brings the cigarette to his lips. Andy, like Paul, has blond hair and a Slavic face, but while Paul's fine features and delicate hands might have belonged to Count Vronsky, Andy resembles a younger, hairier, more dashing Nikita Khrushchev.

"*Tovareeshch?* What the hell does that mean?" I pull out my new Russian-English dictionary and thumb through it, but before I can figure out where the letter *t* comes in the Cyrillic alphabet, Paul is saying, " 'Comrade.' It means 'comrade.' "

It's June 1991. Paul has invited Andy to move with us to Moscow, where each of us hopes to save ourselves and maybe even each other. Andy is Paul's former college roommate as well as his best friend. Back when they met as freshmen at Princeton, the two had bonded over their shared disdain for Soviet-style communism—Paul because he was Russian and had spent his childhood in Moscow, Andy because his Ukranian father had been a prisoner in Stalin's labor camps. After college, the two drove cross-country together, where they floundered around San Francisco for a few months until Paul's departure for Paris, but Andy stayed and never really stopped floundering. He's spent the past year smoking pot, teaching an SAT prep course to pay the rent, and growing more and more despondent. When Paul called him to suggest the move to Moscow, he filled out the paperwork for his Soviet visa that very same afternoon. Andy hopes that by spending time in Moscow, he can finally make peace with some of the demons of his father's past, the ones that still haunt his own present.

Paul, meanwhile, is going to Moscow in hopes of beginning a new career as a journalist. He recently quit his Paris-based job as a partner in a French-Soviet trading firm when he realized he could no longer differentiate between the mobsters and the mid-level Soviet bureaucrats he had to deal with every day. He'd joined the firm in the early, heady days of Gorbachev's *perestroika* with the naïve yet idealistic notion that he could teach a country run by apparatchiks about the benefits of capitalism. That ended quickly, after about the fifth payoff.

In the Soviet Union of 1990, almost everyone, from the lowly to the powerful, could be bought. The price was never very steep—a few hundred dollars, a bottle of whiskey, a pack of Marlboros. All around him, Paul was watching Western businessmen surrender their souls to the intoxicating power of being hard-currency gods amongst ruble-carrying mortals. He started to realize that if he didn't get out of the business soon, the elixir would destroy him, too.

The turning point came when Paul and his two partners, Serge and Philippe, were arrested in Moscow by the KGB. It seemed that Serge, a megalomaniac Russian émigré who could play ten chess games simultaneously in his head, had neglected to return approximately $90,000 that had been mistakenly transferred from a Soviet client. Philippe, the bean counter of the group, a straight-laced École Polytechnique graduate with an amazing collection of silk ties, saw the mistake and instructed Serge to send the overpayment back. But Serge, being Serge, refused. So the angry Soviet client called the "friends" he'd purchased at the KGB, the KGB roughed up and arrested Paul and his partners, Serge surrendered a few crisp one-hundred-dollar bills, and with the circle of corruption now complete, the three men were finally released, with only a few small bruises to show for their physical travails.

Mentally—well, that was a whole different story. After the arrest, Paul had trouble sleeping. He would bolt awake sweating, shouting Russian words I didn't understand. So, at my insistent urging and because he knew he had to, he quit.

However, he refused to give up on the idea of Moscow altogether. It is his birthplace, he says, his heritage, and he feels like he still has a lot of reacquainting yet to do. He also says he wants to show me his old apartment building on the Ulitsa Krasnaya Armayskaya—Red Army Street—and maybe even look up his long-lost father.

A few days before quitting his job, he came up with our current plan. With the Bush-Gorbachev summit coming up in Moscow, Paul is sure that some news organization or another there will be able to pay him for his bilingual skills. Then, in his spare time, he'll produce a documentary. He says he wants to focus it on the effects of *glasnost* and *perestroika* on Soviet youth. It's an interesting topic, but for Paul it's also a highly personal one. He knows that were it not for the vagaries of fate, he'd be the one selling *matrioshka* dolls and Lenin pins on the Arbat.

"I just don't get it," Andy says, squeezing himself between the seat and our suitcases. Every inch of floor space in the train compartment is filled with Paul's and my worldly possessions—some clothes, a boom box, thirty CDs, a purple floral bedding set, a pot, a pan, a teakettle, a wooden spoon, a serrated knife, my guitar, my cameras, three hundred rolls of film, two cartons of Marlboros along with a pink and blue Tati bag filled with cheap cosmetics for bribes and a collapsible drying rack. When I suggested we lighten our load and simply buy another drying rack in Moscow, or better yet, dry our clothes at the nearest Laundromat, Paul actually laughed in my face.

"I mean, think about it," Andy continues. "How can the entire Eastern bloc fall apart while Gorby's left standing? It doesn't make sense. At some point, there's got to be a revolution. Don't you think?"

Paul says he doesn't think so. He thinks the reforms of *perestroika* will gradually lead to a capitalist economy. I'm not so sure. I'm certainly no expert on the Soviet economy, but I do know that if my country were a place without Laundromats or even drying racks, I just might be tempted to revolt.

Which frightens me.

See, I'm going to Moscow to escape things like revolutions. After Gad was shot, I made a promise that I would stay away from any stories involving guns and tanks. It was a solemn and spoken promise: I actually opened the windows of our apartment and stared up into the gray Parisian sky, directing the words to Gad. It sounds melodramatic in retrospect, but at the time it didn't feel that way.

Instead, I've decided to shoot a nice, calm, black-and-white photo-essay on Russian women. I stole the idea directly from a book on the subject by Francine du Plessix Gray, which I read after Paul and I moved in together. I'm not sure any magazine will actually be interested in such a photo-essay—in fact, I'm not even sure it will hold my interest for very long—but I don't really care. It's not dangerous. I'll get to use my beloved Tri-X and think in shadows again, and for now, that's enough. I can always freelance for *Newsweek* or *L'Express* on the side, and, besides, our living expenses in Moscow will be negligible.

Andy looks at me and laughs. "I'm not saying the revolution will happen now. But someday it will have to. Communism failed. We all know that. Gorbachev knows that. But if he thinks his fellow *tovareeshch* will be happy with a couple of lame *perestroika* reforms, he's even stupider than I thought. *Pechenyeh* anyone?" He holds out a box of Déli-Choc cookies he bought back in Paris.

Paul grabs one of the chocolate-covered wafers and starts to explain. "*Pechenyeh* is—"

" 'Cookie,' " I say, interrupting him. "That one I could get from context."

Paul puts his arm around my shoulder and beams. "How did I ever find you?" he says, full of friendly sarcasm. He takes a bite of his cookie.

I give him my usual response. "Does it even matter anymore?"

We both laugh. The rejoinder has become our private joke, a sardonic tribute to the gods of chance and fate. It started at a Grateful Dead show we saw in Paris last fall, a few months after we met. The band was crooning "Touch of Gray," and I was watching the skin on the back of our friend Josh's neck melt when I felt Paul squeeze my hand in his. I turned to face him. "How did I ever find you?" I said, not exactly meaning for the sappy words to escape.

Paul took my entire face in his hands and kissed my forehead. His pupils, black from dilation, stared into mine. His face looked angelic, even while dripping. He started to laugh. "Does it even matter anymore?"

I felt my cheeks slowly rising up into my eye sockets, surrendering themselves to the smile. "Of course not," I said, "it doesn't matter at all." The two of us doubled over with laughter after that, howling in that particularly psychedelic way over the absurdity of deconstructing serendipity. We were in love. This seemed certain. Or at least as certain as it could ever seem.

Everything else was just narrative detail.

THERE WAS NOTHING REMARKABLE about the message Paul left me on my answering machine that April 1990, while I was living with Doru in Bucharest. It was the typical "Hi-I'm-a-friend-of-a-friend-of-a-friend" thing I always got from post-collegiate Americans passing through Europe: "Uh, yeah, hi. Romania, huh? Funny message. Your poor parents. Anyway, this is Paul. I'm George's twin brother, you know, Brett's Penn roommate George's twin brother. I think George told me he met you a couple of times. Brett gave me your number. I'm in Paris, just got here, wanted to see if you'd like to have lunch one of these days. Give me a call when you get back."

Yeah, right, I thought, as I scribbled down the message. Not only was the link tenuous—the twin brother of my childhood friend Brett's roommate—I had less than two weeks in Paris before I had to head back to Romania. During that time I was supposed to find Matthew some job leads, I had a long-standing date planned with Luc, a smart, nimble-handed, Rimbaud-loving war photographer I'd originally begun to see for hygiene but who'd gotten under my skin and was now wanting something deeper, I needed to edit my film and print up some of the black-and-white orphan pictures, *L'Express* wanted me to go to Lille to shoot welfare recipients, *Libération* wanted me to come in and meet with the journalist I'd be working with back in Bucharest, *Actuel* needed me to shoot a quick story on French rap artists, my dirty laundry was, as far as I could tell, sprouting mushrooms in the back of my closet, and Doru was expecting me to show up in Geneva with a thousand dollars for his car, which he then needed me to drive with him back to Paris so he could show his work to a slew of French photo editors in the back-to-back meetings he'd asked me to prearrange. In fact, had it not been for Marion, I would have just ignored Paul's message altogether.

Marion couldn't stop crying. She'd just heard about her boyfriend's indiscretion, the one that would soon turn him into a father.

I figured if I introduced her to Paul, it might take her mind off of things. Because I'd briefly met his identical twin brother, George, I knew three basic facts about Paul before going in: 1) he was a Russian immigrant, 2) he moved to the U.S. as a child and 3) he was attractive. Back in college, during a weekend visit to Penn to see my old friend Brett, I had taken a snapshot of George sitting barefoot on a windowsill, reading a book with a corona of light around him. Christopher, my professor, spotted the image on my contact sheet and suggested I print it up for class. "There's something ethereal about this photo," he said. "Let's blow it up and take a look." Later, while I was printing it in the darkroom, two of the women who'd been working alongside me stopped what they were doing to stare at the photo of George floating in the fixer tray. "Who *is* that?" they asked, in full-throttled italics.

"Friend of a friend," I said.

"Exquisite," said one.

"I'd do him," said the other.

I was secretly hoping Marion would have the same response. That she'd find him exquisite and want to do him and then she'd forget all about stupid Philippe. And that's why, despite my insane schedule, I called Paul back and planned a brunch in the Marais for the three of us.

On a cool spring Sunday afternoon, Paul met me in the lobby of my building. He looked exactly like his twin, with a few exceptions. Instead of standing tall and erect, like George, Paul had a casual, unself-conscious stature, as if he had not quite figured out how to display his plumage. His smile, too, was much more open, unguarded, even slightly goofy. And unlike his brother, whom I remembered as an impeccable dresser, Paul was wearing rumpled clothing at least one size too big for him. But the face was clearly the same—boyish, fair and Russian, with high cheekbones and a strong, angular chin. "Hi," he said, shaking my hand. "I'm Paul."

"I know," I said. "You look just like your twin brother."

He laughed. "Really? What a coincidence."

"Sorry. My sisters are identical twins. I should know better."

"That's good." Paul smiled, holding the door of my building open and motioning me outside. "Then you're not going to ask me, 'So, if I hit you, does your brother feel it?' "

"No. I promise I will never ask you that. And I won't ask you about your secret language or playing tricks on teachers or swapping dates." Though the air still had a slight nip to it, the *terrasses* of the many cafés lining the streets of Les Halles were filled to capacity and beyond with beautiful people wearing denim and leather, blowing smoke into the clear blue sky. At the Châtelet fountain, a lone street performer was belting out a mournful "April in Paris."

"Thank God," said Paul, "that makes things much easier." He seemed to be only half joking.

We picked up Marion and walked through the narrow streets of the Marais until we reached Le Loir Dans la Théière, a neighborhood restaurant with large, comfy armchairs, old wooden tables and lots of magazines piled up here and there. As the three of us gobbled down our omelets together, Paul regaled Marion and me with funny stories about trying to do business between Russia and France—flying from Moscow to Kiev carrying trash bags filled with rubles, the thugs his partner had to hire to drive them around and "protect" them, the Muscovite prostitutes who threw themselves at Western businessmen for a chance to change their miserable lives.

As he spoke, his dirty-blond forelock flopped over his left eye, and he rocked back and forth whenever he became particularly excited about something. If for some reason he became *really* excited, his Doc Martens would start to bounce along, too, as if his body couldn't contain all the crazy plots and thoughts ricocheting inside him. At one point, he became so animated he choked on his espresso, which came spewing out of his mouth and dribbled down the threadbare button-down shirt he wore under his equally frayed tweed jacket. This made him laugh. Clearly, Paul liked to laugh, especially at himself.

"So, what'd you think?" I asked Marion afterwards, as we walked down the rue des Rosiers. Two Hasidic men with their black hats and side curls were laughing in front of the kosher pizza shop.

"He was nice." She eyed me suspiciously. "Why?"

"Oh, no reason. Just wondered what you thought. I mean, did you like him?"

Marion laughed and said if this was my thinly veiled attempt to cure her of Philippe, I could forget it. That I should warn her next time I wanted to set her up with someone. That Paul seemed like a perfectly respectable and decent guy, if a bit short.

"Short?" I said. We were approaching the Centre Pompidou, its mass of blue tubes sticking out amidst the staid Parisian cityscape. The French love to deride the Pompidou, but I think it's one of the greatest buildings I've ever seen. "He wasn't so short. He was adorable. And so funny. Didn't you think he was funny?"

"Yes, yes, he was funny." She looked at me. "You like him."

"No, I don't."

"Yes, you do. I know you. I can tell." She was laughing now.

"No, I don't." A bare-chested man in the sunken plaza in front of the museum was blowing gasoline-fumed flames into the air, each burst whooshing like a blowtorch. "Besides, that's the last thing I need right now."

Okay, so maybe Paul *had* charmed me, I thought to myself, but I meant what I said. The last thing I needed was yet another man to complicate my already far too complicated, compartmentalized, episodic, nomadic, tank gun blood war crazy fucking life.

There was Doru to consider, first of all. We'd been fighting, sure, but some part of me still thought we could make it work, that the chasm separating us could be crossed. There was Luc, who delighted in reading to me from *Une Saison en Enfer* and who had recently suggested we go off and shoot the world together, all the wars, all the strife, all the death. There was Matthew, who'd be arriving in less than a month to live with me. During my last telephone conversation with him, he'd sounded ecstatic about coming.

Each man said he loved me. In fact, I'd never had so much love directed my way, at a time in my life when the barbed wire was loosening, when it was finally starting to dawn on me that what I really needed— more than adventure or a few good rolls in the hay or some well-composed photographs to one day hang on my wall—was love. Real love, the kind of love that spurs sonnets and melts two separate, selfish beings into a single euphoric pot of goo.

It is so simple, the woman on the bus in Zimbabwe had said. *So simple.*

Well, yes. And no. Being loved is one thing. Finding true love is quite another: $n^2 - n + 2 = x$. The variables—the n's—were endless. Like sharing the same language (*Doru and I will never be able to find a common tongue.*). Or having the same goals (*I'm not sure I really want to spend the rest of my life chasing wars with Luc. Or with anyone.*). Or being able to trust (*What if Matthew finds another long-legged blonde from Nantucket to kiss?*).

After dropping Marion off at her apartment, I decided to spend the rest of that Sunday afternoon wandering alone through the streets of Paris, my Leica around my neck. I walked north, meandering through the crooked streets and narrow sidewalks of the Sentier. I passed through Pigalle, the famed red-light district, pausing to shoot a picture here and there. Click. Men entering a strip club. Click. Men exiting the strip club. Boring, boring, boring. Waste of film, even. I climbed up, feeling the muscles in my thighs tighten with each ascending stride along the steep passage from Pigalle to Montmartre. The route was unfamiliar, but I kept the white domes of the Sacré Coeur church in my sights as a beacon, to guide me up and away. I'd visited Pigalle many times while living in Paris, and I'd always loved the visual irony of the Sacré Coeur hovering in the sky above the strip clubs. It was like one-stop Catholic shopping: sin, climb, beg for forgiveness.

Just before the summit, I spotted an old woman, wrinkled beyond recognition, feeding a baguette to some pigeons. *"Vencz ici! Vencz ici, mes petits amis!"*—"Come here, my little friends!"—she said. As she spoke her cheerful words, the pigeon brigade grew, climbing onto her shoulders, sitting on her lap. One of the pigeons grasped the lady's right forefinger with his claws. This bird she pulled close to her chest, nuzzling her nose in the feathers on his wings.

I approached the woman, my camera to my eye. *"Ça vous dérange?"*—"Is it okay?"—I asked, pointing to the camera.

"Pas de quoi!"—"No problem!"—she responded. "Take as many pictures as you like. They are my life, these pigeons. My only children. I bring them a baguette every day, and every day they come to visit me. I love them. They love me. It's a good arrangement."

I was shooting like a maniac now, circling the woman carefully so as not to disturb the warbling pigeons. Click. A bird flies out of frame. Click. The woman throws some crumbs. Click. Click. Click. I'm thinking to myself, with pained resignation, That's going to be me. If I'm not careful, that crazy old lady talking to the birds is going to be me. Alone. Relatively happy, but incomplete. A baguette-wielding, postmenopausal surrogate mother to a bunch of French pigeons.

I climbed up the stairs leading to the Sacré Coeur just as dusk was approaching and sat down on a step amidst the other tourists chatting, smoking, kissing, playing guitar, staring out over the city and sighing at its beauty. Paris lay below us, a muted gray sea of tiny white buildings and diagonal boulevards, the Tour Montparnasse popping its awkward head out in the distance. A few dense clouds were blocking the sunset, turning the sky into a vast domed ceiling of slate. Before long, everyone knew, the sky would darken, the lights of the City of Lights would begin to twinkle, the day would end. A deferential hush fell over the crowd.

Suddenly, at the last possible minute, a few rays of sunshine managed to sneak between the lowest hanging clouds and the buildings. These were followed by the sun itself, shooting out its amber beam like a giant klieg light on the horizon. Gray Paris was no longer gray. It was flaming, warm and orange, filled with shadows and texture, pulsating with light. All around me, the tourists seemed to gasp in unison, holding their breath. A couple of them grabbed for their cameras.

I knew better. Beauty—hope!—like that cannot be recorded. It must be savored the moment it happens. I inhaled the rays, sucked them right into my memory, and kept the camera in my lap.

PAUL CALLED AFTER our Sunday brunch to invite Marion and me out to dinner the following Friday night. The three of us met up at the Père Tranquille as planned, but in the middle of the meal, Marion turned green and had to excuse herself to go throw up in the bathroom, after which she apologized and went home. Ever since she'd heard the news about Philippe's indiscretion, Marion was unable to keep anything down.

After dinner, Paul suggested a movie, and after the movie, he suggested a walk, and because I was enjoying both his company and our post-movie conversation, I said sure. The movie, *The Music Box,* was about a daughter coming to terms with her father's Nazi past, which led us to a discussion about the Holocaust.

"Did you know," he said, "that when the Nazis would come into the gas chamber to dispose of the bodies, all of the Jews would be piled on top of each other, rammed up against the door?"

"Yes. I mean no," I said, suddenly confused. "I mean, I don't know if I heard that once or read about it or if it's just something I dream about." Too late, I thought, as the words slipped out. Now he's going to think I'm a freak.

Paul smiled. "You dream about being gassed?"

Nailed. I nodded.

His smile widened. "Me, too. I mean, sometimes. Other times I'm in an empty village, and the Nazis are hunting me down."

"Really?"

"Yeah, really."

I hesitated and then asked him, "Do you dream about this stuff . . . a lot?"

"Yeah, a lot," he said.

"Wow." I smiled. "Me, too." We walked on.

And that's how we found ourselves well after midnight sitting on the stone steps leading down to the Seine from the Pont Neuf, the oldest bridge in Paris, talking about our lives.

Paul described his childhood in Moscow, the way he used to fall asleep listening to the sounds of his mother's fingers tapping away at the type-writer, churning out samizdat copies of books written by banned, imprisoned or exiled Russian authors. Her name was Rachel, he said. Everyone called her Raya. Raya was forty-two years old when she found out she was pregnant with Paul and his brother. She had never been able to get pregnant during the years she spent with her husband—Moshe? Yasha? Paul could never remember his name—so she'd just assumed she was infertile. Then, when Moshe/Yasha/what's-his-name died, she met Pavel.

Pavel was handsome and young and seventeen years her junior. He was on a home leave from the army. The two had an affair. Raya discovered she was pregnant. She told Pavel. Pavel's mother, a writer and renowned anti-Semite, forbade her twenty-five-year-old son from having anything more to do with the middle-aged Raya or with his future Jewish sons. Pavel fled back to the army. On April 2, 1966, Raya gave birth to her twins. She named them Pavel and Yegor.

"Hey, that's . . ." I counted in my head, subtracting eleven from thirty-one and adding two, "that's three weeks after I was born. Our moms were pregnant at the same time . . ." The fact seemed significant to me. "Except my mom was probably cruising the supermarket aisles shopping for Ho Ho's to feed her cravings—"

"And mine was standing outside in the snow, waiting in a long line to buy a couple of potatoes and a jar of *smyetana*." Paul laughed. I laughed too. He'd finished my joke. No, not only had he finished my joke, he made it better, adding in that funny word *smyetana*. I would have just stopped at the potatoes.

And he dreamed about Nazis. Often.

Stop it, I thought. Be strong. You don't need this right now. You definitely do not need this right now. Your life is already too complicated. But I couldn't stop looking at his face. It seemed almost synthetic, like wax, idealized and sculpted too perfectly to be real. That's it! I decided. He's a golem. Or perhaps a robot sent down to earth to test me. Later that night, he'd pull off his face, show me the wires underneath and we'd both have a good laugh. There was no way someone that beautiful could also be intelligent, witty and obsessed by Hitler. "What's *smyetana*?"

"It's like sour cream, I guess. A Russian sour cream. Anyway . . ."

Paul continued his tale. After he was born, Raya supported her new family by working as a book editor. She found it increasingly difficult to raise two boys, all by herself, in the Russia that was stagnating under Brezhnev, and she dreamed of a better life for her sons. Because she was a Jew—not a practicing Jew, but a Jew nevertheless—she could apply for political asylum based on religious persecution. She filled out the forms and, like all Jews who sought asylum at the time, she became a *refusnik* and was promptly fired from her job. To make ends meet, Paul and George started acting in Russian films, landing a shared starring role in a film called *Telegramma* when they were seven years old. A little over a year later, when Raya was granted permission to emigrate, the boys' names were expunged from the film's credits.

"Hey, I was in a film once. Four whole lines!" I bragged. "Of course, it was made in America, and my name's still in the credits, so it's different," I said, then, suddenly feeling stupid, added, "Sorry for interrupting. Go on."

"No, I'm sorry," Paul said. "It's a long story." Finally, he explained, at the age of nine, Pavel and Yegor became Paul and George and moved to New York City with their mother. "But my mom never got used to our American names. She kept calling us Pasha and Yegorushka."

"Diminutives," I said. "I like Pasha."

"How do you know about diminutives?" he asked.

"I don't know. *The Cherry Orchard?*"

Paul beamed. "You read Chekov," he said.

Jewish charities rallied to Raya's aid, helping her find a studio apartment in Washington Heights, supporting her, finding her odd jobs here and there, donating winter coats and boots to keep her twin sons warm. When things became tight, Raya went on welfare.

Because his mother never learned to speak much English, the burden fell on Paul's shoulders—he was ten minutes older than George, "the responsible one," he laughed—to pay the family's bills, when it was possible, to call the repairmen and to read and translate the notes that came home with him from school. Raya's letters to friends back in Moscow at the time, a few of which Paul was able to read much later, express the sadness and frustrations of starting a new life as an immigrant in America, made especially difficult by her age (fifty-one), by the language barriers, by poverty and by her status as a single mother. Nevertheless, she kept up a good front for her young sons, imparting to them the excitement of living in a country that cherishes freedom above all else.

She carted Pasha and Yegorushka around to every museum, cultural event and public park in New York and made them read all the books she had not been able to get her hands on in Moscow, not only the Russians, like Tolstoy and Dostoevsky, but O. Henry, Jack London, Thomas Mann, Shakespeare. "I've never read so much in my life as I did during those years after we arrived in America," Paul said. As he spoke, he looked down at the dark waters of the river below, as if watching the petals of his memory float by.

"Where's your mom living now?" I asked.

"Oh, she's not alive anymore. She died a while back." Paul lifted his head. He looked straight into my eyes, awaiting my reaction, the inevitable response.

"Oh, God, I'm so sorry, I didn't mean to—"

He cut me off. "It's okay. She died a long time ago, now. I was fifteen."

"Fifteen? What did you and George do? Where did you live? How did you . . ." I was trying to imagine myself in the same situation. A fifteen-year-old orphan, in a strange country with no family. At fifteen, my only real concerns were getting my period and my learner's permit, in that order.

He continued his tale. Told me about the night he and his brother were picked up from summer camp, driven back to New York and told the news of their mother's death. About the fight for custody of the boys that ensued between family acquaintances, one Russian, the other Jewish. About how the fight ended when a sleeping pill was slipped into one of the Russian's many shots of vodka that evening. About the Belgian Orthodox Jews—an older couple, one a Holocaust survivor, with three grown kids of their own—who eventually took him and his brother in until they were old enough to go off to college. About the frequent feelings he had of being displaced, abandoned, rootless.

I want him, I thought. It's not logical or sane, but I want him. I want to rescue him, to kiss him, to cradle him, to hold him. I want to take him home with me and feed him and write him twelve perfect lines in iambic pentameter. I want to show him that sunbeams can break through big old skies of slate. Okay, so Doru was expecting me to pick him up in Geneva in three days, and Luc and I had another date planned for the following night, and Matthew would be arriving from the States in a few weeks. It all suddenly seemed so trivial, small details I could iron out later.

As Paul continued to speak, a *bateau mouche*—one of the many tourist boats that float along the Seine—approached, its blinding lights hitting the stone embankment of the river and the surrounding buildings, turning night momentarily into day. Its passage seemed perfectly timed, as if the captain had somehow known that at that exact fraction of a second, even though I had no camera, I needed to see Paul better, to have a sufficient amount of light flashed onto his face that I might record the image for posterity. Click. There it was, to be filed away in that drawer in my brain. My very own picture of love's first submersion.

Why that precise moment? I don't know. Was it the man or his story? I have no idea. I can't divide my feelings into neat little piles like that. It was both. It was neither. It was Paris. It could have been anywhere. It was, like everything else, random, a fissure of timing and chance, a splash of alchemy I honestly cannot explain, except by conjecture.

Perhaps it was the way he could laugh at the various tragedies of his life in the same way I tried to laugh about mine. Or the openness of his face, how it invited me inside—the way he kept looking at me, blushing, smiling, beaming. One week earlier, I'd seen a disemboweled orphan whose heart lay limp on a wooden plank. Did I think to myself, Here's an orphan I can save? Yeah, sure, maybe. Did the fact that he was Jewish come into play? Well, of course. It was April 20. Hitler's birthday. As good a day as any for two Holocaust-obsessed Jews, who instinctively understood that they could never be complacent, who were angry about all the Jews who were ever tortured, starved and murdered, to fall in love.

Paul held out his hand to help me stand up, and though it was fairly dark, I could see his cheeks flush as our fingers met for the first time. "I'm hungry again. Let's see," he looked at his watch, "it's two in the morning. You up for another dinner?"

"Sure," I said, suddenly famished.

"Well, okay then. Let's go."

As we made our way across the Pont Neuf, holding hands first tentatively, then as tight as our intertwined fingers would allow, for the first time in my short life I could actually begin to imagine what a happy ending might look like.

After our second dinner, we stepped outside the restaurant, stopped and turned to face each other in the middle of the tiny rue St. André-des-Arts. There, amidst the traffic and the late-night revelers, our lips finally met. It was a ravenous kiss, a desperate, gasoline-soaked, fiery kiss, a kiss I would remember for the rest of my life. The kind of kiss whose energy, if harnessed, could have probably sent tiny pieces of shrapnel flying all the way down the street to the Place St. Michel. Then, once again clutching each other's hand, both keenly aware of dawn's proximity, we hurried back across the Seine to my apartment, anxious to start filling the voids.

The sun woke me a few hours later. I peeled Paul's arm off my shoulder and scooted just far enough back so that I could stare at the play of early spring light on his sleeping face. I watched his eyes darting around beneath his closed eyelids, his undulating lashes casting centipede shadows onto his cheeks. I watched the folds in the sheets move up and down as his chest expanded and contracted, felt the rhythmic puffs of air from his nose. I watched his mouth form a half smile and then relax into a boyish pout.

It was as if some sort of internal aperture were closing down inside me, forcing everything that was once blurry and nebulous and incomprehensible into sharp f/16 focus. Then, quietly, I wept for joy. There he was, lying next to me. Perfectly illuminated. My own tiny ray of sun.

Darkness might have fallen during the rest of that weekend, the days might have had their normal ebb and flow, but we were never aware of it. During lunch that Saturday afternoon, Paul and I decided to figure out which of our own features we'd like to pass on to our future progeny, as if that were the most natural topic two people who'd barely known each other for a day would choose to discuss.

"Your nose," I said.

"Your eyes." He laughed.

"Your lips."

"Oh, yeah?" He paused, pursing his lips in an exaggerated manner, studying me. Then he smiled. "Your heart."

Later that evening, as we were holding hands and walking to a movie theater near my apartment, Paul suggested we try an experiment.

"Okay, so we have not left each other's side for approximately twenty-four hours now, right?" he said.

Our date with Marion the night before felt like a lifetime ago. "Twenty-three, I think," I said.

"Fine. Twenty-three. Here's my idea. The movie theater is just over there." We were standing in front of an enormous pair of red, water-squirting lips, one of the whimsical, rotating sculptures built into the colorful Nikki de Saint Phalle fountain, just south of the Pompidou. He pointed north across the Pompidou's sloped cobblestone plaza to the movie theater, a few hundred yards or so in the distance. "Let's separate," he said. He suggested we each walk around opposite sides of the museum and meet up again in front of the movie theater.

I looked at Paul and laughed. "You're joking, right?"

"No. I'm not joking," he said, trying to keep a straight face. Then he giggled.

"Yes, you are!"

"Okay, okay." He squeezed my hand. "It's sort of a joke, but play along with me. I want us to see what it feels like to be alone again, without each other."

Since we'd just realized over lunch that in less than a week our work schedules were about to separate us for nearly two months anyway, I didn't really see the point of Paul's little exercise. But he seemed eager to try it. "All right," I said, "let's do it."

Heat evaporated from my palm as our hands disconnected. I watched Paul walk away, watched him turn to watch me walk away. Suddenly, his figure disappeared into the crowd and behind the blue tubes of the Pompidou. Even though I knew it was artificial, I could feel my body react viscerally to the absence. I was sweating, breathing faster. My chest even grew tighter. I could sense my feet carrying me across the cobblestones, but they had turned to lead. The empty space between me and the movie theater seemed to grow, expand exponentially, as if the few hundred yards had suddenly transmogrified into a lifetime. I began to panic. I will never make it without him, I thought.

The loneliness will kill me.

And then, suddenly, from behind the Pompidou, I could see Paul again. He was running, sprinting, actually, his eyes fixed on mine. As soon as I spotted him, my feet also took off. The people standing in line at the movie theater must have thought we were either actors in some sort of bizarre Gaumont Cinémas publicity stunt or simply what we were, two love-starved lunatics, rushing toward each other with outstretched arms and silly grins plastered from ear to ear. The only thing missing was the *Chariots of Fire* theme song.

But we didn't care what anyone thought. And, besides, it was pure con-

jecture to assume that the movie these people were about to pay to see—
something French and *lourd,* as I recall, with Sophie Marceau or one of
her brown-haired, pouty lookalikes—would be any less insipid.

"Deb," he said, lifting me up and twirling me around, "let's not play
that game ever again." He littered my face with kisses.

I held his cheeks in my hands and smiled, relieved to be touching his
skin again. "I think that's a very good idea," I said.

One of the moviegoers standing in line clapped. We took a small bow.

And that was that. It was time to clean house.

I was not looking forward to the task. That Sunday, with Paul sitting in
my apartment and urging me on, I called Matthew to tell him to cancel his
trip to France. I didn't give him details as to why, but I promised I would
explain everything in person when I returned back to the States for my sister's graduation from Harvard in a month's time. When late one night,
face-to-face, I was finally able to tell him what had happened—that I'd met
Paul, fallen in love with him, actually—Matthew clutched his stomach,
walked away from me, disappeared into the darkness, and threw up into
the Charles River. I felt guilty. I knew that Matthew, who was feeling aim-
less, was perhaps equally if not more upset about not having any plans
than he was about losing me. Nevertheless, I had selfishly toyed with his
emotions, created false hope. The vengeance I had secretly prayed for long
ago now felt empty, even cruel.

As for Doru, on the Monday following that first weekend with Paul, I
took the train to Geneva, paid for his new car, and drove it back to Paris
with him the following day. We argued during most of the trip. Doru said
it was impossible to fall in love with someone during a single weekend. I
said it wasn't. On the night he arrived, I handed him a set of keys to my
apartment, packed my bags and moved into Paul's place in the Sixteenth
Arrondisement.

Three days later, after an emotional good-bye with Paul, I returned
with Doru to Romania to cover the elections. The four-day cross-country
drive to Bucharest through Central Europe was most unpleasant, if picturesque. In Germany, we argued constantly, about nothing and about
everything. In Austria, which really does look like the set for *The Sound of
Music,* we kept getting lost. In Hungary, during a rare moment of peace, I
tried patting my hand on top of Doru's knee while he was driving. It was
nothing more than a gesture of friendship, but he recoiled, pushed it away

and told me never to touch him again. "Save it for your new boyfriend," he said.

Then, a week or so later in Bucharest, just before Marion's arrival to celebrate her birthday, I ran into Luc, who was also on assignment. He reacted to my sudden new devotion to Paul like a true Frenchman, that is to say sadly but stoically, with a lengthy philosophical monologue concerning the meaninglessness of love in a life whose inevitable end is always death, followed by an invitation to spend the night in his room. I told him I'd come up for a drink, nothing more, and when I did he dropped this small bombshell: "One of my old lovers called me. She might be HIV-positive."

"What?!?" I felt like I was choking. Luc and I had been intimate together fewer than a half a dozen times, but a couple of those times we hadn't used a condom.

I *tried* to be fairly conscientious about using condoms. The summer I'd worked at Magnum in 1987, feeling doses of both liberal guilt and morbid curiosity, I'd volunteered a couple of evenings a week—whenever I could get away, really—at Bailey House, an AIDS hospice in Greenwich Village. There I saw, firsthand and in Technicolor, the havoc wreaked by that still-new, still-mysterious disease: the Kaposi's sarcoma, the blindness, the nausea, the slow and steady wasting away. I held hands that felt like chicken's feet. I brushed hair that was falling out. I saw the ambulances and the hearses arriving in equal numbers, helped load gurneys into one, watched a coffin go into the other. I helped to clean out the rooms, disinfected them until their odors of decay were barely perceptible to the endless streams of new arrivals. Only afterwards, as I would wind my way through the cobblestone streets of the Village on my way to the Christopher Street subway station, would I break down and cry.

But did it stop me from playing Russian roulette with my own sex life? Of course not. Sometimes, making arbitrary judgment calls in the dark, I'd allow myself get swept away by a latex-free moment, which I know is inexcusable and stupid, but there you have it. AIDS was something other people got. Invisible Kryptonite.

Or so I told myself. But sitting there in Luc's hotel room in Bucharest, listening to him speak, realizing that I could be touched by the same, well, *plague!* as those poor wretches in Bailey House, I became inconsolable. "What do you mean *might?*" I said.

My mind raced immediately back to Paul: sitting on the banks of the

Seine with him, running around the Pompidou, waking up early every morning for six days straight just to stare at his sleeping face. Luc held my hand, smoothed his fingers gently through my hair. "I mean she had a test six months ago which came out negative, but she just found out *her* ex-lover is positive. She's going tomorrow for a new test."

"This can't be happening," I said. "Not now." Not when I'd finally found love. Not when I'd finally understood how beautiful my life could be, any life could be. Oh God, *no!* I thought. "Goddamnit!" I screamed. I punched my fists into Luc's chest, yelling obscenities, furious and manic. Then I cried myself to sleep in his arms.

A few days later, we found out that the woman's test had come out negative. So did the tests I took over the next two years just to make sure. But the whole mess was yet another wake-up call: even with proper precaution, love could be just as risky, just as deadly as war.

When I returned to Paris, Paul had already left on a five-week trip to Moscow, but he'd borrowed my keys from Marion, sneaked into my apartment and left a gigantic, treelike yucca plant standing in the corner with a note attached to it. *Take care of me,* the note said. *I need lots of water, sunlight and, most of all, love. Yours forever, Pasha.* He'd adorned the note with a cartoon sun, some water droplets and a heart.

I detached the note, sat on my bed, and broke down again, my tears staining the felt-tipped words.

Later that summer, when Paul and I moved into our new apartment on the rue St. Joseph, the first thing we carried over the threshold was that plant. We held the clay pot between us, taking tiny sideways steps, careful not to let the top-heavy trunk topple over. "Here's a good place to put it," he said, motioning with his head and leading me to the window.

"Yeah, that looks perfect."

We set the plant down by the open window and stepped back to admire it. Paul spoke first, giving voice to the words already percolating in my head. "It's growing quite nicely," he said. The leaves were rustling in the wind, dappled in a pool of midsummer light.

"Yeah," I replied, squeezing his hand. "It really is."

"I CAN'T DRINK IT. It's disgusting," I say, spitting out the sugary Russian juice with the distinct taste and texture of sediment into the kitchen sink. Paul and I waited in line for over an hour today at a drab Soviet *produkty* store to buy it. While we were waiting, I asked Paul if *produkty* was the Russian word for "juice." He laughed.

"No, it means 'produce,' " he said, "but it was an honest mistake." Besides the juice and some flaccid-looking pickles, the shelves in the store were empty.

The line to buy juice stretched toward Pushkin Square, where a much longer line was snaking around Moscow's newly constructed, first and only McDonald's. We carried eight enormous bottles of juice back to our apartment past happy Russian comrades sitting down to trays literally overflowing with Big Macs and french fries, all of us, in our own way, proud, bison-toting hunters.

"What do you mean you can't drink it? It's *sok*. I grew up on the stuff," Paul yells from the bedroom, where he's getting dressed for our dinner party. We've invited only our Russian friends over tonight because the last time we tried to mix in a bunch of expatriate Americans, the two groups didn't get along. The Americans, being typically American, were unintentionally patronizing. In return, the Russians, being typically Russian, were intentionally rude.

"Yeah, well, I grew up on Spaghettios," I yell back to Paul, rinsing my mouth out with tap water, "but that doesn't mean I'd want to eat them for dinner tonight." I spit the tap water into the sink. I refuse to swallow it because a few people now have told us it's contaminated with fallout from Chernobyl. It might be just a rumor, like most information around here, but why risk it? Tomatoes the size of small volleyballs have started to appear in the outdoor markets, and I've seen more than a dozen shoppers testing produce, when they can find it, with their very own Geiger counters.

Paul bounds into the kitchen, barefoot and shirtless in his jeans—a sight that, after more than a year together, still makes me dizzy—and grabs a swig of *sok* from my glass. Licking a few drops of juice from his top lip, he pronounces it delicious.

"It's delicious if you like pond scum," I say.

"I love pond scum," he deadpans, kissing me on the cheek.

Paul returns to the bedroom to finish dressing while I sneak a peek outside through the curtains in the living room. The curtains are drawn, as per our landlord Misha's request, so as not to arouse the suspicions of snooping neighbors, who might accidentally or perhaps intentionally let it slip to someone they shouldn't that three foreigners have taken up illegal residence at Number 10, Ulitsa Malaya Bronaya. By Soviet law, Andy, Paul and I should not be living here but rather in specifically designated foreigner housing called *diplomatichisky corpus* (*dip corpus*, for short) where the KGB can keep a good eye on us. Unfortunately, *dip corpus* apartments rarely become available, and when they do, they're expensive. So Misha, a friend of a friend, has agreed to let us live in his apartment while he spends the summer with his wife, Tanya, and five-year-old daughter, Sasha, in their dacha. It's a good arrangement for everyone. We get a cheap, nice place to live, Misha and his family get $100 cash every month—between four and five times the average 1991 monthly Soviet salary—and if we're all careful, none of us will get arrested. Even with all the rule bending going on in Moscow, it's still hard to know how far one can push the bounds of *glasnost* until someone cries foul.

The other great thing about the arrangement is that every other weekend, Misha and his family come into Moscow to do their laundry (in a makeshift plastic contraption they hook up to the bathtub) and to buy food, which means that Paul is in charge of watching Sasha. He lives for those afternoons with her, and she, in turn, worships him. They go on long walks together, throw bread crumbs to the ducks in Patriarch's Pond, talk about life. Seeing them bond like that makes me even more crazy with love for him. Clearly, Paul will be a good father one day, despite being abandoned by his own. We decide that if we should have ever have a daughter, we'll name her Sasha.

Misha's apartment, our illegal sublet, is on the second floor of a beautiful, old building in the center of Moscow, just steps away from Patriarch's Park, made infamous as the spot where Berlioz slips and falls under the tram wheels in *Master and Margarita*. It's also one block away from the fish store that never seems to have any fish and two blocks away from the bakery that sometimes has bread.

Like all stores in Moscow, the stores in our neighborhood are marked only by the name of their alleged commodity: "Fish," "Bread," "Shoes," "Meat," "Gifts," "Produce." There are also a couple of stores marked "Purse repair," but I've never seen anyone ever go in or out of them.

I have my nose and right eye pressed against the glass of the window to try to assay the length of the line at the bakery down the street. It's a block long. I yell to Paul in the bedroom and tell him to hurry over to the bread store so he can get back before our guests arrive. They're scheduled to show up soon, but Russians are notoriously late, always by at least an hour. This is not because they're rude. It's just that here in Workers' Paradise, time has no intrinsic value.

Paul yells back that he'll be out in a minute and asks if Andy's come back with the vodka yet. We sent Andy out two hours ago on his favorite mission, vodka search and retrieval. When we first arrived in Moscow in June, he had to run all around the city looking for vodka trucks that happened to be off-loading new shipments through the back-alleyway entrances to the stores; he'd slip the drivers ten extra rubles over the selling price, and they'd slip him a couple of bottles.

But now, with the new kiosks sprouting up all over town, it's getting easier and easier to use rubles to buy not only vodka, but scarce foreign goods as well—things like Marlboros, bananas, pineapple juice, lighters, cognac and an end-of-the-summer glut of down jackets from China. At the kiosk near Metro Universityet, I even found a couple of old (pre–toxic shock pamphlet) boxes of Tampax.

The problem with the kiosks, however, is that you can never predict which one will have which merchandise on any particular day. And sometimes, if your favorite kiosk proprietor hasn't paid off the right person, your favorite kiosk will explode into flames, leaving a pile of burnt wood and ash in its place the next morning.

There are two Western-style, foreign-owned grocery stores that carry most of the basic food items we could ever want to buy, so long as we buy them with hard currency. But with a box of granola selling for two or sometimes three times its normal rate, we can only rely on these shiny establishments as our stores of last resort. Even so, for tonight's dinner, we went to the new one off Mayakovsky Square and splurged on fifteen dollars' worth of Italian tortellini.

All told, it will have taken the three of us almost an entire day to scavenge for tonight's food and alcohol, not counting the two hours I had to wait yesterday for Dima, my black market contact at the *podarky* ("gift") shop on Kutoozovsky Prospect, to show up with the two large tins of black caviar he'd promised me.

By the time our Russian friends arrive, Paul's come back with two loaves of bread, Andy's made it back home having only finished off half a bottle of the seven bottles of vodka he found and the caviar is on the table. Our guests include two filmmakers, a journalist, an actor, an editor and other various Russian intelligentsia who all hang out in the same *tusovka*—which roughly translates as "gang" or "clique," but is more of an intrinsic philosophy of Moscow social life.

Though the conversation is held in Russian, I'm sloshed enough to at least partially understand and even participate in the discussion, which becomes more and more animated with every new shot of vodka consumed. Our friends spend the evening both reveling in the fact that they are eating tortellini and smoking Marlboros at a Russian apartment rented for dollars (albeit illegally) by Americans as well as worrying with an almost preposterous fear that something will somehow happen in their ill-fated country which will close the golden doors of *glasnost* that Gorbachev has finally pried open.

"It can't go on," says Katya, a documentary filmmaker, the daughter of a famous Russian actor, and the de facto anchor of her *tusovka*. "They'll find a way to beat us down yet."

I try to argue, in my infantile Russian, then in English with Paul as my translator, that it's fatalistic to assume something dire will happen. A few of our guests start to laugh and shake their heads. "Look at Czechoslovakia," I say, trying to sound smart, "look at Poland—"

Katya cuts me off. "You don't understand this country," she says, the tone of her accented English pleasant, factual and decidedly nonjudgmental. She takes a long drag on her cigarette for extra emphasis. "This is not America. Or even Czechoslovakia or Poland. There is no logic here. We are Russians, doomed by geography and history to live miserable, dark, cold, snowy and pathetic lives." She pours another round of vodka shots for all of us, emptying the fourth or perhaps fifth bottle of the evening, and holds her own glass aloft. *"Na zdarovyeh!"*—"To our health!"—she says, her voice soaked in irony.

"HOW CAN I SAY THIS POLITELY? They're boring," says Bob.

It's 9 P.M. in the middle of August, and I'm talking on the phone with Bob Pledge, the president of Contact Press Images. I joined Contact, the agency that had represented my pictures of the Afghan war, a few months after the Romanian orphanage picture debacle at Gamma. Bob was very excited about my Soviet women project when we talked about it in Paris, but now that he has the contact sheets in front of him, he's reconsidering.

"How boring?" I ask.

"Pretty boring," he says.

"Great." I'm having a bit of a career crisis. I've spent so long staring at a viewfinder filled with grim images that I seem to have forgotten how to frame a normal picture. The camera has begun to feel strange in my hands, heavy around my neck, like an extra appendage I no longer need. Shutterbabe, or at least the idea of her, is slowly dying.

I had an assignment to shoot the Bush/Gorbachev summit, but it bored me silly. Grip and grin, they call it, those handshakes between heads of state that are set up specifically for the cameras. I had to spend an entire week leading up to the summit sweet-talking bureaucrats from the Foreign Ministry, taking them out to lunch at the new Pizza Hut in order to procure the proper accreditations and press passes to the most sought-after events—the treaty signings, the press conferences, the visit to the tomb of the unknown soldier, the "casual stroll" through the Kremlin grounds—while making sure to keep myself off the lists for the peripheral pools—Raisa and Barbara visit hospitals, Raisa and Barbara sit down for a cup of afternoon tea, Raisa and Barbara dedicate a bronze duck statue.

Once I snagged the good passes, I then had to show up at the Foreign Ministry at the appointed time, only to be shuttled through metal detectors, loaded on to a bus and dumped into a room or inside a roped-off outdoor space for a good hour or two before the two presidents were scheduled to arrive for their three-second handshake/stroll/salute. When George and Mikhail would finally show up, it was all I could do not to get trampled by the other photographers, who would suddenly turn into a flashing pack of mad, rabid dogs. Many times, I ended up missing the picture altogether, getting shots of snarling Secret Servicemen or Bush's left ear instead.

"Why don't you shoot some street scenes? All the magazines keep asking me for current Moscow street scenes," Bob is saying, his voice scratchy over the endlessly clicking international line. Another journalist told me he thinks that the KGB records every international phone call, which would explain the clicking if it's true. Whenever I'm on the phone with my parents, I picture an enormous room filled with KGB agents, all sitting at their metal desks with earphones and notepads, frantically scribbling

down every word out of my mother's mouth—*"Can you believe it? Your fa-*
ther started snoring right in the middle of the bar mitzvah. . . . Yes, I swear
to God! . . . Richard, please, turn down the TV, I'm trying to talk to Deb-
bie."

"What kind of street scenes?" I ask Bob.

"You know, breadlines, babushkas, street peddlers, Red Square,
Lenin's tomb, whatever. Leave the Soviet women project alone for a month
or so. I don't think it's working."

"Okay," I say, actually relieved to unburden myself of the project. It
was a dumb idea for a photo-essay anyway, born only out of a desire to do
something safe and interesting on an intellectual level, not a visual one. A
photojournalist, especially a photojournalist whose livelihood actually depends on selling photos, has to choose her subjects carefully. Lots of things
that are intriguing to read and learn about do not necessarily translate visually. Like computers. Or early cognitive development. Or quarks. Or Soviet women.

Then there's the more fundamental problem: I've realized I don't love
doing portraiture. I can't be Annie Leibovitz, with her truck full of lighting
equipment and industrial fans, her stylists, hair and makeup people all
fluttering about her, fulfilling her festooned visions of famous faces. I can't
be Richard Avedon, with his stark white backgrounds and his large-format
eight-by-ten Deardorff camera, collecting human torsos in a vacuum. I appreciate their work, but I'm starting to understand that what I love most
about photography are the contextual accidents, the "decisive moments,"
as Cartier-Bresson called them—images with irony, with narrative juxta-
position, with stories to tell.

In fact, my favorites among my own photos were never actually produced on assignment. They were accidental, serendipitous street shots,
homages to photographers like Cartier-Bresson, to Gary Winogrand or
Robert Frank, not to Leibovitz or Avedon. Like the time I was shooting two
Gypsy girls in Nîmes and a gust of wind blew their miniskirts up at the
precise moment a priest stepped into the background. Like the old man I
was shooting in a Parisian park who, as he was pushing his twin grand-
children in their stroller, suddenly stopped and placed his head in his
hands as if he were either crying or giving up, while the stroller kept
rolling ahead. Like the bulldog I shot whose owner, holding the leash
proudly above him, shared the exact same jowls.

NÎMES, FRANCE, 1990

PARIS, FRANCE, 1988

PARIS, FRANCE, 1988

Bob's right. I need to get back to the street. "I'll have twenty rolls for you by the end of the week," I say. "Okay?"

"That's my girl," he says.

I hear keys jingling in the front door and the sound of laughter. When the door finally opens, Andy is standing there with his arms around two leggy Russian women. I recognize them and their cleavage from the footage Paul has shown me of his documentary. They are Irina and Svetlana, and they are hard-currency prostitutes, which, even if I hadn't seen Paul's footage, I could have easily figured out from their Western-style clothing and thick makeup. One dark, one fair, they both have the kind of lithe bodies and delicate facial features that might have earned them Ford modeling contracts had they been born in Duluth instead of Dneprope-trovsk.

One of the unusual by-products of *glasnost* in Moscow is the loosening of the definition of the word "prostitution." I was surprised when I found out that the typical Soviet hard-currency prostitute is not a streetwalker, and she is not the kind of woman who asks for payment up front. She's what we Americans would simply call a gold digger. She's pretty. Often quite smart. She expects gifts in return for her good company: makeup from France, clothes and shoes from Italy, plane tickets to London. She also expects a liberal powdering of pocket change, which can take the form of any hard-currency denomination, but should preferably come in tidy stacks of either dollars or deutsche marks. In fact, her standard of living is now so much better than the rest of the Soviet population's that in a recent survey of twelve-year-old Russian girls who were asked, "What do you want to be when you grow up?" hard-currency prostitute topped the list.

"*Champanskoyeh*, Debrichka! Drink, drink . . ." Andy's holding out a wobbling, half-drunk bottle of Russian champagne to me and slurring his words. Ever since we've arrived in Moscow, Andy has concentrated his daily efforts in two parallel directions—drinking and getting laid. The latter seems to agree with him, even though he's too broke to sustain most of the girls' interest for long, but the drinking is starting to take its toll. Paul, ever the optimist, keeps thinking he can save his friend from this downward spiral. He even managed to get Andy a ten-dollar-an-hour job working with him as a desk assistant at ABC. But Andy arrived hungover and two hours late on his very first day and was promptly fired. A few nights later, he returned home at 4 A.M. with vodka breath, two black eyes and a bloody nose. When we asked him what had happened, he couldn't remember.

I take one look at the scantily clad girls and tell Bob I'll call him back. Then I grab Andy and drag him into the kitchen, leaving the women by themselves in the living room. I admonish him for being drunk and for bringing Irina and Svetlana back to our apartment. "Andy, you promised," I said. While I have no problem with Andy's sexual proclivities, I do mind the excessive drinking, and I don't like it when he brings these women back to our apartment. Not only is it against our landlord's slightly paranoid rules for keeping us all out of jail, it relegates me to the tiny bedroom I share with Paul, often for hours on end. He promised Paul he would try to look for his own apartment when we arrived in Moscow, but after three months, he's still sleeping on the living room couch, our own renegade teenage son.

Andy just smiles sheepishly. "I'm sorry," he says, looking down at his feet. "I won't do it again. This is the last time. I promise." He hugs me, tells me he'll make it up to me. Then he stumbles back over to the couch, where the two women have saved him a place between them.

I drag the phone into the bedroom and dial Paul's number at work.

"ABC News," he says, proud of his new job. He was hired on the spot less than a week after our arrival, and he has already distinguished himself as smart, capable and able to leap through the type of bureaucratic hoops that could easily cripple even the most seasoned Moscow-based journalists. Once, when it was 1 A.M. and two 747 jetfuls of TV equipment that had just been flown in from New York got stuck in customs at Sheremetevo Airport, Paul simply hired five Russian army trucks, convoyed them to the airport, figured out which customs agents required bribes, and transported the entire payload back to the ABC bureau before daybreak.

"Pasha, it's me," I whisper.

"What's the matter? Why are you whispering?"

"It's Andy," I say. "He's brought home two new women. They're the ones from your video. They're in the living room. And he's drunk again."

Paul and I do not fight often, but Andy has become a bit of a thorn between us. I've grown to love Andy, warts and all, but I'd love him a lot more if he weren't living in our apartment. The last time Andy pulled a stunt like this, I told Paul if it ever happened again, he'd have to choose between us. "Shit. Okay," Paul says. I can here the sound of an edit deck rewinding in the background. "I'll be home as soon as I can. I just have to finish up a story."

I bar myself in the bedroom and try to study some Russian, but I can't concentrate with all the grunting and laughter seeping through the open transom. I try to picture the scene on the other side of the door, wondering if the women are actually enjoying themselves as much as their squeals would seem to suggest. Andy's a kind man. Though fueled by the hormones of a teenage boy, he has the heart of a child. He likes to laugh when he's getting laid, as if sex were an amusement park ride, the kind that spins you around really fast and then drops the floor out from under you. And he's gentle, even when drunk. Does that make sleeping with him any easier to justify?

An hour later, when I smell the postcoital cigarettes and hear Paul's keys in the door, I walk out into the living room. Andy is playing our Roxy Music *Avalon* CD, and he's sitting with Irina and Svetlana on the couch, drinking beer and stubbing out a butt. There are at least seven empty bottles and a full ashtray on the coffee table in front of them, along with the now empty bottle of Russian champagne. Andy's shirt is off. The women are dressed, though Irina's nipple is peeking out of her aquamarine spaghetti-strap top. She kisses Andy's neck while Svetlana gently strokes his chest. I greet Paul at the door. He gives me a quick kiss on the cheek and marches over to the living room couch.

"Okay, girls," he says to the women, his voice firm but gentle. He's clearly uncomfortable in his role as policeman, and he shoots me a look of frustration. I raise my eyebrows and stick out my neck to urge him on. "It's late," he continues. "Time for you ladies to go home."

"Oh, Pasha, let 'em stay. They're not hurting anyone." Andy has his aw-shucks innocent face on, the one he uses when he knows he's been caught doing something naughty.

Paul is usually a sucker for that face, but this time he says, "No, Andy. It's time for them to leave."

"Oh, but Pasha—"

"No, Andy." He bids the women farewell and shuts the door behind them. Then he walks over to the couch to sit down next to his friend. I go into the kitchen, where I can still watch and eavesdrop. "Andy, this is not working," Paul says, his arm draped paternally around Andy's still-bare chest. "Deb and I, we're trying to build something here together . . ." He waits a beat. ". . . and it's not a brothel." Paul's gentle laugh defuses the tension and, taking his cue, Andy joins him.

Then he adopts a more serious tone. He tells Andy we like having him, but that we're not his parents. That he has to grow up, cut down on the booze. That if he wants to have drunken ménages à trois with hard-currency prostitutes, he'll have to find another living room in which to conduct his business.

I can hear Andy's voice start to crack. "But I like it here with you guys. . . ." His words trail off.

"Andy," Paul says, unable to look into his friend's welling eyes, "I think it's time for you to . . ." But before he can get to "move out," Andy is slumped over, passed out on the couch.

I go into our room and bring out the spare bedding. Paul thanks me with a glance and puts the pillow under Andy's head. Then he spreads the blanket on top of him. "Andrushka," he says, using the Russian diminutive of Andy's name, the affectionate version an adult would choose to address a beloved child, "what are we going to do with you?"

ON A COOL AUGUST MORNING, at around seven-thirty, I am awoken by a call from another Andy, Andy Hernandez, my friend and fellow Moscow-based *Newsweek* photographer. "Get dressed and get your butt outside," he says. "Gorbachev's missing."

"Missing? What do you mean missing?" I try to rub the sleep from my eyes, briefly wondering if I'm dreaming. I see Paul in a half doze next to me. The phone feels cold against my ear. I'm awake.

"Missing as in no one knows where he is. Rumor is he's been arrested."

The words sink in, and I sit bolt upright in bed. The president of the Soviet Union is missing. This can't be good. I rouse Paul. He looks up at me with that squinty-eyed, drowsy morning face. I tell him what I've been told. He has the same reaction as I did. "Missing? What do you mean missing?"

"I'm not sure," I say, as the two of us hastily throw on our clothes. Though it's only August 19, there's already an autumn chill in the air. I grab my leather jacket, shove a couple of rolls of film in the pockets, hang two cameras around my neck, and try to swallow. Presidents don't just up and disappear without political consequence. At least I don't think they do.

Who would have arrested him?

Paul's head emerges from his sweater. He's smiling, unable to contain his excitement. "I bet it's the KGB," he says, reading my thoughts as usual. "Or hard-line communists. Either way, there'll be a reaction." He's practically giddy with anticipation.

"Great," I say, feeling nauseous. I sit down on the bed to get a grip.

Paul stops dressing. "Oh, come on, Debs," he says. "This isn't the Gulf War. Gorbachev's missing. That's all."

When the Gulf War started, I was sick with the flu, Paul and I had recently moved in together and I had a vaguely foreboding feeling about the whole thing. From where I stood, far away from the amber waves of grain, Bush's obsession with Saddam seemed scripted, the buildup of American troops looking more and more like a very expensive and dangerous publicity stunt. Gad called me in Paris, wanting to know when I'd be leaving for the Gulf, if I'd like to work with him when I got there, share car and hotel expenses with him. I blew my nose and told him I wasn't feeling well, that I was on antibiotics, that the war was crap, that our movements would be restricted, that Bush was a nincompoop and that I would probably just sit this one out. I told my editors at Contact the same.

Though these excuses were all true, I was too embarrassed to tell anyone, even Paul, another equally important reason for my ambivalence. At the time it seemed too wimpy, too *girlie*. I mean, what was I going to say, that I was in love with Paul, and suddenly the thought of dying in a war seemed much less romantic? My self-image was at stake. So was my career. I was supposed to be a photojournalist; I was supposed to be brave, scrappy, fearless, on a plane the moment a bomb drops, as full of macho bravado and testosterone as the boys. I was supposed to be Shutterbabe, intrepid superhero. But ever since I'd met Paul, I couldn't even menstruate without contemplating the loss.

Luckily, Paul had understood this without being told. He brought me soup and nursed me back to health. He sat with his arm around me on our couch in our cozy apartment on the rue St. Joseph, watching the smart bombs falling on CNN and playing the clown to make me feel less guilty. "Now tell me," he'd say, pointing to the SCUD falling on the TV screen, his intonation mimicking a third-grade teacher's, "which is better—A) sitting here with me or B) standing under one of those? And no fair choosing 'none of the above.' "

Later, when I broke down after I heard about Gad's execution, when I collapsed and started shaking and screaming because I couldn't deal with the dissonance between my fury over Gad's death and my elation at having eluded the same fate, Paul let me sob into his shoulder until his T-shirt was soaked.

But today, here in Moscow, with Gorbachev missing, Paul wants to see the news, not watch it on TV. Which, because it's the sentiment by which I used to live, I understand. "Come on," he's laughing, tickling me and pulling me off the bed. "Gorby needs us."

I tell him if it's all the same with him, I'd rather just stay home and organize my socks. But then I stand up, and Paul says things like "That's my girl" and "It's probably no big deal," even though I can tell he feels otherwise. If it were really no big deal, he wouldn't be carefully arranging his Hi-8 camera and microphone in his bag and unloading an extra battery from its charger. He peeks into the living room to check on Andy while I finish checking my equipment. "Not home yet," he says, which doesn't alarm us anymore. He scribbles a note for his friend, and we head out the door. *The revolution has begun,* it says.

I'm still slightly queasy and my heart is pounding as we run down the stairs of our apartment building, two by two. But when we step outside onto the sidewalk, we both stop, silent. The early morning sun is streaming down Malaya Bronaya. Birds twitter in the trees. An old lady with a broom made from twigs is going through the motions of street sweeping. It's 7:45. Moscow is still waking up.

Paul starts to laugh. "See, told you," he says, as we walk down the street. "Nothing's happening."

That's because everyone's still drunk, I think to myself, but in deference to Andy I keep my mouth shut.

We decide to head to Red Square, for no other reason than it seems the most logical place to hold a demonstration if a demonstration were to be held. We go on foot, taking Malaya Bronaya to Pushkin Square, walking past the McDonald's and the statue of Pushkin, and then slowly making our way down Gorky Street until we reach the Intourist Hotel. Nothing seems amiss. Gorky Street looks like it always looks at this hour, mostly empty, too wide and haphazardly dotted with idle street sweepers, stumbling alcoholics (*Is that Andy?*), and shuffling workers in their gray imitation-leather shoes and permanent scowls, carrying empty plastic bags that they hope to later fill with loaves of bread or slices of pig lard.

We stop the first person we run into. He's a middle-aged man, wearing a windbreaker to match his melancholia, and we ask him if he's heard the news about Gorbachev. He looks at us as if we've just told him the funniest joke he's ever heard and walks on.

We ask a few more random pedestrians if they've heard any news about Gorbachev. They, too, think we're nuts and walk on. Holding my hand, Paul leads me down a set of stairs, into the underground walkways beneath Manezhnaya Square, and then out and up the cobblestone plaza of Red Square toward St. Basil's Cathedral. "Maybe they've got Gorby locked up in there," he says, pointing to the cathedral and smiling conspiratorially. "Like Rapunzel."

"Good theory," I say, playing along. I glance skyward. "Except, of course, Gorbachev is bald, so . . ."

We are trying to giggle the tension away. For the moment, it's working.

St. Basil's looks resplendent in the morning light, its multicolored onion domes sprouting skyward like gigantic dollops of psychedelic soft-serve. Legend has it that after St. Basil's was built, Ivan the Terrible—true to his sobriquet—had the architect's eyes gouged out so that he should never again be able to design something as perfect or beautiful.

I've been meaning to shoot some stock images of St. Basil's, so I step back into the middle of the plaza to frame my shot. I'm in the middle of snapping off a few when I see Paul run over to shoot a small group of demonstrators who've just taken up a position between St. Basil's and the entrance to the Kremlin. The only words I can make out on their Cyrillic signs are *Gdyeh Gorbachev?*—"Where is Gorbachev?"

Now that's stupid, I think. Didn't they learn anything from Tiananmen? Unless a banner is written in English, it might as well be a tree falling in one of those peopleless forests. I explain this to one of the men, and he takes out a black marker and writes, "Stop coup d'état," on the plastic bag slung over his shoulder.

I hold the video camera for Paul while he conducts an interview with the demonstrators, but it's clear they don't know any more about what's going on than we do. We mill about Red Square for another couple of hours or so, growing ever more bored by the minute. A few more people have now joined in with the demonstrators, and they're all gathered in a polite circle around a small and scarcely audible transistor radio. It's tuned, but just barely, to the BBC World Service, but the BBC has no news either. Onlookers multiply. They stand in small clumps and try to peer into the tinted windows of the black Zils—the Soviet equivalent of Cadillacs—that drive in and out of the Kremlin gate, shuttling apparatchiks from here to there, from there to where? To find Gorbachev? The whole thing seems so preposterous. The president of the Soviet Union can't actually be "missing." It must be a hoax.

But the curious crowds continue to grow, and then, sometime around noon, from somewhere in the distance, I hear a faint, low rumble.

"Did you hear that?" I ask Paul.

"Hear what?" he says.

"Shhh. Listen."

The rumble grows louder. It seems to come not from a particular direction but from everywhere. The ground underneath us starts to shake. Pedestrians are now stopped in their tracks. A mother leans down to scoop up her child. "Yeah," Paul says, "what the hell is it?" His laughing voice is suddenly nervous. "It feels like an earthquake."

I fall to my knees and put my hands, then my ear on the ground. I can feel the smooth cobblestones of Red Square trembling in my palms. I stand up. What is it? The sound, now closer, has a metallic quality to it. It's mechanical, sort of like . . . *Hey, wait a minute!* I know that sound.

Holy shit.

Suddenly, I can feel my heart bouncing like a paddle ball inside my chest. "Tanks," I say to Paul, choking on the word. "Not an earthquake. Tanks. Come on, let's stick together." I take his hand in mine. I tell him if we lose each other, I'll come find him at the ABC bureau.

"Holy shit," says Paul. We run down the cobblestones, in the direction of the loudest sound, together.

As we enter Manezhnaya Square, the first column of tanks appears at the top of Gorky Street, a long green snake winding its way south toward us, pushing its way through the normal flow of traffic. "Oh my God," Paul says, "APCs. BTR60s, driving down Gorky Street. What the fuck is going on?"

Paul, with his early Soviet education—which included a school-wide drive to collect scrap metal for the Soviet war machine, along with bake sales to help the napalmed children of North Vietnam—knows the names of every tank, fighter plane and warship ever created. He's just never seen them in action.

This worries me.

"Armored personnel carriers, tanks, what's the difference? Just don't get in their way," I say, practically screaming over the now tremendous din.

But Paul isn't listening. He's staring at the young soldiers, at the way their torsos and guns pop out of their hatches like armed gophers. The soldiers stare back at him, at us, at everyone. Their eyes are wide open, their eyeballs shifting back and forth in their sockets, surveying the crowds now instantaneously streaming out of buildings and subways and walkways and cars and buses and storefronts. One of the soldiers shouts something in Russian I don't understand, but from his gestures I figure it must be "Move out of the way."

Now larger tanks appear, the kind with caterpillar tracks and enormous gun barrels. They are careening into the center of town, spewing black smoke and grinding up chunks of pavement in their wake.

Paul takes out his video camera and, his hands shaking, turns it on. "Now *those* are tanks," he says, holding the camera to his eye. "T72s. That's it. *Glasnost* is over."

All of the vehicles are moving quickly now, converging and heading straight toward us. My body feels stuck in the cracks between paralysis and flight, but I manage to pull out another camera from my bag and begin shooting wide shots. Because my hands, too, are uncontrollably trembling, I set the shutter speed to 1/250th of a second to avoid blurring.

Manezhnaya Square, like most public spaces in Moscow, is freakishly oversized, normally dwarfing the continual stream of cars passing through it. But now, as the plaza starts to fill up with hoards of angry Russians, as the tanks begin to muscle their way into its center, for the first time the space appears to have been built to scale, as if all along it had been designed not as a traffic circle but as a staging ground for a coup d'état.

The noise of all those engines sputtering and clanging up close is overwhelming, supersonic, like the Surround Sound thunder of an action film with the volume set too high. Layered underneath are the cries of the rapidly expanding, deeply enraged and slightly confused throngs, who are now coming in closer, surrounding the tanks. Fists are waving in the air. Brave babushkas (literally "grandmothers," but used to describe all aging Russian women)—many of whom are old enough to have been alive during the revolution in 1917—are throwing themselves in front of the metal monsters and maternally tsk-tsking the soldiers, yelling, "Boys! Boys! We're all on the same side. What are you doing? Go back to your barracks!"

or "Who's giving you your orders? Where's Gorbachev?" or simply "You should be ashamed of yourselves!" One old woman, a tiny woman, is standing on the side of a tank, brandishing an old umbrella at its commander, the loose flesh under her arm shaking vigorously. "What are you going to do, shoot me?" she asks, only half joking. Teenage boys and girls, grown men and women are all either crying or screaming or running or yelling or doing some sort of combination of the four.

I'm shooting pictures like a maniac, burning through an entire roll of film in less than two minutes, but when I finally take my eye away from the viewfinder, I realize that I've lost Paul. "Paul! Pasha!" I scream, but my voice is barely audible amidst the cacophony. I jump up and down to try to peer over the heads of the crowd. It's no use. I've lost him. I panic, my chest tightening like a tourniquet around my heart. Please, Paul, I think, don't do anything stupid.

By now, the gigantic plaza is filled to capacity with flesh and metal. The tanks are effectively stalled, no longer able to move in any direction unless the soldiers intend to run over bodies, which, at this point, seems as likely as not. They are angrily revving their engines, sometimes lurching forward just far enough to elicit the full-throttled screams of the crowd: "Stop! You'll kill us!" they yell. At this point, because I'm so small, I can't see anything other than limbs, chins and clouds, along with the wheels of a single tank obscured through a sea of denim jackets. I'm frantically, claustrophobically scanning my eyes beyond the perimeter of the plaza, searching for a lamppost or a pole or anything sticking out above the crowd that I might climb on to get an unobscured view, a better shot, a breath of air. Maybe even a glimpse of Paul.

But Manezhnaya Square is so open and vast, and I'm so tightly crammed into its center, I have only one recourse. Exhaling deeply, I push my way forward through the sea of people until I reach the nearest idling tank. I can feel the vibrating metal in my hands as I attempt to pull my body up, but it's too high. I can't gain a proper foothold. I'm about to give up when a babushka standing next to me sees the camera around my neck and realizes what I'm trying to do. "Help her up!" she yells, her voice loud and admonishing. "Somebody help her up!" Suddenly a thousand arms are hoisting me off the ground and into the sky. "Good, good," the old woman says, obviously relishing her role as director. "Be careful. Don't hurt her." When I'm finally standing on top of the tank, I look down at the woman and notice that she's crying. "Shoot, young lady! Shoot!" she pleads, the tears seeping into the deep crevices of her wrinkled face. "Show the world what is happening here!"

"Uh, okay," I say, holding the camera up to my eye, knowing that under the circumstances, this is pretty much the only thing I have to offer. Other protesters follow my lead, and now the tops of the tanks are covered with their writhing bodies. Like maggots on a corpse.

Suddenly, the tank lurches forward, almost throwing me to the ground. I grab on to a handle sticking out near the hatch, bend my knees for balance, and try to shoot one-handed. Unfortunately, this does not allow me to rotate the focus ring, so I go for a slower shutter speed, close down my aperture and pray. My viewfinder is filled with dozens of tanks and thousands of tiny heads, receding in the distance to mere pointillist specs of life. Snap. So this is what history looks like. This is how the wave swells. I usually arrive, like the rest of the press corps, just as the foam has started to recede.

I'm feeling euphoric, pressing the shutter, winding the film with quick flips of my thumb, when all of a sudden, my camera attacks me. Slams me right in the nose. For a second, I'm confused—is my Nikon alive?—but then I feel a hand clenched around my upper arm, shaking it violently. I whip my head around to investigate. The hand belongs to a red-faced tank commander. His head has popped out of the hatch on top of the tank, and his lower jaw is hanging wide open in stunned disbelief. He starts cursing at me in Russian, his eyes bulging out in fury. *"Dyevuchka!"*—"Young lady!"—he yells, his voice an equal mixture of machismo and rage. *"Shto ti blyet zdyes sidyish?"*—"What the fuck do you think you're doing?"

Oops.

"Fotografirovat," I say, still shaky with my Russian grammar. *"Ya malinki. Ya nichevo nye ovidyet,"* which even though it means, "To take pictures. I'm little. I to see nothing," gets the point across that I'm using his fancy armored personnel carrier as a step stool.

"Fotografirovat?" he screams, beside himself. *"Fotografirovat!?* Get the FUCK OFF MY TANK!"

Now he's shaking me, trying to push me off the tank. The crowd hisses, the men threatening to kill the soldier, the babushkas admonishing him to be polite and keep his hands to himself. I'm yelling, in English now because he's hurting my arm and because I can't think straight, things like "Get off me!" "Leave me alone!" and "Stop it, ouch!"

While this is happening, although I don't see it, an Associated Press photographer and a CNN camera crew climb up on the tank directly behind me. They start to shoot our silly altercation.

CNN will run the footage later that day, *USA Today* will splash us across their front page and hundreds of other newspapers and magazines worldwide (including *The New York Times* and *Paris Match*) will publish the photo of the tank driver grabbing my arm, his mouth clenched in fury, my face stunned in disbelief. The captions accompanying the picture will range from misleading—"A woman climbs on a tank on Moscow's Gorky Street to argue with its driver"—to completely false—"Russian woman defends her city against oncoming tanks." A journalist from a German magazine will even manage to track me down a week later to ask if she can send over a photographer and makeup artist to take a follow-up picture of me, the hero of the putsch. ("Just like that guy in Tiananmen!" she'll say.)

"Wait a minute!" I'll scream, to anyone who cares to listen. "It's not what you think. I was just trying to get a better view!" But nobody wants to hear the truth when the myth is so much better.

THE NEXT SEVENTY-TWO HOURS of the coup are a sleepless blur. I'm mostly just running back and forth between Sheremetevo Airport, where I send off my film with willing passengers, and the Byeli Dom—the "White House," home of the Russian parliament and ground zero for antiputsch activity. The burly cab drivers who chauffeur me between these two points curse out the putsch leaders, calling them things like money-grubbing Jewish horn-headed corrupted motherfuckers. Then, as usual, they make me pay them twenty dollars over the ruble fares on their meters.

During this time, Yeltsin is holed up inside the White House, strategizing with his cronies, while outside the White House, Soviet citizens are busy constructing antitank barricades out of old bed frames, steel girders, barbed wire and just about anything else they can lay their hands on. Even though the TV news has been preempted by *Swan Lake*, everyone understands the basics of what's happening, that a group of hard-line communists have decided to overthrow Gorbachev and with him, their country's newly emerging freedom. Within hours of the start of the coup, I run into our filmmaker friend Katya, who only a week earlier had made her doomsday predictions at our dinner party. I find her milling about the plaza outside the White House, shaking her head and clutching her mother's hand. When we talk, she tries to make light of the situation, flashing a mischievous smile while saying, "Yeah, well, it's only a matter of time before they start shipping us all off to labor camps again," but I can tell by her white knuckles that she's not convinced of the humor in her joke.

On that first day, I spend the afternoon shooting some of the barricade-building. Four men hoist a cement barrier. Two girls carry over an old ladder. One kid throws his bicycle into the mix. The whole scene reminds me of old Soviet propaganda films, except instead of happy Russians dressed in overalls, tilling the fields in perfect collective harmony, I'm watching happy Russians dressed in black market Levi's collectively building a freakish-looking wall against communism. "Higher, higher," one man yells, "we must build it higher."

"Dima, go get that park bench. . . ."

"Lyosha, Shura, we need some of those metal barriers from the police station. . . ."

"Here, take my truck. It'll stop a tank, and the piece of shit doesn't work anyway. . . ."

I've never seen so many Russians getting along so well together.

Soon the trolley car drivers start arriving, parking their blue and white trams in the middle of the street while the burgeoning crowds hoot and cheer. The mood is festive, even hopeful. "I'm here to help," one says.

"Where should I park this one?" asks another.

The taxi drivers decide to show their solidarity by ceremoniously tossing their fare meters into a big pile on the pavement. It's a pretty lame gesture—Russian cabbies never use their meters anyway, and it's not like a pile of small metal boxes would ever stop a tank—but I guess it's the thought that counts.

I'm shooting the pile of meters, wondering if anyone back at Contact or *Newsweek* will have any idea what they're looking at when they edit my film, when I hear my name called out. "Deborah! Deb!" I look around, but can't figure out where the sound is coming from. "Up here! Over here! Look up!" the voice says. I look up, and there, atop a barricade jerry-rigged

MOSCOW, USSR, 1991

out of park benches and chunks of cement, planks of wood and an old trolley car, is my roommate Andy.

He's sitting on the roof of the trolley, swinging his legs back and forth. He has his arms wrapped around his fellow demonstrators, the attractive female ones, at least, and in one hand he holds a partially consumed bottle of vodka. He takes a big swig and smiles, happier than I've ever seen him. "They sent my father off to Siberia," he yells down, his voice brimming with pride, "but they're sure as hell not going to get me!" He repeats himself in Russian for the sake of his new buddies, and they all erupt into defiant cheers.

"Andy," I shout back, "what the hell are you doing up there? This is not your revolution. You're from New Jersey."

"Who cares?" he says, taking another shot of the vodka and wiping his mouth with the back of his sleeve. "I'm staying. They can try to run me over, but I'm staying!" The bravado is pure John Wayne, and it elicits even more cheers from his fellow barricade-sitters. He passes around his bottle for all to enjoy. I tell him to be careful, but I also understand that for the first time since arriving in Moscow, Andy has found something to believe in.

"You seen Paul?" I ask. He hasn't. It's been hours since we lost each other in the chaos of Manezhnaya Square, and I'm dying to run over to the

ABC bureau to see if I can find him. But the word on the street is that the putsch leaders have scheduled a press conference, and the word from the *Newsweek* bureau, where I briefly checked in, is that I'm on assignment, so I say good-bye to Andy and run over to shoot the press conference. Besides, I'm not really worried about Paul's or about anybody else's safety at this point. Since those first scary hours when the tanks rolled into Moscow, the army presence in the streets has turned from menacing to benign. In fact, with soldiers and tanks occupying positions on every major Moscow artery, somehow the city feels safer than usual, as if all that artillery and hardware might cause a policeman to think twice before stopping us foreigners, under the pretense of a traffic violation, to extort our money.

When I arrive at the press conference, the place is brimming with Betacams and wires, tripods and tungsten lights. It's late enough in the day that all the usual suspects, at least the ones from European cities with up-to-date Soviet press visas, have had time to jump on their various planes and find their way to Moscow. Of the two hundred or so journalists here, I must know at least half. I say hello to some colleagues who've just arrived from Paris, most of whom greet me with a warm kiss on either cheek and some version of *Can you fucking believe it?*

The putsch leaders enter the room, led by Gennadi Yanayev. The others—Yazov, Pugo, Kryuchkov and Pavlov (all, ironically, Gorbachev appointees)—take their seats on the dais with him. Not one man is smiling. In fact, all of them seem scared, like criminals on a firing line. "Gorbachev is ill," Yanayev says, his hands shaking violently. The reporter sitting next to me shakes his head and says, "Yeah, right," under his breath. When it is later suggested that Gorbachev might be allowed to retake control if and when he ever gets "better," the guy has to put his hand over his mouth to keep from laughing out loud.

"That's it," he whispers to me. "They're doomed."

After the press conference, I finally run over to the ABC bureau to look for Paul. When I arrive, he's being interviewed by *Nightline* as an eyewitness to this afternoon's chaos. He sees me, smiles, gives a little sheepish wave and mouths the words "Give me ten minutes" while pointing to his watch. The bureau is crowded with people and equipment, so I make myself at home on the floor and start writing up my captions while waiting for him to finish. "How do you spell 'Yanayev'?" I ask one of the producers.

Without turning around from his editing deck, where he's furiously logging press conference footage, he laughs and says, "I'm not sure, but try *d-e-a-d-m-e-a-t*."

When his interview is over, Paul comes up from behind me and kisses me on the neck. "I heard you climbed up on a tank," he says. "You really are the little revolutionary girl of my dreams, aren't you?"

I blush. "Little, yes. Revolutionary, no," I say. "Anyway, it wasn't a tank. It was an APC."

Paul looks up at the ceiling, his hands clasped together in mock prayer. "Thank you, God. She's perfect."

IT'S THE THIRD DAY of the coup, and though it's drizzling, the crowds outside the White House are still growing larger. The barricades have become a giant *tusovka,* with young people banding together in happy, soggy groups to drink and to mingle, to hang out and to make out, all in the name of defending democracy. Surrounding this merry gathering are soldiers and tanks from the Taman division, all of whom decided as early as the first night to switch over to Yeltsin's side and to take up defensive positions around the parliament. For an extra photogenic flourish, they've covered their tanks with signs of support and with Russian flags, and they've plugged up the barrels of their Kalashnikovs with red carnations.

Mothers now bring their young children to the barricades, not so much to protect the White House as to use it as a playground. The kids climb up onto the barricades and jump down the other side. They mount the tanks and swing upside down from their cannon barrels. I'm shooting this, trying but failing to frame that perfect child-on-tank picture, when another photojournalist I know, a boorish guy with his gut hanging out, comes over to join me. "Don't waste your film," he says, shooting off a few frames of his own just in case. "That kind of photo's been done to death."

I disregard him and continue to shoot. "You're so wrong," I say. I circle around to the other side, where the kid is now peeking his head down the hatch. I'm frustrated. Can't get a good shot, no matter where I stand. Then the boy jumps off, and I've lost my opportunity. Exasperated, I look my colleague in the eye. "Innocence meets evil will never be done to death," I say. "It's at the heart of everything."

"Ooh, excuse me," the photographer says. He pulls out a cigarette, takes a puff and flicks the ashes on my shoe. "Is that what they taught you at your fancy university?" There is hairy blubber peeking out between his shirt and jeans.

"No," I say, slowly backing away from him. "It's what I've taught myself."

I wander off, zigzagging through the column of tanks, pausing to shoot when the occasion presents itself. I spot a babushka with a plastic bag, and I start to salivate. The babushkas, never ones for sitting on the sidelines, spend their time walking from tank to tank, carrying old plastic bags filled with sandwiches, bread and bottles of *sok* to feed the turncoat soldiers. "What do you have for me today?" one of the soldiers asks, as the old lady approaches with her bag of goodies.

"A little cheese, a little pig lard. Impossible to find ham today," she says, looking somewhat ashamed and apologetic.

"Don't worry," the soldier says. He bites into a sandwich, wipes his mouth with the back of his sleeve and smiles. "As soon as we get rid of Yanayev and those other pigs, the stores will be filled with ham." He winks at her. The babushka giggles flirtatiously and gives him another sandwich.

I have not had a real meal since the night before the coup. I try to resist the urge, but the sight of all those sandwiches becomes too much for me to bear. I walk over to the babushka and beg her for one. "Of course," she says, handing me a cheese sandwich and filling my pockets with two more. "You're still a growing child. You need to eat, get big and strong."

I'm about to explain that I'm actually twenty-five years old, that I stopped growing, oh, probably nine years ago and that I doubt her cheese sandwiches will boost me up anywhere near five-three, but instead I just smile and thank her. I bite into the sandwich, ravenously ripping off huge chunks and washing the whole thing down with a swig of *sok*. Then I kiss her cheeks the customary three times. "Thanks again," I say, catching my breath. "I was so hungry."

As the drizzly day melts into a wet evening, the mood around the White House intensifies. Rumors of planned late-night attacks ricochet from barricade to barricade. Some even say the Spetznaz troops have been called in to finish Yeltsin off. One of Paul's Moscow drivers, from his days working with Serge, used to be a Spetznaz soldier. A stocky, jocund veteran of the war in Afghanistan, he'd often regale us with stories of being dropped by helicopter behind enemy lines, into the heart of the Hindu Kush. There, he would execute Afghani soldiers using only his bare hands. "You've never felt power," he'd say, his eyes growing wistful and vacant, "until you've felt another man's neck snap in the palms of your hands."

I'm wandering around the White House, not really shooting much. It's too dark, nothing is happening and besides, I want to conserve my Quantum flash battery, which is fading, in case the Spetznaz really do attack. Normally I carry around a few spare double-A batteries as a backup, but I haven't been able to find any recently in the kiosks.

Sometime before midnight, I run into Paul wandering near one of the barricades. He looks exhausted. Tells me he's spent the past twenty-four hours running around inside the White House with a bunch of his ABC colleagues, trying to procure an interview with Yeltsin for Ted Koppel. Ted, he says, waited dutifully on the floor in the corridor outside the Russian leader's office, at one point taking off his shoes and laying down for a nap when he grew tired. Paul hugs me, puts his head on my shoulder. "Don't mind me," he says, speaking quietly into my neck, "I'll just take my own little snooze right here."

"Poor baby," I say. "Maybe we should just go home. I'm toast, too." I've slept only four hours since the first day of the coup, and those were spent curled up in a fetal position on the floor of an ABC editing room while my flash battery recharged.

Paul lifts up his head. "Yes," he says. "I can barely stand."

A misty rain is falling as we wander our way back home through the crowds, between the Taman tanks, over barricades and around the parked trolley cars blocking the path between the White House and the Ring Road. I can't put my finger on it, but something about tonight feels different than the two previous nights. More intense. The demonstrators, growing ever more agitated, have linked arms to form an enormous human chain across Kutoozovsky Prospect. Swaying back and forth, they are shouting anticommunist slogans and singing old Bolshevik revolutionary songs, completely unfazed by the contradiction.

Paul and I look at each other, sigh and take out our equipment. "So much for sleep," he says.

I take a few pictures of the human chain, my flash popping here and there, but then I notice that, like me, my detachable flash battery is truly on its last legs. When it's fully charged, its line of green diode dots are all illuminated. Now, only one dot remains lit, the one lone soldier still standing, which means that even if something were to happen tonight, there will soon be no way to record it.

"Forget it," I say to Paul, pointing to the spent battery. "It's useless. I can't even shoot. Let's just go home."

It's after midnight as we start home, our necks bent down against the increasing rain. I lean my head into the hollow space between Paul's chest and his clavicle bone and, just for a moment, allow myself the indulgence of shutting my eyes.

And then, just as my muscles start to relax, just as I can practically taste the pleasure of sleep, a man comes running up to us out of nowhere. He's panting, his face glistening with rain, sweat, and fear.

"You two, with the cameras! Come with me! Run! There are tanks on the Ring Road." He's speaking so fast, I can barely understand him. The only other word I can make out in the avalanche of sound coming out of his mouth is *stryelyayut*—"they are shooting." Paul breaks into a sprint. I follow, the sudden rush of adrenaline obliterating both the tranquil moment and any lingering fatigue.

When we reach the overpass above Ring Road, we both see and hear them. A column of tanks is exiting the underpass directly below us, its path blocked by a massive barricade of abandoned trolley cars parked closely and densely together. "Let's stay up here for now!" I scream at Paul, partly out of fear, partly because I have no idea what's happening and partly so he can hear me over the now familiar din of metal tracks on pavement. On either side of the sloping walls leading out from the underpass, a crowd of people has started to gather. Someone yells, *"Fascisti!"*—"Fascists!"—and then someone else yells, "Go back where you came from!"

It's dark, the scene lit only by the streetlights above and by their reflections in the wet puddles below. Dammit, I think, remembering my flash, and then I start cursing out loud, banging my flash battery against the wall of the overpass in anger. It's the Murphy's Law of photojournalism: just when you need them, every battery that can go dead will. *Fuck!* I have only enough juice for two, at the most three or four more pictures.

I decide to start with pictures I can shoot without a flash, like a compressed overall shot. I take out my 180-millimeter lens, attach it to my Nikon and place the camera on the overpass wall to steady it during the long exposures. I open my aperture as wide as it will go and shoot off ten

MOSCOW, USSR, 1991

pictures of the tanks approaching the trolley car barricade at various shutter speeds, bracketing for safety—1 second, 1^1/$_2$ seconds, 2 seconds, 2^1/$_2$
seconds, etc.—hoping the vibrations from the tank engines and my shaking fingers don't blur my photos.

Two gunshots ring out, and we duck. Paul is crouched down right next
to me, holding his video camera at his side and muttering, "Ohmigod
ohmigod ohmigod," under his breath.

A minute or so later, we stand up to assess the situation. There are
now hundreds of shouting, angry spectators gathered around the tanks,
their jumbled cries growing louder and louder. Paul and I seem to be the
only two journalists around, the others dutifully waiting back at the White
House for the purported Spetznaz attack. But then I spot a single reporter
scribbling frantically into his notebook. "Follow me," I shout to Paul, and
we run over to ask the guy what's going on.

He stares up from his notebook, his eyes wide and scared. "Fuck if I
know!" he snaps, his pen now poised helplessly in the air.

Suddenly, as if to answer our question, the first tank in the column
starts to accelerate forward, crashing forcefully into the side of a trolley car.
The crowd lets out a collective howl.

"Come on," Paul says, grabbing my hand, "let's go."

I hesitate. I shouldn't be here. I promised Gad. I promised myself. I love Paul. My flash isn't even working. But the moment passes. Give a well-intentioned, recently reformed heroin addict a junk-filled needle—just one, just for old times' sake—and watch what she does with it.

Breaking into a sprint, we head down alongside the outside of the underpass wall until we reach the barricade. We make our way through the trolley buses and enter the blockaded area. Suddenly, we are on the Ring Road. Boxed in. Surrounded on two sides by the underpass walls, on another side by the barricade of trolleys and everywhere we look by tanks, lurching, clanging, belching black smoke. A few demonstrators are inside with us, dodging tanks, yelling at the soldiers, running from here to there and back again across the glistening wet pavement.

The first tank tries once again to push its way through the barricade, backing up and ramming forward. "Watch out!" I scream to Paul, who has his camera glued to his eye, and he jumps out of the path of the tank's backward trajectory just in time. Another man is less lucky. We hear screams and cursing, and out of the confusion run five panicked men, carrying out a bleeding *tovareeshch* in their arms. "Move, move! Get the fuck out of the way! He's injured!" they scream. I shoot a few pictures of this, but the flash goes off only once.

What I wouldn't give right now for a fresh pack of double-A batteries. And a lobotomy.

"Shoot, little girl, shoot some more!" the spectators are yelling at me, and I'm pointing to my flash and yelling back, "It doesn't work!" and they're yelling back, "Yes it does!" and I'm yelling back, "No it doesn't!" and then someone calls me an idiot and I give up trying to explain the vagaries of my flash battery while I pray for the Quantum to recycle, which it does, but while it's recycling I hear a couple more gunshots go off, and all I can think is, Oh God, what am I doing here anyway? Shooting pictures? This is insane! Where's Paul? There he is. Watch him. Watch his back. Why am I here? Come on, you goddamned flash. Work! Why am I doing this? What's the point? It's too dark anyway. What kind of life is this? I can't focus. I can't focus. IT'S TOO FUCKING DARK. AND I CAN'T FOCUS! "Ahhhhrrggghhhh!!!!" I shout, full of addict's remorse, holding my head between my hands, trying to silence it, still waiting for that one remaining diode to appear.

The percussive beat of metal hitting metal punctuates the clamor of mass chaos as the first tank finally rams its way through, leaving a huge gap where a trolley used to be. More demonstrators appear, running out of nowhere to try to close the gap, rocking the displaced bus back and forth in hopes of moving it back into position. "Are you insane?" someone shouts. "You can't move a fucking bus!"

"Fuck your mother!" someone else yells. "Let them try!"

A few civilians have now climbed onto the second tank to try to keep it from getting through the newly exposed hole in the barricade. Others are throwing large wooden sticks and scraps of metal underneath the caterpillar tracks to try to stop it, but the sticks snap in two like matches and the metal scraps are no more effective than dough under a rolling pin. The men who've climbed up onto the tank are cursing and yelling and trying to open the hatch. Suddenly, the tank lurches back, and one of the men is thrown to the ground. Before he can get up, his body disappears, crushed effortlessly underneath the tracks of the tank. Everyone watching this, including me, screams. We are helpless, lost in collective horror. "You're killing him! You're killing him!" the crowd wails, but by the time the tank has finished traversing his body, the man is already quite dead.

A flock of bodies and lights and flashes encircles the bloody corpse a few feet from where I'm standing, and I know I should get over there and join the twinkling vultures, but I can't move my feet. It's not that I'm having a self-righteous epiphany. I figured out the parasite thing a long time ago, and it still hasn't kept me from working. It's just that I'm so scared, I'm barely holding it together. It's the way I should have felt in Israel and Afghanistan, had I been less of a first-time hack. The way I should have felt the moments before being stabbed in my hotel room in Zurich, had I not deemed myself wholly invincible. The way I should have felt when I was dropped all alone into the jungles of Zimbabwe, had I understood jungles and my own smallness in them.

It is vertigo, the sick, hollow, air-sucking kind that strikes when you gaze down from the tightrope you've been casually traversing and suddenly realize there's no net after all, when the enormity of what it is you stand to lose finally—*finally*—hits you.

A man pushes his way through to the corpse and, sobbing, bends down to scoop up the mangled body. He cradles it in his arms and begins to rock back and forth. Is he a stranger? A brother? A friend? Does it matter? His clothes are being soaked with the dead man's blood, and he's crying and screaming and rocking and shaking and shouting obscenities at the soldiers. "You've killed him! You've killed him, you fuckers!" he wails.

The tank backs up quickly along the wall, shooting sparks as it scrapes the concrete not ten feet from where I'm standing with my back pinned against it.

Now the crowd of onlookers, which has swollen to well over a thousand people, becomes infuriated. From their semisafe vantage point behind the underpass wall, a few of them start to yell, "Killers! Fascists!" and then they all join in the rhythmic chorus, their fists raised angrily in the air, crying, *"Fa-sci-sti, fa-sci-sti, fa-sci-sti . . . ,"* each pounding syllable a drumbeat against the dread of their own fragile mortality.

And then someone lobs a Molotov cocktail over the wall, which explodes on the ground, and then another Molotov cocktail is tossed, this time hitting the top of the tank. A few seconds later, the tank—this massive hulk of metal, this heavy behemoth monster—jumps two feet into the air as it bursts into flames.

"Holy shit!" I can hear Paul yelling through the reverberating boom, but in the seconds that follow the explosion we are separated by people and fire and pandemonium and darkness. I panic and start screaming his name, but, once again, he is gone.

"Oh, God, oh, God," I'm crying. "NOOOOOO!"

The crew of the burning tank bails out and, agitated and frightened, they start to fire their Kalashnikovs into the crowd. *Pa-pa-pa-pa-pa-pa-pa! Pa-pa-pa-pa-pa-pa-pa!* The bullets are ricocheting everywhere, the wall behind me separating the underpass from the road leading to the overpass is too high, I'm too small to scale it, I'm boxed in, I'm screaming, I drop to the ground, in a puddle right next to the wall, my cheek in the dirty water slick with oil, my arms covering my head. "Paul!" I yell. "Oh God, PAAAA-SHAAAAAAA!!!!" and then my voice is choked with sobbing while my convulsing body makes tiny ripples in the water, and I'm staring at the ripples because only a fool would look up, and I'm thinking to myself while the rain hits my neck and the bullets pierce the air and the water soaks my knees and the ripples flow out, *This is what fear looks like.*

The machine-gun fire is unrelenting, coming in angry spurts and cackles, crackling over the voice of the enraged tank commander, who's shouting Russian words I either don't or no longer understand. "Paul!" I scream again, raising my head for just a second to let the sound escape, and just as I do, I see a man no more than a few yards in front of me fall to the ground. Blood squirts out of his skull and onto the pavement. It mixes with the rain and flows in small, quiet rivulets down the gradual slope of the pavement to where I lie paralyzed.

I open my mouth to scream, but the sound that comes out is nothing like I've ever produced before. It's guttural and shrill, a moan more screeching tire than human, and it comes from a place inside my body I don't want to find again.

Somehow, I get up the courage to crawl on my stomach, inching forward with elbows and knees toward the trolley cars, but they are now engulfed in flames, utterly impassable. If I could just get over the wall behind me, I'd be fine.

I will beg.

Still crouching, the gunfire to my back, my hands stretched beseechingly into the air, I start to shout. *"Pozhalsta! Pozhalsta!"*—"Please! Please!"—I yell up to the people behind the wall, and within seconds I am lifted up and over, skinning my knee and the side of my face against the wall on the way up.

Stunned and in an oddly calm, psychotic daze, I wander aimlessly through the crowds on the other side of the wall after that, my hair falling out of its braid, my clothes soaked with mud, rain and the blood of an unlucky stranger. When the remaining tanks finally retreat, and the demonstrators joyously take over the one they set ablaze, I shoot a picture of a euphoric man in front of the burning trolley cars, his hands raised victoriously in the air like a quarterback's after a touchdown. This is the photo *Newsweek* will choose to run as a double-page spread in their next issue, accompanied by three various others I also shot. I practically step on another man, whom I think I recognize as the one who got the bullet, but I can't be sure. It was so dark back there, and he's lying on the other side of the wall from where he fell. Whoever he is, half of his forehead is gone, and someone has just left him lying here all alone on the side of the road, his brains leaking out of his skull. In his pocket is a pack of cigarettes. He won't be needing those anymore.

I fall to the ground behind the man's head and pull out my camera. Looking through the viewfinder, I make a vague attempt at proper framing, but not for *Newsweek*'s sake. Pictures of bloody heads missing big

MOSCOW, USSR, 1991

MOSCOW, USSR, 1991

chunks of flesh are not published in America. No, this is more of a souvenir photo, a small keepsake to remind me of the darkness.

I press the shutter. My flash goes off. I press the shutter again, then again, waiting to hear the high-pitched whir of a recycling flash, knowing full well that without the flash the pictures will come out completely underexposed. I take my eye away from the viewfinder and look down at my battery. It is finally dead.

PAUL AND I MANAGE TO find each other amidst the residual flames and anarchy, and when he hugs me I begin crying all over again. "You're covered in blood," he says.

"I know," I say, giving in to the sobs. "I lost you back there." My tears soak his shirt.

"No you didn't. I'm right here, see?" He takes my hands and puts them on his cheeks to prove his point, and when I don't laugh he lets me cry a little more, using his thumb as a squeegee. A few minutes later he says, "Let's go," and I want to just stay there hugging and bawling and chewing on life, but I know we have to get Paul's footage back to ABC within the next hour or so, and I need to call Contact on the satellite phone to tell them about my photos, otherwise what the hell were we doing back there boxed in between tanks and bullets? There had to be a reason.

We walk quickly, both still dazed and disoriented, clinging tightly to each other as we make our way on foot back to the bureau. At first we try to speak, to make sense of what we saw—"That was pretty intense, wasn't it?"—but after a while we submit to the silence that descends when words become impotent.

It's after 1 A.M., and yet the streets are still choked with people, their umbrellas, their smoldering cigarettes, their outrage. Because of the blood on my clothes and my scraped cheek, we are stopped periodically by curious barricade-sitters, who ask us to explain what we saw back there on the Ring Road, but our imprecise answers inevitably disappoint. Everyone wants numbers. *How many died?* We don't know. We saw two, but we heard there were more. *How many injured?* A few. *How many tanks were there?* Five, maybe six or seven. *How many shots were fired?* A lot.

Death is so much tidier when it's reduced to statistics. Numbers are safe, empirical. Three dead, eighty dead, a thousand dead: these are the facts we crave, the stuff we can understand. Sure beats imagining one man, lying all alone in the rain, his brains slowly oozing out of his skull.

Even six million is fathomable as a number. It is large, horrible and awesome in scope, but conceptually much easier to stomach than the thought of a single person—someone just like us—standing naked, cold and abandoned, waiting for the gas to be turned on.

Paul and I finally arrive at the ABC bureau. When we open the door, both of us out of breath, we see a sight so incongruous with the madness we've just survived that it makes us stop and stare. There in the middle of the room, sitting on a foldout metal chair with her head upside down between her legs, is Diane Sawyer. Impeccably dressed, with perfect little pointy shoes, she is vigorously brushing her famous blond hair, tousling it, stroking it, making it perfect. When she finally flips her head up, the hair falling flawlessly around her face, she sees us staring at her and gasps. "Oh, my," she says, her signature voice mellifluous and deep. "What happened to you two?" She addresses the question not really to us, but rather to the bustling room at large, which makes her query feel like one of awkward celebrity politesse, not curiosity.

Paul, never one for catching subtleties in conversation (is any man ever?), starts to explain—"Well, you see, we were on the Ring Road . . ."— but before he can get another word out, a producer appears yelling, "Live shot!" and two tungsten lights go on, and last-minute makeup is applied, and there's some discussion about a flyaway strand of hair, and then Diane says, "Okay, I'm ready." She quickly blots her lipstick one last time.

IT IS DAWN by the time we make it back to our apartment. The door has been left unlocked, and an acrid smell of melting plastic—and, what is that? metal?—is wafting from the apartment into the hallway. "Jesus, what's that smell?" Paul says, and then he sees the smoke coming from the kitchen and runs inside to investigate while I dash into the living room to check on Andy. I see him lying naked, fast asleep on the pullout couch, his arm around a new and equally naked conquest. There are empty beer bottles, champagne bottles, vodka bottles and a half-drunk bottle of Jack Daniel's spread haphazardly on random surfaces throughout the room.

On the coffee table, pushed aside to make room for the foldout bed, are two ashtrays, both of them brimming with butts and bottle caps.

"Goddamnit, Andy!" Paul yells from the kitchen, angrier than I've ever heard him. "Debs, come here, I need your help. He left the burner on. It melted the fucking teakettle."

I run into the kitchen. The teakettle looks like the watches in those Dalí paintings, only worse, melted flat and gooey and drippy all over the burner. Paul has filled a bowl with water, which he is throwing onto the smoldering mess to cool it down. He hands the bowl to me, tells me to fill it again and douse the area with water. Then he marches into the living room, his footsteps like thunder, and tries to shake Andy awake. "You idiot!" he says, his voice acrimonious, frantic.

I throw some more water on the burner and then step into the living room, where I prop my tired body against the wall and yawn. "Relax," I say to Paul. "It's fine. We'll clean it up later." I notice the naked girl open her eyes, then, seeing me, she quickly shuts them closed again, covers herself and pretends to sleep. Andy is still drunk, barely able to rouse himself, even with Paul helping him. He makes a valiant effort to sit up but then slips back down, a giant, brawny rag doll, his head falling limp on the pillow. Paul, shaking his head in disgust, muttering "Idiot" once again, this time more quietly, stands up and wanders over to the window. He rubs his bloodshot eyes and stares out blankly at the peaceful street, the new day unraveling below. "You could have died," he says to Andy. To himself. To no one in particular.

FOUR DOZEN OR SO babushkas are lined up along the brick wall, sitting on chairs or milk crates in their threadbare dresses and flowered head scarves, sunning themselves with closed eyes and skyward-tilted faces in the courtyard of the apartment complex on Krasnaya Armayskaya Ulitsa, Paul's childhood home. It's the end of summer. Snow will be coming soon.

"You think he still lives here?" I ask Paul, as we wander from doorway to doorway, poking around. Looking for clues.

"This is Moscow." He laughs. "No one ever moves."

We are searching, if half-heartedly so, for Paul's father, the one he never knew, the one whose anti-Semitic mother sent him back to the army when she found out her son had impregnated Paul's Jewish mother. "Well, why don't you just ask one of those ladies if they know him?" I say, pointing to the tidy row of shrunken apple-faced sunbathers.

"Yeah, yeah, okay," he says, and he walks over to talk with the nearest old lady. *"Vih znayetye Pavel Sokolov?"*—"Do you know Pavel Sokolov?"—he asks her.

"Znayoo," she says, answering in the affirmative and looking slightly miffed at having her afternoon tanning session interrupted. *"Konyechno znayoo"*—"Of course I know him."

I try to make sense of the rest of the short, rather curt conversation, but it involves words such as "doctor," "stomachache," and "appointment," which confuses me, and then they're on to *Thank you, do you have his telephone number, I'll call, sorry to bother you, good-bye,* and then Paul is grabbing my hand, dragging me away from the babushka.

"What the . . . what happened? Who was she?" I ask, completely befuddled.

"Who, that old woman?" Paul says, making a game of it just to drive me crazy. He glances over his shoulder at the babushka, then returns my gaze with a smirk of irony. "Yes. Well. That was Grandma."

"What!"

"My grandmother," he says, stifling his giggles and shushing me with a finger to his mouth. He pulls my hand even harder, dragging me farther and farther away from the courtyard with quick and purposeful strides. After two interminable minutes, when we've gone far enough away from the strange little wrinkled woman that she has already become nothing more than a strange little wrinkled memory, he stops in the middle of the sidewalk and explodes with laughter. "We pick one babushka out of the forty-five sitting there, a total stranger, and it has to be *my* friggin' babushka. The anti-Semite!" He's laughing so hard, he has to bend over.

I start laughing, too, as I watch Paul, hysterical now, practically hyperventilating, trying to fill in the details between breaths. He tells me he was so flummoxed when the old lady said that Pavel Sokolov was her son and that he was *right upstairs* in the apartment that served as his office, he didn't know what to say. He knew his father was a doctor, so he made up some story about having a stomachache and not having time to stop by just now and that he'd call and make an appointment for tomorrow.

"So, are you going to make an appointment?" I ask, still laughing, but then I stop and so does Paul.

He sighs and catches his breath, that ever-present smile stretched across his face. He takes my cheeks in his hands, then rubs his fingers down my nose. He kisses my forehead, but tenderly, like a father. Like a man defining for himself the concept of family. "No," he says. "I won't. I don't really feel the need to anymore." He puts his arm around me, and as we walk away he holds his face up to the sun. "Come on," he says, "let's go home."

BETHANY BEACH, DELAWARE, 1997

JACOB

THE SUN IS RISING. Tom Brokaw is sleeping, his chair reclined as far back as it will go. A producer and freelance cameraman, seated next to each other in the back of the bus, are trading western hemisphere war stories. Standing in the aisle a few rows up, leaning his elbow on a headrest and surrounded by his minions, Bryant Gumbel is holding forth on the proper garlic-slicing method for a squid-ink pasta dish he recently discovered. And me, I'm sitting across from Tom, staring out the window at barefoot Dominican children and ramshackle houses passing by, trying not to barf.

"These voodoo guys were fuckin' carrying machetes, and we were like 'See ya . . .' "

"You have to cut the cloves into paper-thin slices, not crush them. Then you sauté the tomatoes . . ."

I don't know if it's the talk of machetes, Bryant's garlic, the bumpy bus ride, last night's chicken dinner on the plane down here or some combination of the four that is forcing the bile up my esophagus, but I do know that if this bus doesn't stop soon, Mr. Brokaw and his sporty field jacket will be covered in my vomit.

It is mid-September 1994. Paul and I have just celebrated the first anniversary of our wedding (a lovely affair in a D.C. hotel, nice flowers, good dancing, lots of friends, funny toasts, many tears and an outrageously expensive white silk dress now embalmed for eternity in my closet). We live in New York City, on the Upper West

Side, where we moved at the beginning of 1992, leaving our expatriate lives and snowy Moscow far behind. I work in television now, for *Dateline NBC*. I tried continuing with the photojournalism once I got back to the States, even went up to New Hampshire to cover the primaries, but my heart was no longer in it. I still loved the "photo" part of the equation—the street shooting, taking pictures of my friends, hanging out for hours in the darkroom—but the "journalism" side, the one that paid, was no longer appealing: the political rally grip-and-grins, the random portrait assignments from *Newsweek*, the daily attempts to find visually compelling, marketable stories that did not involve danger, guns, violence, war, drugs or even extended trips away from Paul.

So when Paul decided he wanted to go to film school, and the task of supporting us fell on my shoulders, I unceremoniously sold off my beat-up Nikons (not the Leica, never the Leica) to a used-camera shop and took what I thought was a very safe and impressive-sounding senior production associate job at ABC News's *Day One*. This led to an associate producer position at *Dateline*. Which, ironically, led to this bus trip across the Dominican Republic to the Haitian border, where an armed conflict threatens to erupt.

President Clinton has just announced he will send fifteen thousand American soldiers into Haiti to restore order, which basically means he's finally decided to oust Raoul Cedras and pave the way for Jean-Bertrand Aristide's return. It also means no commercial flights are allowed to land in Port-au-Prince, so a group of us from the various NBC news shows (*Today, Nightly News, Dateline*) chartered this bus in Santo Domingo, where we all arrived by plane—some late last night, others, like me, in the wee hours of the morning. Boarding the bus with everyone before dawn, I felt like a kid setting off on a school field trip, except instead of bologna sandwiches, Fritos and room-temperature milk cartons, our specially catered boxed lunches contain gourmet chicken salad, individually wrapped blondies and big bottles of cold Evian.

"No way we'd have all this food if Tom and Bryant weren't here," one of my colleagues whispers to me. Her name—weirdly enough—is Pascale. *Plus ça change, plus c'est la meme chose.*

Pascale's got a point about the food, but I'm more impressed by the fact that we're riding a chartered bus to cover an insurrection. "Here, have mine," I say, handing her my lunch. "I'm too nauseous to even look at it."

To pass the time and to concentrate on something other than my gurgling stomach, I start flipping through the black loose-leaf notebook I was handed as I sped out of the *Dateline* offices. The notebook's filled with recent wire stories and press clippings about the current situation, meticulously prepared by some poor, overqualified, Ivy-educated underling. It's collated. Highlighted. Striated with yellow dividers and anal-retentively labeled tabs: "CLINTON: statement 9/1/94," "CEDRAS: reply," "ARISTIDE: *NYTimes* article," "POLITICAL OVERVIEW: *Time* mag." As I perfunctorily thumb my way through it, not really attending to the meaning of the words, my mind wanders back to the crumpled mess of ripped, espresso-stained Afghan war clippings I shoved in my camera bag before heading on a plane to Peshawar to meet that other Pascal, the mean one. The memory of that trip, though painful, now makes me smile.

Like Afghanistan, Haiti is one of those countries whose political upheavals and murderous atrocities I've never been able to keep straight. In fact, the real reason I'm on this bus to Haiti is because I speak fluent French, not because of my expertise on the Duvaliers or the troubled history of the island. Plus my boss, Neal Shapiro, the executive producer of *Dateline* and a decent, good man, was desperate and asked nicely. Plus I knew Pascale would be going, and she's pleasant company as well as half Haitian. Plus I'm one of the few journalists on staff with actual war experience.

Because of the extremely hierarchical structure of a typical newsmagazine show, most television journalists do not begin their careers doing what most people would consider actual journalism. Instead, a majority of them go straight from college into jobs with such diverse titles as "desk assistant," "production secretary," "production associate," or "assistant producer," which all mean, essentially, professional photocopier, coffee fetcher, phone answerer, tape logger, correspondent hand holder, archive-footage searcher, flight and hotel-room booker and punching bag/blame taker if a story doesn't make it to air on time. When I started at ABC, I was shocked by the amount of drudgery I was expected to perform. At the end of some days, my hand would ache from spending eight, nine, even ten hours scribbling—we had no computers—such inanities as "01:02:35: wide shot of tornado. 01:02:47: medium shot of tornado. 01:03:04: close-up, windshield wipers."

The four years I'd spent as a professional photojournalist counted for nothing. Even worse, since the world of television journalism is all about paying your dues, those four years I'd spent not fetching coffee, not logging tapes and not making copies were seen as wasted time.

I'd had such high hopes for my new job. It had a salary. A cubicle with file drawers, an engraved nameplate and an earnest outgoing voice mail message linking my name with that of ABC News. The potential to do good journalism with a plush safety net of cash, collaborators and state-of-the-art equipment. Elevator rides with Barbara Walters. But most of the time I hated it. It wasn't journalism so much as indentured servitude, each day slowly melting into the next in a foggy haze of phone calls, busy work and ass kissing. Even the field work tended to be boring. Because of the lights and equipment, each interview required two hours of setup time. Then there was the b-roll, which most of the time consisted of telling Mr. Expert on Train Safety or Ms. Expert on Chinese Diplomacy to look busy at their computers, or to make a phone call, or to walk gracefully, and without looking at the camera, through a train yard or down a picturesque college campus path, while your cameraman complained that if he didn't have lunch soon, you'd be in violation of union rules. *Yes, yes, we'll break for lunch right after this shot. Okay, Ms. Expert, I know you have a class to teach, but could you please go back to that brick building and walk toward us once again? And this time, could you swing your left arm a little more vigorously?*

To be fair, there were a few good things about that job at ABC. Working with lazy producers meant getting to produce stories by myself. I met Al Gore. I traveled to China. I was able to work closely with John Hockenberry, a smart correspondent—normally an oxymoron—and an old friend of mine from our days covering the *intifadah*. The editing room process pleased me to no end, and a story I had a large hand in cutting about an Amtrak train crash won an Emmy. But these highs were scattered amongst so much tedium, they were hard to appreciate.

I missed photography. I missed the immediacy and instant gratification of a picture well taken. I missed my blue jeans and not having to wear grown-up clothes every day and the blissful solitude. I missed my freedom and the darkroom and the adrenaline and the adventure. I missed cataloging, compressing and translating the world inside a perfectly composed rectangle.

On the other hand, I didn't miss the danger. Or the uncertainty. Or the periodic poverty. Back then, as a senior production associate, my $32,000 a year income was moderate (for New York City, that is) and steady. It paid for our small one-bedroom apartment, for Paul's NYU film school classes and for the opportunity for us to lead a relatively safe, conventional, normal life together. And being safe, conventional and normal, after everything we'd lived through, was all that really mattered.

Which, in a roundabout way, is the real reason I agreed to go to Haiti. *Dateline* hired me away from ABC at the beginning of 1994 to produce stories for them, with a caveat: I'd be what *Dateline* management jovially—and covertly—refer to as a "cusper," an associate producer who produces. The world of the cusper is a nebulous production neverland wherein I rarely have to log someone else's tapes or fetch his coffee, but I still get paid as if I do. Where I'm responsible for producing my own stories, yet often do not have the luxury of an assistant. Where when I hand over my business card after interviewing people such as congressmen, CEOs, college professors and celebrities, they balk, look down their noses and say, "Well if you're the AP, who's producing the story?" Where macho cameramen, the kind who brag about covering the Gulf War even though the closest they've ever come to conflict was when they argued over pool positions during hotel press briefings in Dahrain, will ask me with mock deference what shots I need and then shoot the exact opposite. Where one of the correspondents I produce stories for will talk to me in the tone she reserves for children, her housekeeper and people with Down's syndrome because she assumes I don't know what I'm doing and will therefore compose irrelevant questions for her, write her a bad script and/or make her look fat.

So when Neal asked me to go to Haiti, I knew if I said yes, I'd be showing the kind of unquestioning loyalty that inspires speedy promotions. Which, for lack of a more noble career objective, is what I'm after.

At the tender age of twenty-eight, I've become an unapologetic pragmatist. Simply put, Paul and I want to make babies. We want to make babies so badly it's all we can talk about lately. We love each other. We've done the run-off-and-see-the-world adventure thing. We've witnessed death up close (too closely, perhaps), and we are both aware (too aware, perhaps) of our own mortality. We're ready to give, to relinquish a bit of our selfishness. We're curious to see what our babies will look like. We're becoming more domesticated—staying home more often, nesting. We think we'd make good parents, and we want to be young enough to enjoy our kids, see them grow up, get married, have babies of their own. Then there's the whole Holocaust thing. As far as our reasoning goes, two Jews who get married have a moral responsibility to populate the world with more Jews. Add on top of that the fact that Paul has no blood relatives save his twin brother and that I've started to weep at both the sight of frolicking children and cotton commercials, and, well, it's time. Parenthood beckons.

But a baby, we know, requires more than just mental preparedness on the part of its parents and a promise of undying love. A baby will require money. And time. This is where things will get tricky for us. Paul is still finding his employment footing—he's now working on a documentary for ABC and earning very little—and I'm being underpaid with an AP salary for the job I'm actually doing, which is producing high-quality, well-researched and extremely lucrative stories for NBC News. I know if I could just earn that silly producer title, my now $65,000 salary would increase by at least 33 percent. More important, although there's no precedent at *Dateline* yet for part-time producer work, I hear that at ABC's *20/20*, they've started to allow producers to job share. Which would mean, if I could petition NBC to do the same for me (i.e., a 33 percent salary increase for the title minus a 33 percent salary decrease for lopping off a day or two of work), I could spend time with *and* afford to house, clothe, educate and feed a small critter or two in an expensive city like Manhattan, the first place I've ever lived that feels like home.

Okay, so perhaps a trip to Haiti at this fragile juncture in her history is an odd way of achieving this goal, but the logic is all there: go to Haiti, get promoted, have baby, work part-time, find perfect work/family balance, be happy. Simple. Besides, I work in television now. I'm not actually expected to go out and record violence and bloodshed up close. Even if all hell breaks loose, I'll most likely be booking interviews, writing scripts and feeding tape from satellite trucks while the cameramen are out there risking their macho little butts.

Then again, you never know. A lot of weird stuff has happened since Paul and I left Moscow, despite our attempts at "normalcy." On our way back through Paris, the entire stairwell and first floor of the narrow, five-story apartment building we were staying in caught fire in the middle of the night, stranding us to luck and near-fatal levels of smoke inhalation on the top floor while the *pompiers* in the street below yelled at us to stop screaming, close the windows and stay calm.

Then there was the whole Dima and Anton fiasco. When we finally made it to New York at the beginning of 1992, Dima and Anton, two beefy, thick-necked Russian actors whose portraits I'd shot in Moscow on assignment for *L'Express,* showed up on our Upper West Side doorstep and asked Paul and me to help them find jobs working in gyms. What we didn't realize back in Moscow, when the two actors politely called and asked us to help them get tourist visas to the U.S., was that the director of their film, Pavel Loungine, often chose his actors according to how closely their real lives intersected with their roles. Loungine's film, *Luna Park,* was about the Russian mob. In it, Dima and Anton played bodybuilding mobster thugs, because they were, in fact, bodybuilding mobster thugs. And the reason they wanted to work in a gym was that they'd smuggled an entire trash bag filled with illegal steroids into the U.S., which they hoped to sell to muscle-worshiping Americans for a tidy hard-currency profit. Unfortunately, Anton was also using some of the stash himself, which led to violent outbursts like the one that prompted him to drag Dima under the boardwalk in Brighton Beach and stab him eight times in the heart.

Dima survived the stabbing, if barely, and while drifting in and out of consciousness he gave the police our names and numbers as his only contacts in America. We wound up spending the next two days either in the Brighton Beach police precinct answering questions or wearing flak jackets up in Spanish Harlem to help the cops look for Anton or in the hospital where Dima lay recovering but in critical condition, helping to sort the whole mess out. In retrospect, the NYPD abused our cooperation. They sent Paul as unarmed bait up the stairs of Anton's rooming house, while they followed at a safe distance behind him with their guns drawn. Then they arrested Anton in front of Paul, made him realize that Paul had betrayed him. They also made Paul translate and recite to Anton his Miranda rights once they booked him, because the one—one!—cop on duty in Brighton Beach who was supposedly fluent in Russian couldn't get beyond *"Kak vas zavoot?"* ("What is your name?")

Anton was eventually sentenced to seven years in jail for aggravated assault and battery. A few months after his incarceration, he started sending us menacing letters from an upstate New York prison with cartoons of himself toting multiple assault rifles and dressed like Arnold Schwarzenegger in *The Terminator,* replete with thought bubbles coming out of his head that read, "I'll be back." The police assured us that Anton would be deported to Russia after he got out, but they could not promise us that once he got there he wouldn't just immediately turn around, take the next flight back to New York and seek his revenge.

Then there was Serge, Paul's former partner from his Russian business days in Paris. Philippe, Paul's other partner, had recently flown into New York to meet privately with us. He told us that he was now fairly certain that Serge had surreptitiously started buying and dealing Ukrainian arms during the time the three of them had worked together, that he had perhaps stepped on many toes he shouldn't have. There were rumors about a contract on Serge's life. Philippe urged us to be cautious because of the earlier business alliance. After that meeting with Philippe, any time we heard Russian spoken on the streets of New York, especially behind us, especially the crude, cursing Russian of would-be thugs, we'd panic.

Indeed, in a year's time, Serge would be killed by an assassin's bullet through the glass door of his new apartment on the Avenue Foche in Paris. His murder would be the first confirmed Russian mafia hit on French soil.

Then there was the winter after we got married when ABC sent me to Moscow. I was going back there to collaborate on a couple of stories, one about the decrepit Russian space program, the other about a newly popular Jew-hating fascist named Vladimir Zhirinovsky. Our team's fixer, who oddly enough had gone to kindergarten with Paul, agreed to help me locate Paul's biological father, Pavel, during the few hours of downtime I had before my scheduled flight back to New York. Now that Paul and I were officially married and thinking about children, I had a vested interest in checking out the roots of the family tree. But even more important, as Paul was helping me in the cab the day I left for Moscow, he'd suddenly said, "Find my dad."

Though Paul had lost the scrap of paper with his father's phone number on it, Pavel Senior was not hard to track down. Russia may no longer have been communist, but Moscow still had enough of an apartment shortage to keep most people put. I just went to the same complex of buildings on the Ulitsa Krasnaya Armayskaya where we'd stumbled upon his anti-Semitic grandmother back in '91 and asked around. "I was only twenty-five. A boy. So stupid. We all make mistakes," the poor, shocked man lamented through glistening eyes, sitting with me at his kitchen table, sucking on a cigarette and gulping down yet another stiff shot of vodka. He promised to write to his son, to explain the inexplicable as best he could. My fixer took a few souvenir snapshots of the two of us together to show Paul. Then I left for Sheremetevo Airport, never to return.

You know, just your standard weird stuff. The kind of stuff that makes you crave a normal life. And while I do not exactly know what a "normal" life is, I definitely know what it is not. It is not a life riddled with near-death experiences. Or a life where a thug who knows where you live stabs his best friend and brings you down with him and sends you threatening letters from an upstate New York prison. Or a life where your ex-colleague gets murdered by the mob. Or a life where fathers don't stick around to love and take care of their children.

THE BUS FINALLY ARRIVES at the Haitian border, a dusty, middle-of-nowhere strip of land bifurcated by a simple chain-link fence and guarded by armed border police. Today, the fence is alive, crawling with anxious, cursing journalists trying to connive, sneak or force their way past it. Jack, the *Today* show unit manager, whose role seems to be that of our cruise director, runs off with our passports, paperwork and manifests to present to whichever armed man looks to be the most in charge. Pascale volunteers to accompany him and help with translation. "Shit. How do you say 'manifest' in French? Or 'bat phone'?" she asks me.

I don't know what a bat phone is in English, let alone French, and my nausea is peaking. *"Le téléphone bat?"* I say. "I have no idea. Just wing it." Then I exit the bus, clutching my stomach. I manage to make it twenty yards before retching. I'm definitely sick, no doubt about it. Then again, I'm not too concerned. Ever since the dysentery in Afghanistan, my stomach has never been the same. Especially when I travel.

If only it were morning sickness. Paul and I have been actively trying to get pregnant for the past six months, but just before I left I took yet another one of those E.P.T. home pregnancy tests, and, once again, the magic red line never materialized. Which means I should be getting my period, which is now five days late, any minute. Which means, if history's any indication, I'll start bleeding right here in the middle of nowhere.

I'm wiping off my mouth with a tissue when I feel a hand grabbing my shoulder from behind. "Come with me, young lady. You're under arrest." The hand and the German-accented voice (*Nazi!*), whispered into my left ear from behind, startles me. Makes me shriek and jump, even, but then I turn around and see my old friend Klaus, a photojournalist colleague from my Moscow days. He's wearing the usual costume. Photographer's vest. Two Canon EOS cameras, now the de rigueur camera for all photojournalists. Dirty clothes. Benignly devilish smile.

"Klaus, what the fuck! You scared the shit out of me." I can feel my heart pumping at double speed in my chest.

Klaus is bent over, laughing. "I know, I know," he says, catching his breath. "I saw you standing there and couldn't resist. Anyway, are you sick? What are you doing here? Where are your cameras?"

I take a deep breath and compose myself. "I'm fine, working, and I sold them," I say. Around my neck, where my cameras used to hang, is a fancy, laminated press pass dangling on a long silver chain, the kind TV producers collect and string from thumbtacks on their office bulletin boards to show how cool they are. Klaus reaches out to grab it with a quizzical, almost sad expression on his face. "Ooh, 'NBC News in Haiti,' " he says, reading the press pass. "Such pretty colors. How impressive."

"That's nothing. Wait until you get a load of our air-conditioned bus."

Klaus laughs. "So you've gone over to the other side," he says with a smirk. "Expense accounts. Drivers. Blow-dried correspondents . . ." Photojournalists and TV producers have always had a friendly, mocking rivalry. Photojournalists pity the producers' reliance on others, their need to work in teams of three or more, their cumbersome equipment, their inability to really live and breathe the story. But they also envy the producers' muscle, their access, their infrastructure and their abundant resources. TV producers, logically enough, pity the photojournalists for their need to cram together into hotel rooms or even camp out in their rental cars to save money. They pity the financial and emotional burden of never knowing whether a photograph taken, especially a photograph shot in a dicey situation, will ever help pay for the photographer's trip or even see the light of day. But producers envy—really and truly envy—the whole photojournalist-as-cowboy thing. They envy the photographers' freedom to move around where they want when they want and with whomever they choose. They envy the way a photojournalist's end product, a still photograph, is the sole vision of a single, curious mind.

As for me, having now been on both sides of the visual journalism divide, I no longer envy either one. Though I miss photography more than I'd ever miss television if I quit, I think the aspects that are enviable about each profession are outweighed by the pitiable ones. Having the name, power and money of network news means very little to me when the end product, be it a five-minute story or a fifteen-minute story, is so often diluted, sensationalized and mediocre—not to mention fleeting—by the time it airs. And who cares about running around the globe making "art" if part of what makes the art great is being a scrappy, reckless loner with no permanent ties or responsibilities to any other human being?

If I were to envy anyone in the profession of information gathering, it would be the newspaper reporters. They usually know the native language of and live in or near the places about which they write. In the field, they carry nothing more taxing than notebooks and pens, and they have the freedom of movement that working alone provides. Their expenses are paid, they're not constantly changing reality by sticking cameras in their subjects' faces, and their idea of "getting close to a story"—as Julian once explained to me way back when in Harare—doesn't mean placing themselves in the middle of the crossfire to get a good shot. Their idea of getting close to a story means standing back. It means examining the big picture, figuring out the larger implications before dealing with the specifics. It means reporting and understanding the story well enough to write it.

But that's only *if* I were to envy anyone out here today. Actually, at this very moment, the only people I really envy are the men and women I see in my Upper West Side neighborhood, the ones gliding up and down Broadway every evening pushing grocery-laden strollers or carrying tiny infants in those new, navy-blue Swedish baby carriers with the little anchor appliqués. The ones walking their cherubs to school in the morning before heading off to their own places of work, or strolling *en famille* on the weekends to check out the dinosaurs at the Museum of Natural History. And I want to know what kind of jobs these men and women have that allow them to live comfortably and happily without always having to jump on a plane at a moment's notice to fly away to politically unstable places like Haiti. I want to know how they pay for their mortgages, their baby-sitters, their tuitions and all of those grocery, clothing and pediatrician bills while still having time to push their kids on the swings. I want to know if they even *like* these jobs, and if so, I want to know how I can sign up for the same kind of balanced life. Assuming, of course, that I can actually get pregnant.

Put simply, I want the life my mother's generation of women were, for the most part, denied. Paul and I have discussed it in detail. We've decided that when we have kids, at least one of us will need to have a flexible work schedule. Since I want to be the one with such a schedule, and Paul doesn't, the choice is easy. I'll work part-time, he'll work full. Shouldn't be too hard, right?

Klaus and I catch up. I tell him about moving back to the States, about the soul searching that made me quit photojournalism, about the desire to lead a simpler, more mainstream existence. He nods and says a lot of uh-huh's, as if he understands, but I can tell by his eyes that he thinks I've gone bonkers. "Well, at least come say hi to all of your old pals. We missed you in Bosnia," Klaus says, leading me over to a shady spot where all the usual camera-toting news junkies are standing around in their regulation circle, comparing equipment, shooting the shit and smoking.

"Yeah, sounds like it was a real party," I say.

When the other photographers notice me approaching, they gasp. As if I had died. As if I'd come back as a ghost.

Then slowly, one by one, they embrace me and offer their very real, very warm greetings. Much warmer, in fact, than when we used to all work together.

"*Salut!*"

"How the hell are you?"

"*Comment ça va?*"

"You haven't changed a bit."

Now it's Alain's turn. "*C'est pas vrai!*"—"Say it isn't so!"—he says, hugging me and kissing me on both cheeks. Alain is one of the few Gamma photographers whose company I really enjoyed during my tenure there. Then again, he came to France from Vietnam, I came from America, and this bonded us as confreres more than anything else in a country like France, where xenophobia is as woven into the fabric of the nation as foie gras. Alain also has the distinction of being one of the last people to see Gad alive. After hearing the gunshots that ripped through Gad's body, Alain and a *Village Voice* reporter hid out in a ditch for as long as they could. Eventually, they were captured and interrogated by Iraqi soldiers.

But Alain doesn't like to talk about that.

"*C'est vrai,*" I say, smiling. "How are you?"

"Fine, fine," he says, pulling out his pack of Marlboros and offering me one.

"No, thanks," I say, "I quit." An awkward silence descends. It's clear from Alain's body language that the mere act of saying "I quit" has constructed a waist-high wall between us. I enjoyed smoking, in the same way I enjoyed shooting pictures in nutty places, but I can't justify doing either one if I'm committed to having a baby.

"You quit, huh," he says. "So what are you doing here anyway? We'd heard you'd quit photography, too. Had a kid. Went back to America to change diapers."

A few dirt-kicking, bent-chin snickers erupt from the all-male group, and I feel my cheeks turning crimson. My former colleagues, some of whom I'd considered friends, are clearly making fun of me. Laughing at my expense.

"You heard wrong," I say. I am annoyed at the implication. Never mind the truth, that I'd gone back to America and started an entirely new career. So what if I'd gone back to have a couple of babies instead? Would that have been so horrible? I see what photojournalism did to a friend and mentor back in Paris, one of the few older women I know who still works in the field. I understand the steep price she paid because I was there at her dinner table on the day she turned forty, when she announced with brimming eyes that she'd had dozens of important exhibitions and awards but no children.

I see the middle-aged single women who work in my new profession, the often angry and sad ones who were born late enough to reap the early benefits of feminism but not late enough to give up on the whole notion of pretending to be a man in order to succeed. These women have offices crammed with Emmys, but homes with rooms barren of possessions and memories save their own.

I see the one successful female producer I know of that generation who actually did manage to spawn a few kids between Emmys. I see the way she prides herself not only on having returned to her job within days of her first child's birth but on having covered a war when she was eight months pregnant with her third. I do not wish to begrudge any woman her choices, especially the pioneers, but neither of these two feats strikes me, personally, as particularly prudent. Yes, I know men return to work within days of their children's births, but men don't have lactating breasts or post-partum recovery issues such as uteruses hanging out of their vaginas. And yes, male journalists cover wars no matter the gestational age of their fetuses, but men don't have to carry those fetuses around in their bellies or protect them from whizzing bullets.

While all of this seems obvious to me, I know it is only my opinion, based on nothing more scientific than my gut. It is also my opinion—and a bizarrely unpopular one, at that—that, be they male or female, journalists with children should not cover wars. Then again, I also don't think they should skydive or shoot heroin or drive without seat belts. Or climb mountains off of which they might fall. A parent dying under such circumstances could really fuck up a kid but good: make him angry, provoke him to act out in ways he shouldn't. Like grabbing a telephone receiver and smashing it into his lover's head.

If such opinions make me a bad journalist and a bad feminist, so be it.

As the assembled group of photographers continue to laugh at Alain's diaper joke, my first cowardly impulse is to say something like "Diapers? Me? Yeah, right," just to fit in, to turn the teasing around. Instead, in a moment of sudden clarity, I ignore the men and their smug laughs and stare directly into Alain's eyes. "I'm not a mother yet," I say, "but if everything works out the way I'd like it to, I will be soon. And then I guess I'll just have to figure out what sort of work I'm able to do afterwards."

The photographers stop laughing. A few even look ashamed, but the invisible wall between us is now firmly cemented, and I'm standing all alone on one side of it. Clearly, I'm out of the fraternity. But it's a club whose membership I suddenly no longer desire.

How many times did I curse my body? How many times did I ponder how much easier my life would have been had I just been born with a Y chromosome instead of an extra X? How many times did I regret the enormous trouble my body caused me, the way it bled and attracted assaults and made me an easy target for any man with a gripe and a will to act upon it? How many times did I wish my body weren't curvy? Or small and weak and useless as a weapon of self-defense?

What an ingrate I was. What a unique gift to have a body that can serve as the vessel of a future life. What a stroke of good design to have breasts that will sustain it. What an important responsibility to be cast as the keeper of the flame instead of the igniter of fires. What ecstasy to feel such a deep, ferocious, overwhelming primal urge, not only to love and to pro-create, but to nurture.

What the hell am I doing here?

The silence that has befallen us all feels uncomfortable. I break it with a "Well, okay, I guess I better get back to my bus," and then the men and I pose for a few pictures with our arms around each other as if we'd actually see one another again to trade snapshots.

An hour later, the photojournalists have all made it across the border. (They always do.) But the only good pictures that will come out of this trip will be taken by a Magnum photographer named Alex Webb, who's famous for his stunning, color-saturated, semiabstract images of Haiti. The pictures he produces on this trip for *The New York Times Magazine,* however, will lean more toward social commentary than art, and their biting irreverence will cause enormous controversy, even vitriol in the photojournalist community, especially amongst those photographers unable to take a joke at their own expense. My personal favorite is a shot of the American troops landing in Port-au-Prince. It's one of those curtain-yanking images that pulls back to show the lights and the wires and the stagehands. In it, struggling against the wind and dust whipped up by the landing helicopters, a massive swarm of photojournalists—one of them with his pants falling off—are all jockeying for position, their cameras poised and ready. Directly in front of them is a massive swarm of soldiers lying prone on their bellies, their guns also poised and ready. But far less convincingly so.

As for us TV people, who are hoping to shoot some good patriotic theater of our own, crossing into Haiti will be more problematic. I can tell by Pascale's downtrodden look that she and John have had no luck getting us and our many tons of equipment over the border. John announces that some of our group, a random assortment of producers and correspondents from the *Today* show and *Nightly News,* will be allowed inside Haiti. Others, whose faxed list of names arrived too late, will have to return with the bus to Santo Domingo. My name is on that list.

Never mind that the following day, Jimmy Carter will broker a peace accord with Cedras, rendering any fears I may have had of getting killed moot, not to mention ruining the story for anyone covering it with a lens instead of a pen. (Except for Alex, of course, but he's a genius.) After throwing up one more time before boarding the bus, I decide that even if our paperwork manages to get through, I'm taking the next plane back to

New York, my career and promotion be damned. My body's message is clear and succinct: get thee to bed.

The bus starts to roll, heading back in the direction from which it came, away from the Haitian border. Pascale, who was looking forward to her first armed conflict, is staring glumly out the window. "Cheer up," I tell her. I know how she's feeling. I can still remember the way I felt when I was left behind by that other Pascal back in Peshawar. How I was desperate to see a war. Any war. How I wanted to inhale that drug, to let it run through my veins and wake me up to what was real. How I wanted to prove I could do it, to myself and to others: *Oh, yes, well, that reminds me of the time I was with the rebels in Afghanistan* . . . But now, six years later, I'm barely able to conceal my glee at the thought of returning home to my cozy apartment in Manhattan.

"Maybe you'll make it inside tomorrow," I tell Pascale. "Or the day after that. And if not, hey, there'll always be another war."

"WE'LL BE ABLE TO TELL if the amoebas are back after we see the results of the lab work, but before I prescribe any of the strong stuff, is there any chance you're pregnant?"

I'm sitting in a gastroenterologist's office on the Upper East Side three days after getting back from the Haitian border. My stomach has gotten worse. I have not been able to hold down any food for days now, and this along with the diarrhea has made me extremely weak and dizzy, to the point where Paul had to literally carry me into a taxi to get me here. "I can't believe you made it out of Afghanistan in this condition," he'd said, as I lay my head on his lap in the backseat of the cab.

"Yeah, well, different time, different place, different body," I'd replied, suddenly grateful to be riding in a warm car with my cheek pressed against my husband's thigh instead of cold and all alone on the back of a donkey.

I tell the doctor that we've been unsuccessfully trying to get pregnant. That even though my period is now over a week late, I'd taken yet another home pregnancy test just this morning and it, too, had come out negative.

"Yeah, well, I never trust those things, especially if you're only a week late." She orders another blood test, and the next day she calls me at home, where I'm still lying in bed, to tell me I have a nasty case of gastroenteritis, but that I can't take any medicine for it because I'm five weeks pregnant.

"What!"

"You're pregnant," she says. "Congratulations."

I cry for a very long time. Then I call Paul at work, and he cries. Then I cry again and drag my vomiting, weak and fluxing body over to Barnes & Noble to buy *What to Expect When You're Expecting.* Just like any normal expectant mother might do.

Then, on my way home from the bookstore, I have a peculiar thought. Or perhaps not so peculiar, on account of the pea-sized miracle now growing inside me. I'm walking up Broadway, on a brilliant, crisp fall day with bright yellow leaves swirling in tiny sidewalk tornadoes, and I'm thinking: Maybe there really is a god. Maybe all that barfing on the road to Haiti was a deliberate sign from my unborn child, some higher power's delicate way of saying *go home.* Maybe the signs are all around us—from the missed plane that crashes to the opening of a tulip, from the murder of a beloved friend in Iraq to the helpful person who finds you sprawled unconscious in Harvard Square and carries you to safety—but we're all just too ignorant, proud and foolish to read them.

I've doubted the existence of a god for so long now, ever since that day I had to swallow and digest Auschwitz. But what if even the Holocaust was meant as a sign? A terrible, incomprehensible and unbearable reminder to all of us who were spared of how precious and precarious our time here is. What if the fact of the concentration camps is the only way of proving to us, by means of comparison, that we are not tattooed numbers but people, each one unique, with a name and a story to tell? That our lives, in all of their frequently mundane, often arduous, and sometimes grossly unfair glory, are worth living.

In fact, who am I to say God—or whatever you want to call something greater than us, beyond our pitiful comprehension—doesn't exist? Even Albert Einstein, that genius of all things quantifiable, could not abide by atheism. I suppose the closer he came to figuring out all of the how's in the universe, the more urgently the why's cried out for answers.

At the end of that November, back in Potomac for Thanksgiving, I decide to attend my ten-year high school reunion. I'm three months pregnant now, hardly showing but finally able to tell people the news. I run into Ellen, the girlfriend who'd helped me memorize fifty digits past the decimal point of *pi* back in second grade, back when we were wandering through the hallways and petals of our flower-shaped elementary school, fidgety, eager for information and mind-numbingly bored. She's a doctor, she tells me, happy with the way her life worked out. "Me, too," I say, and then, after giving her a brief synopsis (job, marriage, pregnancy), I suddenly stop and with a mischievous smile say, "So, Ellen, can you still do it? Can you still remember it?" I begin my recitation. "Three point one four one five nine . . ."

Ellen starts to laugh. "Two six five, three five eight, nine seven nine . . ." She wrinkles her nose. "I can't remember the rest."

I rack my brain. "Three two three, I think it was. Three two three and then, well, it all kinda goes fuzzy."

"Yeah, well, we're getting old," she says, still laughing. "Only *pi* goes on infinitely. But you're right. Definitely three two three." She stares down at my stomach. "Teach it to your kid, you'll remember it again."

I smile. A memory flashes into my head, an image of Ellen and me standing in the playground at school. Her hair is in pigtails. We're young, maybe six or seven years old at most, and we're holding hands. She's wearing a striped shirt, red and blue, I think. Her mother has just died. A heart attack, as I recall. She is crying. I'm trying to comfort her but can't find the words. "I will," I say. I hug her tightly, my eyes starting to water. "I promise I will."

Later, as I'm pointing people out to Paul, as the band is playing "Stairway to Heaven," Gabe, my first love, almost father to my almost child, walks over with some of his friends to hug me. It has been nine years since we've last seen each other, nine years since I took a trip down to his college in Louisiana to see if we could make it work again between us. After a bit of mindless chitchat, after introducing him and the others to Paul, I tell him the news. "I'm pregnant," I say.

Gabe takes in the information, smiles. Puts his hand to his heart then touches it to my belly. "Oh, Debs," he says, "that's so great. I'm so happy for you."

The tempo of the music quickens, something about a "bustle in your hedgerow." What the hell does that mean? "Yeah," I say, "I'm so happy for me, too."

THE CALL COMES EARLY one morning, a few weeks later, on a cold December day. Paul and I are lying in bed, snuggled warmly underneath the covers, watching the ice chunks flow down the Hudson River. To pick up the receiver, he has to take his hand away from my now sixteen-week swollen belly, which he's been gently and proprietarily rubbing. "Do you feel the baby moving around inside you yet?" he asks, reaching for the phone.

"No, not yet," I say. "Who's calling so early?"

Paul picks up the phone. Says hello and then after a pause says "No!" with such softness and pain, I can tell somebody has died. Then he hangs up, sits on the edge of the bed, and starts to cry.

"Who was that?" I ask. I touch his shoulder, but he recoils.

"Andy's brother," he says. "Andy killed himself last night."

We spend the rest of morning in our robes, wandering around our living room, staring blankly out at the ice chunks, reminiscing about our friend and former roommate from Moscow—*Remember when he came home with that bloody nose? Remember when he was building the barricades during the coup? Remember his laugh?* Trying in vain not to conjure up the image of him walking down the steps to his parents' basement, sticking a gun to his head and pulling the trigger.

We'd been feeling optimistic about Andy lately. He'd recently moved back from Moscow to finally get on with his life. He'd found a job with a bank. A respectable suit-and-tie job in midtown Manhattan. He was looking for his own apartment. He made vague promises about giving up the drinking. He was desperate for renewal, he said, for a second chance to prove himself a capable, responsible, trustworthy man.

He lasted at his spiffy, new job less than a month before blowing his brains out.

Paul is pacing around the living room, mumbling, trying to make sense of it all. "I just saw him last week. . . . He was acting so strange . . . drinking again, telling me he loved me, saying bizarre things . . ." He stops in his tracks. "Oh, Jesus. Debs, I think he was saying good-bye." He puts his head on my shoulder and leaves it there, shuddering, for a very long time.

At the funeral a few days later, while staring at Andy's embalmed, serene face, at the shell that used to be our friend lying completely inert in a satin-lined coffin, I feel in my womb the first internal flutterings of the life that will become my son, Jacob.

The signs are everywhere, if you just pay attention.

•

IT IS A FRIDAY AFTERNOON, sometime after five. I'm sitting in my windowless closet of an office at *Dateline,* finishing up some work. I am seven months pregnant with my second child, a daughter, and I am tired. My ankles are swollen. Jacob, my now nineteen-month-old son, is at home with Dolly, his baby-sitter, our savior. This morning, when I promised him that after I got back from work we could light some candles together, he looked up at me as if he actually understood what I was proposing. Light. Calm. The comfort of an ancient ritual, of a mother's presence. It's been a long week for both of us, deserving of candles, with a fruitless two-day business trip to Boston thrown in for good measure.

I turn off my computer and put on my coat, feeling that phantom piece of rope tied between Jacob's chubby wrist and my rib cage growing taut. I'm halfway out the door when my phone rings. It's Jim, the senior producer in charge of assignments. "Don't hate me," he says, his voice appropriately apologetic. "I need you to crash a story for Tuesday."

Shit. So much for candles. "On what?" I ask, with more than a just a slight snap to my tone. Poor Jacob. Poor unborn baby. Poor family.

He pauses. "Tall women."

Now, incredulous, I pause. "*Tall women?!* You've got to be joking."

"No, I'm not."

But wait. I've gotten ahead of myself.

JACOB PAVLOVICH KOGAN was born on a balmy spring day in May 1995 after eighteen hours of labor. Toward the end of the third hour of pushing, when the epidural had worn off and things were looking kind of static and grim, I grabbed Paul by the collar and told him if he didn't eject the fucking "Goldberg Variations" from the CD player and throw on Abba's *Gold: Greatest Hits* instead, the goddamned baby would never come out. Tiny Jacob was finally able to extricate himself from the birth canal in the middle of "Fernando," much to the delight of our nurses, who tried to convince us to name him accordingly. As if birth to Swedish disco weren't bad enough.

Motherhood quickly engulfed me. Jacob had reflux for the first six months of his life, which meant his stomach and esophagus were in con-

stant, burning pain, he cried nonstop, he projectile vomited on every carpet and piece of upholstered furniture in our apartment, he had to swallow
and keep down four servings of Mylanta a day, he could never breast-feed
for more than five minutes at a time and he had to be held upright, even to
sleep, twenty-four hours a day. Which can get pretty tricky. But if I danced
with him with just the right amount of sway to "Son of a Preacher Man,"
or took him on a two-mile walk in the now barf-covered navy-blue Scandi-
navian baby carrier with the cute little anchor appliqué, or threw him over
my shoulder and sang a rousing version of any minor-key song—the Israeli national anthem worked best—or if I just held him close enough and
tight enough and whispered, "It's okay, little duck, it's okay," he'd stop, forget his pain and smile. And when that happened, I could think of nothing
else I'd ever done of equal import. Or any experience or lover or orgasm or
sunset or story or song or substance that had ever, in my entire thrill-
seeking life, made me feel that good.

I took as long a maternity leave as I could. I thought about leaving my
job altogether, even pondered the logistics and seed money I'd need to
start my own baby photography business—which I'd already begun on the
side—but after six months without my steady NBC income, our household
credit card debt was fast approaching the gross national product of some
lesser Third World countries. Paul, meanwhile, was rediscovering his
roots as a computer geek. Though he'd just accepted a job building some
bizarre new thing called a web site, the two of us knew there was no way
we'd be able to survive on his salary alone. Besides, who knew whether this
whole Internet thing would stick anyway? Remember this was 1995. Paul
could be out of a job at a moment's notice.

So I hired Dolly, an angel of a woman from the Philippines, and be-
grudgingly went back to work.

Back at *Dateline,* where I spent the majority of my time missing Jacob
and weeping with my office door closed, I knew I had to figure out a way
to cut back my hours and responsibilities, to trade fewer dollars for more
time at home. Then, two months after my return to work, my then eight-
month-old son was rushed to the hospital with intussusception, a potentially fatal blockage of the intestines. The fourth barium enema Jacob had
to endure, without sedation, cleared the blockage, but timing in intussusception is everything. Had Dolly called me a few hours later than she did
to tell me that my son's diaper was filled with gelatinous blood, I would

have already been on a plane to shoot an interview in D.C. instead of where I needed to be: in the hospital, holding my baby's tiny hand, wiping his tears and praying to whichever god would listen for his survival.

After the ordeal with Jacob, I started earnestly looking into the possibilities of part-time work. Ideally, what I wanted was to be able to work on two or three stories at a time on a three- or four-day-a-week schedule, instead of juggling five stories at a time and having to work not only five days a week, but often nights and weekends just to get everything finished. The all-too-frequent travel was becoming impossible for both me and for Jacob, who in time began crying at the mere sight of my suitcase.

It's not that I didn't want to work. I knew I needed to work, not only to keep us from going bankrupt but also to keep me sane. However, paid work did not, in my mind, have to mean all-consuming work. My gut was telling me that my son and his welfare and the time Paul and I would be able to give him while he was young was equally, if not more, important.

Unfortunately, without that stupid producer title, I was stuck. The NBC brass made it abundantly clear what they thought about associate producers working part-time when they denied the request of one of my female colleagues, another associate producer who gave birth a few weeks after me. She was extremely upset about having to make such an all-or-nothing choice, but she could afford to quit and did. I did not have the same luxury.

Knowing I'd have to suck it up and bide my time, I decided if I couldn't ask for fewer work days, at least I could ask to produce stories that required minimal travel. Unfortunately, I never bargained for the type of pieces this meant I'd be assigned. (Never mind that the travel time and stress were often the same, if not worse in certain cases.) In rapid and increasingly less newsworthy succession, they were as follows: a very boring story about the credit card industry, another very boring story about the credit card industry, a story about wedding dress dry-cleaning scams, a story about a fight that broke out in a sandbox between two toddlers, a story about calming fussy babies, a story about getting your toddler to go to bed. When they tried foisting the picky eaters story on me, I finally rebelled. "Please, no more parenting stories!" I begged. It was hard enough being without my own kid, let alone spending hours upon hours with other people's crying, fussy, sleep-deprived children.

True, I was one of the few producing mommies on the show at the time, but I couldn't help but notice that none of the ample supply of producer daddies was being asked to do stories on topics like picky eaters. And in fact, after I refused to do it, the picky eaters story was passed on to my friend Diana, who was—big surprise—pregnant with her first child.

"I promise. I'll do anything else. Even hurricanes," I said to Jim, desperate to get off the mommy track.

And that's how I finally hit the nadir of my career as a journalist: Tall Women.

"WHAT ABOUT TALL WOMEN?" I ask Jim. I take off my coat, lay it on the back of my chair with the false hope of swiftly retrieving it. I look at my watch and picture Jacob. In thirty minutes or so, if I can reach Paul and tell him he has to *get home now,* my son will be sitting down to a dinner of chicken nuggets and broccoli. Without me. Without candles.

"I'm not sure," he says, laughing. Jim has a gift for turning everything into a joke, even bad news. "But I think it's some zeitgeist thing about how there seem to be a lot of tall female celebrities around now. Call *People.* They'll give you the scoop." I try probing a little deeper, but the only other fact Jim can tell me about my tall women story is that *People* magazine has decided to devote the entire cover of their next issue to the subject. Since *People* and *Dateline* have a new exclusive deal to coproduce stories together, this means that I—all hugely pregnant, swollen, five-two, of me—will have four days to shoot, write and cut a ten-minute spot celebrating everything I am not and do not believe in, not to mention having to live with myself and my feminist guilt afterwards. As if short girls all over America don't already have a thousand other reasons to feel inadequate. "Oh, and it better be good, 'cause Andy'll be watching. He wants these *People* stories to, you know, spice up the show."

Andy is Andy Lack, president of NBC News.

"You mean Andy wants to see tits and ass," I say. I sit down, search around for my notebook and pen. "Tall tits and tall ass." I'm not naïve. I understand a network's need to garner rating points. Each rating point translates into higher ad rates, which, in turn, allows our parent company, GE, to pay all of our salaries, keep us on the air and turn a handsome profit.

Jim, ever the smooth office politician, chokes back a giggle. "Honey, those are your words, not mine."

I turn to a fresh page in my notebook and scribble, *Tall Women.* Then I underline it. Twice. So, I think, it's come to this.

I reach Paul at his office, tell him he needs to get home to relieve the baby-sitter. Then I call Jacob to hear his spunky voice, to tell him I love him and to try to explain to him about the candles. "Sorry, Jakey, we'll light them tomorrow, okay?"

"Okay," he says. Then he starts to cry.

Then I call one of the reporters at *People* to find out her specific angle on the subject of tall women, but she is curt and rushed, in the way even nice people get when it's Friday evening and they just want to go home. "Beats me," she says. "Far as I know, it's just an excuse to put Carolyn Bessette Kennedy on the cover."

Great, I think. There's no way the publicity-shy new Mrs. JFK Junior will ever speak to *People* or to me. Nor, I soon learn, will Brooke Shields or Uma Thurman or Gina Davis or Tyra Banks or any of the other dozen or so tall female celebrities whose PR representatives I am able to reach or leave sheepish messages for that Friday evening (*"Hi, uh, yes, um, I'm calling from* Dateline, *and, uh, we'd like your client to speak with us on the topic of being tall. . . ."*).

The only female celebrity who agrees to do an interview about her tallness on such short notice is Daisy Fuentes, who says she's happy to have the publicity on account of her new calendar, the one with the photographs of her semiclad. So that Monday, with my pregnant belly bulging underneath the tent I'm currently using as a dress, I get to spend the entire morning listening to the long and leggy Revlon model/ex-VJ/actress/calendar pin-up girl rant about the tremendous suffering she endured growing up so horribly tall, thin and beautiful. Then, ignoring my increasingly frequent and uncomfortable Braxton-Hicks contractions, I stay up all night writing the script.

When I arrive home very late the following evening, Jacob is already asleep. The next morning, toddling around in his pajamas, he sulks and ignores me. "Mommy at work," he says, echoing his father. "Mommy no come home."

"Just don't tell him Mommy is crashing a story on tall, naked celebrities so Andy Lack can jack up his Nielsen ratings," I say to Paul, as I rush out the door once again. "It might be hard for any kid to forgive that."

The next day, with Michael Jackson's impending fatherhood dominating the celebrity headlines, *People* decides to shelve their cover story on tall women for a later date. Which means all of the insane hours I spent ignoring my own impending motherhood were for naught.

A few weeks later, now thirty-five weeks pregnant, stressed out and exhausted, I'm putting the finishing touches on yet another similarly insipid, celebrity-driven story assignment when I suddenly go into preterm labor. The story's about the Six Degrees of Kevin Bacon game, which seemed to embarrass Mr. Bacon during his interview as much as it embarrassed me to produce it, but while I'm lying in the maternity ward of New York Hospital, surrounded by worried nurses fluttering about and monitoring my contractions—watching them drop from four minutes apart to three to two (*"Come on! Where's the doctor! We need to get her on terbutaline or she's gonna have this baby tonight!"*)—I can't help thinking about a silly thing Kevin told me off camera.

"I'm a father first, an actor second," he'd said, amongst other surprisingly sane nuggets of familial wisdom. So as I'm watching the painful contractions peak and valley on the graph paper sliding through the monitor attached by a wire to my belly, worrying about the lack of surfactant on my daughter's immature lungs, holding Paul's hand and trying not to cry, all I can think about is when will it be my turn to say the same thing? When will I be able to say I'm a mother first, a journalist second? That is, if I can even call what I've been doing journalism.

My obstetrician finally arrives, after rushing to the hospital in her sparkly black cocktail dress from a party my emergency at the hospital has interrupted. She is livid, but not about missing her party. "What have they been doing to you at work?" she asks wearily, as if she's seen this kind of thing one too many times before. "I just don't get it. Why don't these companies understand that a woman in her third trimester cannot be treated like a mule. That's it," she says. "You're staying in bed until this baby is ready to come out."

Strong prescription drugs and modified bed rest will keep my daughter in utero for another two weeks, just long enough to make sure her lungs will be functional at birth. It's becoming more and more clear to me that one needn't go to war to risk the life of an unborn child. Any asinine story with a strict deadline or a strenuous job with long, irreducible hours will suffice.

Sasha Rachel Pavlovna Kogan arrived three weeks early, minuscule, but thank God healthy in March 1997. She was an easy baby, my little gift, with tiny, delicate fingers that, the moment I saw them, made me think of a line from e. e. cummings: *nobody, not even the rain, has such small hands.*

"WAIT A MINUTE," I say to Paul, pointing at the television screen. "That's Jacques. And there's that guy from Sipa. Nicolas, I think. What the . . . they're being carted off to jail!" It's Labor Day weekend, 1997. I'm still on maternity leave with Sasha. It's after midnight, but Paul and I are awake and sitting in the living room of my parents' house in Bethany Beach, Delaware, glued to CNN. Princess Diana has apparently been killed in a car crash with her lover Dodi El-Fayed, son of Harrod's owner, Mohammed El-Fayed. CNN keeps cutting back to footage of my former photojournalist colleagues sitting in the back of a police van, all of them under arrest and under suspicion of having caused the accident.

"How weird," Paul says.

"Poor Jacques," I say.

I call Marion, who's now working for *Paris Match,* at her apartment in Paris. It's the wee hours of the morning for her, but it sounds as if she's been up all night. I ask her what she's heard. "Oh, Debs, it's just horrible. They have Langevin. And all the others."

I spent some time with Jacques Langevin, a well-respected war photographer known best for his Tiananmen pictures, when we were in Bucharest together covering the elections. He is a decent man, modest and intelligent, definitely not your typical, in-the-face paparazzi photographer. His arrest as a homicidal menace makes no sense.

It's not that I doubt the fact that Jacques had been outside the Ritz trying to snap a few pictures of the princess. The odd assignment like that has always been part and parcel of being an agency photographer, and never more so than during these lean years of dwindling magazine assignments and declining markets for still images of international news. Though it's difficult to pinpoint exactly when it happened, somehow the confluence of twenty-four-hour cable news plus the end of the Cold War plus an international fin de siècle obsession with celebrity have irreparably altered the professional landscape for the photojournalist. Before I got out of the business in 1992, I'd shoot a celebrity photo every now and then to help me finance my other, riskier ventures, sort of like a bridge loan between wars. Now, for the photojournalist, it's come down to shoot Princess Di, or die.

"You should put Jacques on *Dateline*," Marion says, only half joking, "let him clear his name." I explain to Marion that I'm happily still on maternity leave, but if she doesn't mind, I'll give her number to Neal, our executive producer, should he decide to fly a producer over to Paris to do the story. "No problem," she says. "I'll be glad to help."

I call Neal at home. He's not there, so I leave a message on his answering machine, along with Marion's number and a host of other contact names and numbers, all major players in the Parisian photojournalist scene. Then I leave him my phone number in Delaware, in case he has any further questions. The following morning, I get a call first from Jim, then from Heather, another senior producer at *Dateline,* both of whom tell me in no uncertain terms to book myself on the next plane to Paris.

"But, but, but . . ." I try to say. But you can just use my name. But I was just trying to help from afar. But I don't want to get involved. But I'm enjoying myself. But this is my family vacation. But I'm supposed to have another month and a half of maternity leave. But Paul took the week off from work. But Jacob and I are having a great time building sand castles. But I have those annoying Manhattan nursery school applications to consider. But, and I know it sounds blasphemous, I don't really care about Princess Di. But I was looking forward to another week of Kodak moments. But Sasha will only be this young once.

But I have no desire—none whatsoever—to go to Paris.

And then, suddenly, it occurs to me, the biggest "but" of all, and a perfect excuse to boot: But I have not yet weaned Sasha. Four out of her five feedings a day still come directly from my breasts. She's six months old, just like her brother when I weaned him, but she's such a joy to feed—and I don't know if I'll have any more babies, any more chances for the kind of pure and intimate bonding breast-feeding affords—that I want to keep it going for just a little while longer.

I call back Heather and tell her that I don't want to go. That, in fact, I can't go, on account of my breasts. Heather's my friend as well as my superior, and she knows I've been asking my boss for a promotion so I can then try to work out a part-time schedule. "If I were you," she says, "and you know I'm only looking out for your best interests, I would not refuse

this assignment. It'll look bad, and you're right on the verge of that promotion."

I want to hate Heather, but I know she's right. I feel like kicking myself for ever making that stupid phone call. What was I thinking? While
agreeing to go to Paris may not get me promoted immediately, *not* going
to Paris will mean it'll be at least another year of sucking up before I can
lobby NBC to cut back my hours. Which means another year of spending
far less time with my children than I think they deserve. After discussing
it with Paul, we decide that the long-term benefits for our children, if I co-
operate with *Dateline* now, far outweigh the short-term misery of my
daughter's abrupt weaning.

We leave Delaware and head back to New York that day. That evening,
with my body overflowing with milk and regret, I board the plane to Paris.

The trip back to my old stomping grounds turns out to be a professional
success but a personal and physical nightmare. Paris shines as brightly as
ever, but I am unable to appreciate her beauty. I cry a lot. I feel sort of
weaselly begging my old colleagues to go on camera. The pace of the work
is so arduous, I never get more than four hours of sleep a night, and sometimes I get none. My breasts explode all over the city, forcing me to dash
into random *toilettes publiques* when the pressure becomes too painful,
whereupon I must then lean over a sink and manually express them. As I
watch the streams of mother's milk hit the side of the basin and then slide
down the drain, I picture my tiny daughter at home, wailing from the loss.

In a month or so, when I'm back from Paris, a seven-month-old Sasha
will maneuver her way into the underwear drawer at the bottom of my
dresser and remove one of my old bras. She will fondle it, rub it against her
cheek while sucking her thumb, and wear it with the arm strap around her
neck like a necklace. Soon thereafter, it will become her security blanket.

If that's not a sign, then coincidence is a much trickier beast than I
ever imagined.

MY PROMOTION, the one I'd been waiting three years to get, the one I
was counting on to catapult me into the world of part-time work and balanced parenthood, finally came through a few weeks after my Paris trip in
the form of a company-wide e-mail from my boss. Unfortunately, the e-
mail went out on the one day I'd decided to play hooky with my son (sign!).

The circus was in town, and Jacob wanted to see the elephants and eat pink cotton candy, and I wasn't able to come up with any logical reason to say no. Apparently, Neal was looking everywhere for me that afternoon to tell me and to offer his congratulations. As were all of my colleagues, who clogged my computer with messages like "Congratulations!!!!!!!!!!!! Where are you?" or "It's about time. Where are you?" The next morning, sheepishly, I went into Neal's office, apologized for being at the circus instead of at the office ("Ah, well, they're not much different anyway," he'd joked,) and then I blurted out everything that had been on my mind. The dumb stories. The lack of balance.

Amazingly, though he himself was childless, he understood. He promised to keep me away from the *really* dumb stories. He promised to try to create a part-time producer position. He said that even though there was no precedent for such a position at *Dateline,* I could talk to the NBC brass to work out the logistics—hours, days, salary, duties, etc. He gave me a paternal hug, said he was glad I came to him with my problems.

I was sent to meet with one of NBC's vice presidents. Despite having two small kids of her own, she seemed slightly less sympathetic to my situation than Neal had been. It was a phenomenon I was starting to see more and more of in my fellow mothers. Whatever choice they had made for themselves, that was the choice all other mothers were supposed to follow. Friends were becoming enemies over the issue of whether to stay at home or work or do some hybrid of the two. It was subtle—one woman, the mother of teenagers, telling me, "Well, I stayed at home while my kids were little and they benefited enormously"—and sometimes less so, like the time just after Jacob was born when I was talking with a colleague at a wedding. When I admitted my ambivalence about returning to work, she glared at me and said, "That's completely insane. You have to do something for yourself," and then stalked away angrily. Even the playgrounds seemed segregated, with working mothers congregating with other working moms, stay-at-home mothers congregating with other stay-at-home moms, and part-time working mothers misunderstood by both.

The NBC vice president and fellow mom did promise to work everything out. As I turned to leave her office, however, she made me promise not to tell the other women on staff about our negotiations, as if the desire to balance work with child rearing were a contagious disease that might spread and cripple the company. As if no one would notice a pattern to my weekly absences. I promised to keep quiet. Then I waited.

A month passed. Then another. There seemed to be some problems with head count, the VP said. I left her messages. I wrote strongly worded memos, asking for the part-time work to begin immediately. The head count issue, whatever it was, would not go away. My daughter took her first steps in front of the baby-sitter. I wrote more memos, left more messages. After seven months of bureaucratic bungling, with my infant daughter no longer an infant, with my son about to start full-time nursery school, with my travel suddenly increasing, with my work no longer fulfilling, and with Paul now in a position, if barely, to support the household on his new Internet job salary, I finally gave up.

Handing in my resignation to Neal, whom I now considered a friend, was hard. He'd been kind, tried as best he could to be helpful, and he seemed visibly upset at my departure. But with the human resources representative assigned to my case—a stranger, a cog in the entrenched bureaucratic wheel that had failed me—I was livid. At my official NBC exit interview, I said, "You guys better watch out." Women were getting pregnant in record numbers at *Dateline,* I told her, and if the company could not adjust to this changing demographic by offering at least the possibility of part-time work to the women—and men!—who needed it, the show would have no one left to produce stories, to feed the hungry, five-night-a-week machine.

Less than two years after I quit, as I sit here writing this, part-time producer positions at *Dateline* have become a reality. I could be kidding myself, but I like to believe that my angry resignation may have had something to do with it. At least I hope it did.

Meanwhile, my daughter, Sasha, though still alarmingly tiny, has turned into a feisty, pouty, strong, opinionated, flirtatious, fearless and devilish young girl, whose favorite pastime is sticking her fingers inside the mouths of large dogs. She refuses to wear dresses, she prefers upside down to right side up, and when anyone dares to compliment her beauty, she responds with an adamant, clenched-fisted, foot-pounding, "I'm not pretty! I'm handsome!" One day, when I picked her up from preschool and found her wearing a plastic crown, I made sure to tell her that she made a very *handsome* princess. Little two-year-old Sasha scowled at me, already a mortified teenager. "Mommy! I'm not a princess," she said, her hands on her hips and her chin jutting out for added emphasis. "I'm a king!"

She also claims to have a penis. Far be it from me to burst that bubble.

BETHANY BEACH, DELAWARE, 1999

While Paul is convinced that Sasha is a crotchety, fifty-year-old grande dame stuck in the body of a toddler, my parents are convinced that she's their revenge. "Just wait until she runs off to Afghanistan," they say. "Then you'll see." I'm convinced that as long as she does not run there with a camera-toting, bandanna-wearing, skull-clobbering guy like Pascal, she'll be just fine, thank you very much. Especially because I'm hoping that by the time she actually makes it there, the land mines will have been cleared and the Afghanis will have stopped trying to shoot one another.

My son, on the other hand, is deathly afraid of dogs. (His first sentence? "'Fraid of doggies.") Jacob's more of a sensitive soul—a poet, a dreamer. At the age of two, he threw a penny in a fountain and said, wistfully, "I wish to smell a rainbow." He's prone to spontaneous outbursts of both affection and existential angst, incredulous that good can exist side by side with evil. He has fallen in love with one of his classmates, a little girl named Grey who looks enough like him that they are often mistaken for twins. They've decided to get married. They say they will have three children, two boys and a girl, whom they will name John, Steve and Natasha. On the morning it suddenly occurred to Jacob that everyone in the world has to die—he was three and a half, riding the bus to his preschool with me—he stared out the window and cried for a long time. Then, still sniffling, he made me promise that he and Grey would die on the exact same day, so they wouldn't have to live without each other.

You kind of have to wonder why it took my son less than four years to own one of the truths I had to spend more than two decades figuring out. Just ask him. He'll tell you. The secret to a happy life is love.

When he's old enough, when tiny Sasha's old enough, I'll jump on my soapbox and tell them a few more. Simple truths, like the quest is as important, if not more important, than the goal. Like hearts have a surprising resilience. Like war is bad. Like some things in life are inexplicable, and many others are ambiguous. Like not everyone can be saved. Like sex can be either beautiful or ugly but never both simultaneously. Like reading and traveling teach us more than we can ever learn in school. Like girls have it tougher than boys, still, and that owing to such things as body mass and the mechanics of rape, perhaps always will. Like babies should be born only to people who are ready for such a colossal responsibility. Like parenthood—a parenthood sown of planning and love—is by far and away the most profound experience life holds.

IT IS THE SPRING OF 1999, the height of the conflict in Serbia and Kosovo. Jacob, who is not yet four, has grown disturbed after watching a *60 Minutes* segment about the war, which apparently had a parental warning about its explicit contents at the top that we stupidly missed. His drawings, one of which he named his "Guernica," have begun to feature evil creatures named Milosevic, burning houses, corpses and guns. He's started having vivid nightmares in which bad guys burn down our apartment and make him go live in a tent. He finds his way, with increasing frequency, into our bed, shaking and in need of affection.

One night, while Paul and I are tucking him in, he asks, "Why do bad guys fight wars?"

The two of us look at each other, caught off guard as usual, and struggle for an answer he'll understand. We offer many. Because they don't know how to communicate. Because they seek power or revenge. Because they're angry. Because they lack love. Because they don't understand one another. Because they fear anyone different from themselves. Because they're stupid. Because they don't know how to share.

Jacob isn't buying any of it. "But why do they have to kill each other? Killing's not nice."

"You're right, sweetie," Paul says. "It's not." He kisses his son and throws me a fake smile. "Honey, he's all yours." Then he says, "Sorry, Jakey, Mommy's much more of an expert on wars and bad guys than I am. Ask her to tell you about some of the things she's seen."

"Gee, thanks," I say. I fake-smile back.

Paul climbs down from the top bunk, turns on the Pooh night-light and kisses his already slumbering daughter beneath us. Then, after asking whether I want pasta or couscous—"Pasta," I say, "definitely pasta"—he turns off the overhead light and closes the door gently behind him.

I stare down at my son, who's snuggled under the covers in his new cowboy pajamas, smelling of soap. His anxious eyes probe mine. "Mommy, what did you see?" He's clutching Rock, the pink and green batik elephant he picked out himself, his sole talisman against evil, a little too tightly. I crawl under the covers beside him and wedge my shoulder beneath his head. I let my hand wander under his pajama top. Find his heart. It's beating those swift, tiny miracle beats, the ones that always catch me by surprise and make me think about oxygen, God and the thirteen billion years that came before us. What did I see? I didn't expect to have to deal with this question so soon. I start rubbing quiet circles across Jacob's downy, bulbous stomach, searching my head for the right words.

"Well, you see, Jacob, it's like this . . ." I sigh. Hoping to make sense of it all. Not sure I ever will.

Then I open my mouth to begin.

IN MEMORIAM

WILLIAM ALFRED

OVIDIU BOGDAN

ANDY DANIK

JOE GALL

GAD GROSS

JACQUES HAILLOT

SERGE MAJAROW

A C K N O W L E D G M E N T S

MORE GRATITUDE than I could ever fit in this small space goes to Tad
Friend, a friend indeed, who lovingly edited this book in its larval
stages and did not laugh at my ineptitude.

I am also grateful to both John Burnham Schwartz and Phyllida
Burlingame—who were privy to many of these stories as they were
either happening or shared forthwith, over tiny cups of espresso at
Café de Flore—for their unique insight, wisdom, marginalia and
enthusiasm, as well as to David Handelman, for performing expert,
last-minute microsurgery on this manuscript when my eyes were
too tired and tearful to see.

If it were in my power to do so, I'd bestow a lifetime supply of
good karma and chocolate bunnies upon Courtney Hodell, for helping me find my way into the arms of Jennifer Rudolph Walsh,
agent/mom/superhero. Without Jennifer, these pages would have
gathered dust in a drawer. I am also grateful to Mollie Doyle, for
originally acquiring the book, and to Ann Godoff, for her behind-
the-scenes foster-parenting. As for my editor, Kate Niedzwiecki,
who polishes prose with the same ease with which most of us tie
our shoes, I am deeply indebted to her for providing this orphan
with such a loving, stable home.

Thanks are also due to Jennifer Steinhauer, Robin Pogrebin,
Edward Klaris, Abby Pogrebin, David Shapiro, Stephen Dubner,
Ellen Binder, Larissa MacFarquhar, Rebecca Posner, Julie Dressner,

Sara Mosle, Porter Gifford, Anna Forrester, Josh Berger, Joe Flanigan, Brooke Williams, Betsy Cohen, Geraldine Moriba-Meadows, Courtney Rogmans, Sandy Rubenstein, Kammi Reiss, Helen Thorpe, Monique El-Faizy, Kathy Ryan, Elizabeth Beier, Michael Hirschorn, Susan Lehman, George Kogan, Todd and Tammy Yellin and my sisters, Jennifer, Julie and Laura Copaken, for their own thoughts, interest and/or shrewd pencil marks along the way, as well as to Richard Murphy, Lisa Schiffren, Scott Satin, Gilles Peress, Marion Mertens, Pierre Luton, Julian Borger, Doru Iordache, Mauzi Kalousek, Jim Nachtwey, Luc Delahaye, Oliver Phillips, Alex Webb, Neal Shapiro, Dominique Saint-Louis and Jim Gerety, for jogging my memory and helping me sort out names and facts. Evan Shapiro, bless his clever soul, wins the grand prize for coming up with the book's title during morning drop-off at our kids' preschool.

For donating their own private spaces, so that I could write without two active, noisy toddlers underfoot, I must thank first and foremost Maia Samuel, but also Andy Behrman, Suze Yalof and Amie Weitzman. Many thanks also to the Columbia Teacher's College Library, the New York Public Library, the Xando at Seventy-sixth and Broadway, the Starbucks at Eighty-sixth and Columbus and Avenue Restaurant, as well as to all the strangers in those public spaces who, whenever I had to run to the bathroom, agreed to keep an eye on my laptop. But most of all, thanks to Dolly Bisa, for giving me the peace of mind that comes from knowing my two aforementioned active, noisy toddlers would be well cared for, hugged and picked up from school on time in my absence.

For teaching me to love words, I lie prostrate before Tom Gillard; pictures, Christopher James; life, Marjorie and Richard Copaken; motherhood, Jacob and Sasha Kogan.

As for Paul Kogan, my love, my savior—the man who kept pushing me to write down these stories, who supported the family when I decided to finally do it, who tirelessly read every miserable rough draft and weathered every subsequent tantrum—you know how I feel about you. And now, with this extended love poem, so does everyone else.

DEBORAH COPAKEN KOGAN
lives with her husband and
two children in New York City.